DEMOCRACY
AND
POLITICAL
IGNORANCE

DEMOCRACY AND POLITICAL IGNORANCE

WHY SMALLER GOVERNMENT IS SMARTER

Ilya Somin

STANFORD LAW BOOKS
An Imprint of Stanford University Press
Stanford, California

Stanford University Press
Stanford, California

©2013 by the Board of Trustees of the
Leland Stanford Junior University.
All rights reserved.

Printed in the United States of America on acid-free,
archival-quality paper

Library of Congress Cataloging-in-Publication Data
Somin, Ilya, author.
Democracy and political ignorance : why smaller
government is smarter / Ilya Somin.
pages cm
Includes bibliographical references and index.
ISBN 978-0-8047-8608-9 (cloth : alk. paper)—
ISBN 978-0-8047-8661-4 (pbk. : alk. paper)
1. Democracy—United States. 2. Ignorance (Theory of knowledge)—
Political aspects—United States. 3. Voting—United States.
4. United States—Politics and government. I. Title.
JK1726.S67 2013
320.973—DC23   2013013483

ISBN 978-0-8047-8931-8 (electronic)

Typeset by Classic Typography in 10.75/15 Sabon MT Pro

To my Grandparents
The late Ber and Pauline Somin
and
Basya and Nathan Firun

Contents

Acknowledgments

A BOOK AUTHOR NECESSARILY acquires numerous debts that are difficult to repay.

For excellent research assistance at George Mason University and the University of Pennsylvania Law School, I would like to thank Eva Choi, Susan Courtwright-Rodriguez, Ryan Facer, Bryan Fields, Matthew Hart, Marisa Maleck, and Haidee Schwartz.

I owe a major debt to several scholars who read and commented on substantial parts of the manuscript: Bryan Caplan, Jeffrey Friedman, Heather Gerken, Guido Pincione, David Schleicher, and two anonymous reviewers. I am also grateful to other colleagues who gave discrete suggestions on individual parts of the manuscript or earlier works that it built on, including Peter Boettke, Roderick Hills, Sanford Levinson, Mark Pennington, and Donald Wittman.

Thanks are also due to the many scholars and students who gave useful comments at presentations of earlier drafts of parts of this book at the New York University Economics Department, the New York University Law School, Northwestern University School of Law, the George Mason University Economics Department, the George Mason University School of Law Levy Seminar, the IVR international conference on law and philosophy, the University of California at Santa Cruz Economics Department, the University of Athens, the University of Torcuato Di Tella law faculty in Buenos Aires, the Korea Institutional Economics Association, the Cato Institute, the Liberty Fund, and the University of Hamburg Institute of Law and Economics.

Michelle Lipinski of Stanford University Press deserves special thanks for her excellent work in editing the manuscript. Frances Malcolm, also of Stanford University Press, provided valuable assistance in preparing the manuscript for publication. I would also like to thank the copyeditors at Stanford University Press for their invaluable efforts.

Colin Hall deserves credit for suggesting what eventually became the book's subtitle. I should also acknowledge the many other friends and colleagues who made subtitle suggestions in response to my requests.

At the George Mason University School of Law, I am grateful to Dean Daniel Polsby and my other colleagues for providing such a wonderfully supportive atmosphere for scholarship, and to the Law and Economics Center for financial support. My assistant, Katherine Hickey, was extremely helpful in dealing with a variety of logistical issues related to the book.

Acknowledgment is owed to the publishers of previous works for allowing me to adapt some of the material from those pieces. Parts of Chapters 1, 2, and 6 use material from my article "Political Ignorance and the Countermajoritarian Difficulty: A New Perspective on the 'Central Obsession' of Constitutional Theory," *Iowa Law Review* 87 (2004): 1287–1371 (reprinted with permission). Chapters 1, 2, and 4 borrow some material from "When Ignorance Isn't Bliss: How Political Ignorance Threatens Democracy," Cato Institute Policy Analysis No. 525 (2004). Some material in Chapters 3 and 4 is adapted from "Voter Ignorance and the Democratic Ideal," *Critical Review* 12 (1998): 413–58, while "Knowledge About Ignorance: New Directions in the Study of Political Information," *Critical Review* 18 (2006): 255–78 helped inform Chapter 3. Parts of my forthcoming article in *Nomos*, "Foot Voting, Federalism, and Political Freedom," to be published by NYU Press, as well as "Foot Voting, Political Ignorance, and Constitutional Design," *Social Philosophy and Policy* 28 (2011): 202–227 were used in the development of Chapter 5.

My greatest debt is to my wife, Alison, for her thoughtful advice and encouragement, and for putting up with all the disruptions she had to deal with as a result of my work on this book.

Last but not least, our golden retriever, Willow, gets credit for being so understanding when I could not give her as much attention as she was entitled to during the first year of her life with us, due to my having to work on the book. Retrievers are often more rational and perhaps even more knowledgeable than humans.

DEMOCRACY
AND
POLITICAL
IGNORANCE

Introduction

> A popular government without popular information, or the
> means of acquiring it, is but a Prologue to a Farce or a Tragedy;
> or perhaps both. Knowledge will forever govern ignorance.
> And a people who mean to be their own Governors must
> arm themselves with the Power that knowledge gives.
>
> —JAMES MADISON[1]

MUCH EVIDENCE SUGGESTS that there is widespread public ignorance about politics in America. The biggest issue in the important 2010 congressional election was the economy. Yet two-thirds of the public did not realize that the economy had grown rather than shrunk during the previous year.[2] In the aftermath of that election, the majority of Americans did not realize that the Republican Party had taken control of the House of Representatives, but not the Senate.[3]

When President Barack Obama took office in 2009, his administration and the Democratic Congress pursued an ambitious agenda on health care and environmental policy, among other issues. The media covered both issue areas extensively. Yet a September 2009 survey showed that only 37 percent of Americans believed they understood the administration's health care plan, a figure that likely overestimated the true level of knowledge.[4] A May 2009 poll showed that only 24 percent of Americans realized that the important "cap and trade" initiative then recently passed by the House of Representatives as an effort to combat global warming addressed "environmental issues."[5] Some 46 percent thought that it was either a "health care reform" or a "regulatory reform for Wall Street."[6] It is difficult to evaluate a major policy proposal if one does not know what issue it addresses. In 2003, some 70 percent of Americans were unaware of the recent enactment of President George W. Bush's

Medicare prescription drug bill, the biggest new government program in several decades.[7]

The existence of such ignorance does not by itself prove that there is anything wrong with our political system. Perhaps these polls were somehow unrepresentative. In any case, maybe voters do not need much in the way of knowledge. Perhaps they can make good decisions even if they know very little. Still, these examples and others like them are at least cause for concern. If the public really is often ignorant, we might have a serious problem on our hands.

WHY POLITICAL IGNORANCE MATTERS

Democracy is rule by the people. The literal meaning of the original Greek word *democracy* signifies exactly that: rule by the *demos*, the Greek word for the common people. The day-to-day business of government may be conducted by elected officials. But those leaders are ultimately responsible to the public. If they fail to serve the interests of the voters, we can "throw the bastards out" and elect a set of "bastards" who will hopefully do better. In this way, the democratic process is supposed to ensure that we get what Abraham Lincoln called "government of the people, by the people, for the people."[8] The key to the entire system is the accountability of elected officials to voters.

Some political theorists value democratic control of government for its own sake.[9] Others do so for primarily instrumental reasons.[10] Either way, accountability is a crucial part of the picture. But effective democratic accountability requires voters to have at least some political knowledge. Voters generally cannot hold government officials accountable for their actions if they do not know what the government is doing. And they cannot know which candidates' proposals will serve the public better unless they have at least some understanding of those policies and their likely effects.

Accountability is also difficult to achieve if voters do not know which officials are responsible for which issues. If the public schools perform poorly, should the voter blame the local government, the state government, the federal government, or all three? Which officials, if any, can be blamed for economic recessions? Are mistakes in the conduct of the War on Terror the responsibility of the president alone, or does Congress deserve a share of the blame? Answering these questions and others like them requires at least some degree of political knowledge.

Even if an individual voter does not care about political accountability or does not mind if his government performs poorly, he may still have a responsibility to become informed for the sake of his fellow citizens. After all, the winners of the next election will govern not only him but everyone else who lives in his society. Casting a ballot is not a purely individual choice that affects no one but the voter. In the admittedly highly unlikely event that it influences the outcome of an election, it will also affect the lives of thousands or millions of other people. Even the citizen who is personally uninterested in the quality of public policy may justifiably feel a moral obligation to become informed if he intends to vote.[11]

Obviously, it is not enough to conclude that voters need to have at least some political knowledge to make democracy work. We also need to know *how much* knowledge is enough. If it turns out that voters know too little, it would be useful to know why. Even more important, we need to know what if anything can be done to alleviate the harm caused by excessive political ignorance.

These questions are the focus of this book. I doubt that I or anyone else can answer them definitively. It would be arrogant to assume that any one book can settle issues that have been debated for over two thousand years. But I hope to at least make a useful contribution to the discussion.

The first half of the book analyzes the nature and extent of the problem of political ignorance in American democracy. The evidence shows that political ignorance is extensive and poses a very serious challenge to democratic theory. The severity of the problem is exacerbated by the reality that, for most citizens, political ignorance is not the result of stupidity or selfishness. Rather, ignorance turns out to be rational behavior—even for many who are far from stupid and are genuinely concerned about the welfare of the nation. The insignificance of any one vote to electoral outcomes makes it rational for most citizens to devote little effort to acquiring political knowledge. They also have little incentive to engage in unbiased evaluation of the information they do know.

The last four chapters consider potential solutions. While it may be possible to make voters more knowledgeable at the margin, I conclude that a major increase in political knowledge is unlikely in the foreseeable future. Therefore, the problem of political ignorance may be more effectively addressed not by increasing knowledge but by trying to reduce the impact of ignorance.

This can be at least partially achieved by limiting and decentralizing government power in ways that enable citizens to "vote with their feet" as well as at the ballot box. People choosing between different jurisdictions in a federal system or between different options in the private sector often have better incentives to become informed about their options than ballot box voters do. Unlike ballot box voters, foot voters know that their decisions are likely to make a difference. As a result, they are more inclined to seek out relevant information and evaluate it in a reasonable way.

Is Concern About Political Ignorance Paternalistic?

Concern about political ignorance strikes some critics as unduly paternalistic. Perhaps citizens should be free to choose policies and leaders for whatever reasons they wish—even if those reasons are the result of ignorance. A democrat committed to this view might find the issue addressed in this book at best irrelevant and at worst an unjustified attack on the rights of the people. Even if ignorance leads voters to make poor decisions, we would not be justified in imposing constraints on democracy because the voters have a right to rule as they please. As Robert Bork puts it, "[i]n wide areas of life majorities are entitled to rule, if they wish, simply because they are majorities."[12] H. L. Mencken famously satirized the same point when he wrote that "[d]emocracy is the theory that the common people know what they want, and deserve to get it good and hard."[13]

Unfortunately, however, when voters make poor decisions out of ignorance, everyone "gets it good and hard," not just those who voted for the wrong candidates and supported their harmful policies. That is what makes voting different from individual decisions that affect only the decision-makers themselves and those who voluntarily choose to interact with them. As John Stuart Mill put it in his 1861 book *Considerations on Representative Government*:

> The spirit of vote by ballot—the interpretation likely to be put on it in the mind of an elector—is that the suffrage is given to him for himself; for his particular use and benefit, and not as a trust for the public. . . . [D]emocrats think themselves greatly concerned in maintaining that the franchise is what they term a right, not a trust. . . . In whatever way we define or understand the idea of a right, *no person can have a right . . . to power over others*: every such power, which he is allowed to possess, is morally, in the fullest force of the term, a trust. But the exercise of any political function, either as an elector or as a representative, is power over others.[14]

As Mill emphasized, voting decisions involve not simply an individual choice but the exercise of "power over others." For this reason, we are justified in urging constraints on the scope of that choice if ignorance or other factors leads voters to make systematic errors. Such constraints, of course, are only defensible if we have reason to believe that alternative arrangements might handle information problems better. This book makes precisely that argument.

There is a second reason why it is not a paternalistic infringement on voters' freedom to worry about political ignorance and advocate measures to reduce its impact. As will be discussed in Chapter 3, widespread ignorance about politics is in large part the result of a collective action problem. An individual voter has little incentive to learn about politics because there is only an infinitesimal chance that his or her well-informed vote will actually affect electoral outcomes. Political ignorance is therefore an example of rational individual behavior that leads to potentially dangerous collective outcomes.

Economists have long recognized that outside intervention may be needed to address such "public goods" problems.[15] Such intervention is not necessarily paternalistic because it may actually be giving the people that which they want but lack the incentive to produce for themselves through uncoordinated individual action.

In the same way, it is not necessarily paternalistic to advocate the restriction of air pollution. Individual citizens and firms may produce more air pollution than any of them actually want because they know that there is little to be gained from uncoordinated individual restraint. If I avoid driving a gas-guzzling car, the impact on the overall level of air pollution will be utterly insignificant. So I have no incentive to take it into account in making my driving decisions even if I care greatly about reducing air pollution. Widespread public ignorance is a type of pollution that infects the political system rather than our physical environment.

Finally, even if voters do have the right to select whatever policies they please regardless of their effect on fellow citizens, ignorance might still be problematic. After all, a person making a choice based on ignorance might well fail to achieve his or her intended result. If I buy a lemon car based on the erroneous belief that it is in good condition, my purposes in purchasing it are likely to be frustrated if it quickly breaks down.[16] Similarly, voters who support protectionist policies in the erroneous expectation that they will benefit the economy as a whole rather than weaken it will also end up undermining their own goals.[17] Voters may not be able to effectively exercise their right to choose the policies they wish if their choices are based on ignorance.

Political ignorance might be unimportant if public opinion had little or no effect on policy. In that event, voters would not actually be exercising any genuine "power over others" after all. However, a large literature shows that public opinion does have a significant impact on at least the broad outlines of policy.[18] Public opinion is, of course, far from the only influence on policymaking. As will be discussed later in this book,[19] there are often individual issues on which public opinion has relatively little impact because the voters are unaware of what is going on. Such other influences as bureaucratic discretion and interest group lobbying also have important effects. However, there is little doubt that voter opinions have considerable influence over many policy decisions, even if other factors also matter.

Even relatively ignorant voters can influence policy in cases where some effect seems easily traceable to a government action or when the government is rewarded or blamed for some highly visible event.[20] Ignorant voters can also influence policy by creating opportunities for politicians, activists, and interest groups to manipulate that ignorance.[21] These effects make voter knowledge a potentially important input into the policymaking process. Politicians who wish to be elected and reelected must enact policies that win voter support. And the distribution of that support may be affected by ignorance.

Even if public opinion did not influence policy in the status quo, most major normative theories of democracy assume that it *should* do so, at least to some substantial extent. As explained in Chapter 2, these theories also imply knowledge prerequisites that voters must meet in order to exercise that influence effectively.

In focusing on the importance of voter ignorance, I do not mean to deny the significance of ignorance among political elites and expert policymakers. Such elites also sometimes suffer from political ignorance, either because there are some types of information they inherently cannot know,[22] or because they choose to ignore relevant social science data that is readily available.[23] But whatever the knowledge levels of elites, voters have a vital role in democratic political systems, and their ignorance is significant regardless of whether political elites have similar shortcomings of their own.

The Historic Debate Over Political Ignorance

The problem of political ignorance is not a new one. Political philosophers have debated the implications of voter ignorance for democracy since that system of government first originated in ancient Greece, in the city state of Athens. Early critics of Athenian democracy argued that Athens was doomed to failure because its policies were set by ignorant common citizens.[24] In *The Gorgias*, the great philosopher Plato contended that democracy is defective because it adopts policies based on the views of the ignorant masses and neglects the better-informed counsel of philosophers and other experts.[25]

Aristotle was more optimistic about political knowledge than Plato. Although he admitted that citizens usually have little knowledge individually, Aristotle argued that they could access far larger amounts of information collectively.[26] Nonetheless, Aristotle still asserted that women, slaves, manual laborers, and others whom he considered incapable of achieving adequate levels of virtue and political knowledge should be excluded from political participation.[27]

In more recent centuries, even some thinkers sympathetic to liberal democracy have sought to limit the power of voters for fear of giving free rein to political ignorance. The American founding fathers inserted numerous anti-majoritarian elements into the Constitution in order to provide a check on what they saw as ignorant and irrational voters. As James Madison put it in *Federalist* 63, checks such as an indirectly elected Senate were needed "as a defense to the people against their own temporary errors and delusions."[28] John Stuart Mill, a liberal political theorist generally sympathetic to democracy, greatly feared political ignorance and argued that it justified giving extra votes to the better-educated and more knowledgeable.[29]

In the twentieth century, totalitarian leaders on both the left and the right resuscitated Plato's claim that voter ignorance justifies the abolition of electoral democracy in favor of concentrating power in the hands of a small elite. Vladimir Lenin's 1902 book *What Is to Be Done?* argued that workers cannot be expected to develop sufficient political knowledge to launch a socialist revolution on their own. Left to itself, a "spontaneous" working class cannot get beyond mere "trade union consciousness" and will not recognize the need for a full-blown reordering of society along socialist lines. Therefore, Lenin concluded that the transition to communism required firm leadership by a "vanguard" party, whose members would better understand the political interests of the working class than the workers themselves.[30]

Adolf Hitler, too, rejected democracy in part because he believed that voters are ignorant and easily manipulated, a problem that could only be solved by instituting a dictatorship headed by a far-seeing leader. In his view, "[t]he receptivity of the great masses [to information] is very limited, their intelligence is small, but their power of forgetting is enormous."[31]

On the other side of the fence, many modern scholars—economists and political scientists—have argued that political ignorance is unimportant, or easily surmounted through the use of "information shortcuts."[32] "[G] ive people some significant power," writes political philosopher Benjamin Barber, "and they will quickly appreciate the need for knowledge."[33]

Unlike Plato and the totalitarians, I do not argue for a complete rejection of democracy. I accept the evidence that democracy generally functions better than alternative systems of government.[34] Democracies tend to be more prosperous and peaceful than dictatorships or oligarchies, and usually provide greater freedom to their citizens.[35] They are also more likely to avoid major policy disasters, and do not commit mass murder against their own people.[36]

As an immigrant from the Soviet Union to the United States—one with relatives who were victims of both communist and Nazi repression—I am acutely conscious of the advantages of democracy over dictatorship. But the superiority of democracy over other forms of government leaves open the possibility that democracy might function better if its powers were more tightly limited.

DEFINING POLITICAL KNOWLEDGE

Before analyzing political ignorance, it is important to define what we mean by political knowledge. Throughout this book, I focus primarily on political knowledge defined as awareness of factual matters related to politics and public policy. This includes knowledge of specific policy issues and leaders. As we shall see more fully in Chapter 1, many voters are unaware of the elements of important public policies enacted by the legislature. Factual political knowledge also includes knowledge of broad structural elements of government, such as which public officials are responsible for which issues, and the elements of competing political ideologies, such as liberalism and conservatism. For example, the majority of citizens do not know which branch of government has the power to declare war.[37]

It is also important to consider the extent to which voters are unable to rationally evaluate the information they do have. By "rationally," I mean only whether they evaluate the information in a logically consistent, unbiased manner, not whether they reach morally defensible conclusions about public policy. For example, if a voter wants to increase economic growth and she is shown evidence that free trade is likely to promote that goal, her support for protectionism should diminish. However, she could rationally ignore this evidence if she does not value economic growth and instead prefers to maximize the incomes of protected domestic industries, regardless of the impact on the overall economy or the effects on foreigners.

This emphasis on factual knowledge and value-neutral rationality is not meant to denigrate the importance of values and moral knowledge. Ideally, we would want to have voters who are not only factually knowledgeable but also able to use that knowledge to pursue morally praiseworthy goals. We would not want a highly knowledgeable electorate that values cruelty and oppression for its own sake, and uses its knowledge to elect those leaders whose policies are most effective in implementing such perverse preferences.

But factual knowledge and moral decisions are not completely separate. Many perverse moral judgments made by voters are in part a result of factual ignorance. For example, public hostility toward gays and lesbians is in part the result of ignorance about the likelihood that homosexual orientation is genetically determined and not freely chosen or determined by environmental factors.[38] As will be explained in Chapter 5, many early twentieth-century white voters favored policies oppressing blacks in part because they believed that African Americans had inherent criminal tendencies and were likely to rape white women unless they could be cowed by the threat of lynching. These false factual beliefs were not the only cause of racism, but they surely contributed.

Disagreement over some issues, such as abortion,[39] may largely be determined by conflicting fundamental values, with little role for factual information. On a vast range of major political issues, however, differences between opposing parties and ideologies turn primarily on disagreements over how to achieve widely agreed-upon goals, such as economic prosperity, crime reduction, environmental protection, and security against the threat of attack by terrorists and foreign powers.[40] These objectives are widely shared in American society by people across the political spectrum, and are considered to be the most important goals of public policy by large majorities of the public.[41]

Even on those issues for which political conflict focuses primarily on differences in fundamental values, factual knowledge is often still relevant. For example, a voter whose values lead him to support efforts to ban abortion may still need to know whether the government is actually capable of eliminating most abortions, and at what cost.[42] The vast majority of the examples of ignorance considered in this book relate to issues where political debate focuses on competing means of achieving shared values, rather than ones where political disagreements are more likely to be purely the product of differences over fundamental values. Factual knowledge is not the only kind of information relevant to political decisions. But it is often among the most important.

A more fundamental values-based rejection of the idea that political ignorance matters is the claim that it is somehow illegitimate to evaluate the moral decisions of democracies by standards external to the values of the voters. For example, political theorist Ian Shapiro rejects the idea of "some 'birds-eye' standpoint, existing previously to and independently of democratic procedures, by reference to which we can evaluate the outcomes they produce."[43]

Even if it is illegitimate to second-guess the *values* voters bring to the democratic process, it is not clear why it is wrong to point out that inadequate political knowledge might prevent them from realizing those values as fully and effectively as they otherwise might. Such an argument does not challenge the voters' goals but merely points out that they sometimes lack the means to effectively achieve them through the democratic process. To put it in Shapiro's terms, this approach does not adopt "a 'birds-eye' standpoint" on the democratic process but rather judges its output by the standards of the voters' own values and goals.

Yet there is no inherent reason to limit criticism of democratic decisions to the choice of means alone. Unless we become complete moral relativists, we must admit the possibility that voters might sometimes base their decisions on flawed or unjust values such as racism, sexism, or anti-Semitism.

If we do choose to be absolute moral relativists, then we indeed lack grounds for criticizing democratic decisions. But we also lack any basis for claiming that democracy is superior to other forms of government, such as monarchy, oligarchy, or a totalitarian state.[44] If no values are better than others, then there is no reason to believe that the values promoted by liberal democracy are any better than those promoted by the regimes of Hitler or Stalin. We could no more judge autocratic regimes from an external "birds-eye standpoint" than we can democracies.

If, on the other hand, we can legitimately conclude that democracy is superior to authoritarianism or totalitarianism, then the same standards that we use to compare democracy to these alternative regimes can also be used to compare different types of democracies. If democracy is preferable to an authoritarian government because it provides greater freedom, greater happiness, or greater equality, it is also possible that one type of democratic government may be preferable to another for the exact same reasons.

This book does not present a theory of the ideal set of criteria by which political regimes should be judged. But it does assume that some regimes can reasonably be considered better than others.

PLAN OF THE BOOK

The first four chapters outline the scope and nature of the problem of political ignorance in American democracy. Chapters 5 to 7 consider various possible solutions. Some of these are proposals for increasing voter knowledge, while others are institutional adjustments that would reduce the risks posed by a given level of ignorance. I conclude that the problem of political ignorance is a very serious one, and that there is unlikely to be a quick or easy solution. But its effects can to an important degree be mitigated by limiting the size, complexity, and centralization of government.

Chapter 1 summarizes the evidence of widespread political ignorance in the United States. While much of this data will not surprise experts in the field, it is still important to recognize the full scope of ignorance and its remarkable persistence over time. Chapter 2 compares actual levels of voter knowledge to the requirements of several prominent normative theories of political participation. It is not a great surprise that knowledge levels fall short of the requirements of demanding theories such as "deliberative democracy." But they also fall short of the much more minimal requirements of other theories generally considered to be less demanding. The failure of voters to meet the demands of even relatively modest theories of political participation highlights the severity of the challenge of political ignorance for democratic theory. There are unusual cases where political ignorance actually turns out to be beneficial. Overall, however, its vast extent is more a danger to democracy than an asset.

In Chapter 3, I explain why political ignorance is actually rational behavior for most citizens. The core argument is a familiar one to students of political knowledge. Anthony Downs first showed that political ignorance is generally rational in a famous 1957 book.[45] Voters have little incentive to become informed because there is only an infinitesimal chance that any one vote will affect the outcome of an election. This explains why so many remain ignorant about basic political issues even in a world in which information is readily available through the media and other sources. The main constraint on political learning is not the availability of information, but the willingness of voters to take the time and effort needed to learn and understand it.

Chapter 3 also considers the connections between rational ignorance and economist Bryan Caplan's theory of "rational irrationality," which holds that voters not only have incentives to be ignorant but also to engage in highly biased evaluation of the information they do have.[46] The combination of rational ignorance and rational irrationality is a more serious danger than either taken alone. Among other problems, the conjunction of the two makes voters far more susceptible to misinformation and deception than they would be otherwise.

In Chapter 4, I review claims that voter ignorance might be offset by the use of "information shortcuts" that enable voters to cast well-informed ballots despite knowing little or no factual information. Some of these shortcuts have genuine value in enabling poorly informed voters to make better choices. Overall, however, they fall far short of fully offsetting the dangers posed by ignorance. Moreover, some shortcuts actually lead to worse decisions, because they may actively mislead rationally ignorant and rationally irrational voters.

Chapter 5 compares the informational incentives of "voting with your feet" to those of conventional ballot box voting. Instead of seeking redress through electoral politics, citizens who dislike the policies they live under can sometimes pursue improvement by moving to another jurisdiction with more favorable policies, or by making choices in the private sector.

Unlike ballot box voting, "foot voting" creates much better incentives to both acquire information and use it rationally. The reason is simple: for most foot voters, the choice to leave or stay is individually decisive. The would-be migrant does not have to take a vote in which her ballot has only a miniscule chance of making a difference. Rather, she knows that whatever decision she makes she can then implement, subject perhaps to the agreement of a few family members. This simple point has important implications for institutional design in democratic political systems. It strengthens the case for decentralizing political power. The greater the degree of decentralization, the more political decisions can be made by foot voting, rather than ballot box voting alone.

The informational advantages of foot voting also buttress the case for limiting the scope of government authority relative to the private sector. In markets and civil society, individuals can often vote with their feet even more effectively than in a system of decentralized federalism. Foot voting in the private sector usually doesn't carry moving costs as high as those of interjurisdictional migration. In addition, limiting the scope of government could alleviate information problems by reducing the knowledge burden imposed on voters. The smaller and less complex government is, the more likely that even rationally ignorant voters might be able to understand its functions. Smaller government does not make us smarter in the sense of increasing our intelligence. But it can help us make smarter decisions by improving our incentives to make effective use of the intelligence we already have.

Chapter 6 considers the implications of political ignorance for the long-standing debate over the role of judicial review in a democracy. By constraining and (in some cases) decentralizing government power, judicial review can help mitigate the problem of political ignorance. Critics of judicial review have traditionally argued that the power of judges to invalidate laws enacted by democratically elected legislatures must be eliminated or severely constrained. Otherwise, democracy will be undermined, thus creating a "countermajoritarian difficulty." Recognition of the importance of political ignorance greatly weakens this long-standing objection to judicial power. Many of the policies enacted by modern states have little or no democratic pedigree because rationally ignorant voters know little about them, and may even be unaware of their very existence. Even some of those policies voters do know about have been enacted because they do not understand their true effects. By limiting the size and scope of government and facilitating "foot voting," judicial review might actually strengthen democratic accountability rather than undermine it.

Finally, Chapter 7 explores some of the best-known proposals for increasing the political knowledge of the electorate. These include limits on the franchise, improved civic education, changes in media coverage of politics, delegation of greater authority to experts, and proposals for requiring citizens to engage in greater deliberation. Some of these ideas have potential. But many run afoul of the reality that, in a world of rational ignorance, the major constraint on political knowledge is not the supply of information but the demand for it. Even if information is readily available, voters may be unwilling to take the time to learn it.

Proposals to increase political knowledge will also be difficult to effectively implement given real-world political constraints. The very political ignorance and irrationality that necessitates their consideration is a key obstacle to their enactment in a form likely to work. Any reform proposal would have to be enacted by a democratic process that is itself heavily influenced by ignorance. Moreover, it may be almost impossible to increase political knowledge enough to enable voters to cope effectively with more than a fraction of the many complex issues controlled by the modern state.

Given these constraints, we are unlikely to see major increases in political knowledge for some time to come, if ever. We must therefore find better ways to live with widespread political ignorance.

This book does not provide a complete analysis of the appropriate size, scope, and organization of government. Political ignorance is far from the only factor that must be taken account of in any such theory. But it deserves a much greater role in the discussion than it has gotten so far.

CHAPTER ONE

The Extent of Political Ignorance

Nothing strikes the student of public opinion and
democracy more forcefully than the paucity of
information most people possess about politics.

—POLITICAL SCIENTIST JOHN FEREJOHN[1]

THE REALITY THAT MOST voters are often ignorant of even very basic
political information is one of the better-established findings of social
science. Decades of accumulated evidence reinforces this conclusion.[2]

THE PERVASIVENESS OF IGNORANCE

The sheer depth of most individual voters' ignorance may be shocking to
readers not familiar with the research. Rarely if ever is any one piece of
knowledge absolutely essential to voters. It may not matter much if most
Americans are ignorant of one or another particular fact about politics.
But the pervasiveness of ignorance about a wide range of political issues
and leaders is far more troubling.

Many examples help illustrate the point. A series of polls conducted
just before the Republican Party chose Representative Paul Ryan to be
their vice-presidential nominee in August 2012 found that 43 percent
of Americans had never heard of Ryan and only 32 percent knew that
he was a member of the House of Representatives.[3] Unlike Governor
Sarah Palin in 2008, Ryan was not a relative unknown catapulted onto
the national stage by a vice-presidential nomination. As his party's leading spokesman on budgetary and fiscal issues, he had been a prominent
figure in American politics for several years.

One of the key policy positions staked out by President Barack Obama
in his successful 2012 reelection campaign was his plan to raise income
taxes for persons earning over $250,000 per year, an idea much discussed

during the campaign and supported by a large majority of the public—69 percent in a December 2012 Pew Research Center poll.[4] A February 2012 survey conducted for the political newspaper *The Hill* actually asked respondents what tax rates people with different income levels should pay. It found that 75 percent of likely voters wanted the highest-income earners to pay taxes lower than 30 percent of income, the top rate at the time of the 2012 election.[5] This inconsistency suggests that many people supported increasing the tax rates of high earners because they did not realize how high taxes were already.

Despite years of controversy over the War on Terror, the Iraq War, and American relations with the Muslim world, only 32 percent of Americans in a 2007 survey could name "Sunni" or "Sunnis" as one of "the two major branches of Islam" whose adherents "are seeking political control in Iraq," even though the question prompted them with the name of the other major branch (the Shiites).[6] Such basic knowledge is not, perhaps, essential to evaluation of U.S. policy toward the Muslim world. But it would at least be useful.

Equally striking is the fact that in late 2003, over 60 percent of Americans did not realize that a massive increase in domestic spending had made a substantial contribution to the recent explosion in the federal deficit.[7] Most of the public is unaware of a wide range of important government programs structured as tax deductions and payments for services.[8] As a result, they are also unaware of the massive extent to which most of these programs transfer benefits primarily to the relatively affluent.[9]

A survey taken immediately after the closely contested November 2002 congressional elections found that only about 32 percent of respondents knew that the Republicans had held control of the House of Representatives prior to the election.[10] This result is consistent with research showing widespread ignorance of congressional party control in previous elections, though usually knowledge levels were higher than in 2002.[11]

Such widespread ignorance is not of recent origin. As of December 1994, a month after the takeover of Congress by Newt Gingrich's Republicans, 57 percent of Americans had never even heard of Gingrich, whose campaign strategy and policy stances had received massive publicity in the immediately preceding weeks.[12] In 1964, in the midst of the Cold War, only 38 percent were aware that the Soviet Union was *not* a member of the U.S.-led NATO alliance.[13] Later, in 1986, the majority could not identify Mikhail Gorbachev, the controversial new leader of the Soviet Union, by name.[14] Much of the time, only a bare majority know which party has control of the Senate, some 70 percent cannot name both of their state's senators, and the majority cannot name *any* congressional candidate in their district at the height of a campaign.[15]

Three aspects of voter ignorance deserve particular attention. First, many voters are ignorant not just about specific policy issues but about the basic structure of government and how it operates.[16] Majorities are ignorant of such basic aspects of the U.S. political system as who has the power to declare war, the respective functions of the three branches of government, and who controls monetary policy.[17] A 2006 Zogby poll found that only 42 percent of Americans could even name the three branches of the federal government: executive, legislative, and judicial.[18] Another 2006 survey found that only 28 percent could name two or more of the five rights guaranteed by the First Amendment to the Constitution.[19] A 2002 Columbia University study indicated that 35 percent believed that Karl Marx's dictum "From each according to his ability to each according to his need" is in the Constitution (34 percent said they did not know), and only one-third understood that a Supreme Court decision overruling *Roe v. Wade* would not make abortion illegal throughout the country.[20]

Ignorance of the structure of government suggests that voters often not only cannot choose between specific competing policy *programs* but also cannot easily assign credit and blame for policy *outcomes* to the right office-holders. Ignorance of the constraints imposed on government by the Constitution may also give voters an inaccurate picture of the scope of elected officials' powers.

The second salient aspect of ignorance is that most voters lack an "ideological" view of politics capable of integrating multiple issues into a single analytical framework derived from a few basic principles; ordinary voters rarely exhibit the kind of ideological consistency in issue stances that are evident in surveys of political elites.[21] Some scholars follow Anthony Downs[22] in emphasizing the usefulness of ideology as a "shortcut" to predicting the likely policies of opposing parties competing for office.[23] At least equally important is the comparative inability of non-ideological voters to spot *interconnections* among issues. The small minority of well-informed voters are much better able to process new political information and more resistant to manipulation than is the less-informed mass public.[24]

Finally, and important, the level of political knowledge in the American electorate has increased only modestly, if at all, since the beginning of mass survey research in the late 1930s.[25] A relatively stable level of ignorance has persisted even in the face of massive increases in educational attainment and an unprecedented expansion in the quantity and quality of information available to the general public at little cost.[26]

For the most part, the spread of new information technology, such as television and the Internet, seems not to have increased political knowledge.[27] The rise of broadcast television in the 1950s and 1960s somewhat increased political knowledge among the poorest and least-informed segments of the population.[28] But more recent advances, such as cable television and the Internet, have actually diverted the attention of these groups away from political information by providing attractive alternative sources of entertainment.[29] For the most part, new information technologies seem to have been utilized to acquire political knowledge primarily by those who were already well-informed.[30] This record throws doubt on the expectation of political theorists from John Stuart Mill onward that an increased availability of information and formal education can create the informed electorate that the democratic ideal requires.[31]

RECENT EVIDENCE OF POLITICAL IGNORANCE

Data from the time of the recent 2010, 2008, and 2004 elections reaffirm the existence of widespread political ignorance, as does more extensive data from the time of the 2000 election derived from the 2000 American National Election Studies (ANES).[32] Unfortunately, the manuscript for this book was completed too soon to take much account of data from the 2012 presidential election. But, so far, there is no indication of a major increase in political knowledge in that election cycle relative to previous ones, and at least some evidence of persistent ignorance.[33]

Political Ignorance and the 2010 Election

The 2010 election was arguably one of the most important midterm elections in recent American history. The issues at stake included the federal government's handling of the worst recession and financial crisis in decades, the enactment of the Obama administration's historic 2010 health reform bill, and the conduct of ongoing conflicts in Afghanistan and Iraq. The Republican Party gained sixty-two seats in the House of Representatives—the largest swing in the House since 1948, and six in the Senate. In view of the importance of the issues at stake, one might expect voters to have paid closer attention to politics than usual. Nonetheless, survey data show extensive ignorance and confusion even about basic issues.

Table 1.1 compiles data on political knowledge from a variety of surveys conducted during 2010, while the election campaign was ongoing or immediately afterward. The data show that the majority of the public were well informed about a few very basic points. For example, 77 percent knew that the federal budget deficit was larger in 2010 than in the 1990s, and 73 percent knew that Congress had enacted a health care reform bill in 2010. A bare majority of 53 percent knew that the unemployment rate was around 10 percent, rather than 5 percent, 15, or 20.

On many other basic questions related to key issues in the election, the majority of Americans were strikingly uninformed. Perhaps the biggest issue in the election was the state of the economy, which was beginning to come out of the deepest recession in decades. A CNN poll taken just before the election found that 52 percent of Americans identified "the economy" as the most important issue facing the nation.[34] Yet an October 2010 survey showed that 67 percent of Americans were unaware that the economy had grown during the previous year, with 61 percent wrongly believing that it had shrunk. It is certainly true that the economy was in relatively poor shape in 2010. But knowing whether it was growing or shrinking was surely a relevant consideration for voters seeking to evaluate incumbent political leaders' performance on what most of them believed to be the single most important issue. It was not the only information that could have been useful to voters, but it was clearly important nonetheless.

TABLE 1.1   *Political ignorance and the 2010 election*

Question (date of survey)	% Correct Answer	% Wrong Answer	% Admit Don't Know
Knew that the deficit in 2010 was larger than in the 1990s (Nov. 11–14, 2010)	77	12	11
Knew that Congress had passed a health care reform bill in 2010 (July 1–5, 2010)	73	14	13
Knew that the unemployment rate was 10 percent (rather than 5, 15, or 20) (Nov. 11–14, 2010)	53	30	17
Knew that Republicans won control of the House of Representatives, but not the Senate in the 2010 election (Nov. 11–14, 2010)	46	27	27
Knew that U.S. forces suffered more combat deaths in Afghanistan than in Iraq in 2009 (Jan. 14–17, 2010)	43	32	25
Knew that the Obama stimulus bill included at least "some" tax cuts (Nov. 6–15, 2010)[a]	43	54	3
Knew that defense is the largest category of spending in the federal budget (Nov. 11–14, 2010)[b]	39	42	19
Knew that Harry Reid is the majority leader of the Senate (Jan. 14–17, 2010)	38	18	44
Knew that John Boehner would be the new speaker of the House of Representatives (Nov. 11–14, 2010)	38	24	38
Knew the TARP bailout bill was enacted under Bush rather than Obama (July 1–5, 2010	34	47	19
Knew that the economy grew during 2010 (October 24–26, 2010)[c]	33	61	6
Knew that John Roberts is the chief justice of the Supreme Court (July 1–5, 2010)	28	18	53
Knew that David Cameron is the prime minister of Great Britain (Nov. 11–14, 2010)	15	25	60

SOURCES: Data from Pew Research Center surveys, date as indicated, unless otherwise noted.

a. World Public Opinion/Knowledge Networks poll, Nov. 6–15, 2010.

b. The options given on this question were "national defense," "education," "Medicare," and "Interest on the debt."

c. Bloomberg National News survey, Oct. 24–26, 2010.

Perhaps the most important measure that the federal government adopted to try to end the recession that began in 2008 was President Obama's 2009 stimulus bill. Yet 57 percent of the public did not realize that the bill included tax cuts, even though tax cuts in fact accounted for some $275 billion of the total $819 billion in stimulus spending in the bill.[35] Similarly, only 34 percent of the public realized that the Troubled Assets Relief Program bank bailout bill had been enacted under President George W. Bush, with 47 percent wrongly believing that it was enacted under President Obama. Controversy over the effectiveness or lack thereof of the TARP was one of the biggest points at issue between the parties in the 2010 election, with many Republicans criticizing the bill and blaming the Democrats for it.

The Republicans also focused heavily on federal spending as a crucial issue in the campaign. But a November poll taken just after the election found that only 39 percent of the public was aware of the basic fact that defense spending was a larger proportion of the federal budget than education, the Medicare health care program, and interest on the national debt. Understanding the current distribution of federal spending can help voters evaluate what changes should be made in the future.

There was also extensive public ignorance about non-economic issues at stake in the campaign. The majority of the public did not know that the United States suffered more combat casualties in Afghanistan than in Iraq during 2009, which perhaps indicates a failure to fully understand the Obama administration's strategy of shifting U.S. military efforts away from Iraq to Afghanistan. Knowing the relative numbers of casualties might also be useful information for voters seeking to weigh the potential benefits of these wars against their costs.

The 2010 campaign also saw extensive controversy over the role of the conservative majority on the Supreme Court, especially the Court's much-debated decision in *Citizens United v. Federal Election Commission*,[36] which struck down legislation limiting the use of corporate and union funds for election advertising. President Obama and other Democrats repeatedly attacked the Court during the campaign. The role of the Court was also extensively discussed during the summer 2010 confirmation hearings for Elena Kagan, the president's second nominee to the Supreme Court. But a July survey found that only 28 percent of Americans could identify John Roberts—leader of the conservative majority on the Court—as the chief justice of the United States. It is theoretically possible for voters to have a good knowledge of the Court's decisions without knowing the names of any of the justices, and some probably do have such knowledge. However, a citizen who paid more than minimal attention to the extensive press coverage of the Court would be likely to run across the chief justice's name multiple times. Moreover, the performance of the conservative majority led by Roberts was one of the key points at issue in the political debate over the Court's role.

Over 60 percent of the public was unable to identify Senate Majority Leader Harry Reid, a key player in the enactment of the stimulus and health care bills that had been at the heart of the Democrats' legislative agenda in 2009 and 2010.[37] Great Britain continued to be the United States's most important ally in the escalating fighting in Afghanistan, as well as a crucial partner on other foreign policy issues and on coordinating economic policy in the midst of a global recession. But only 15 percent of Americans could identify David Cameron as the prime minister of Great Britain. Knowing the names of Reid and Cameron is not essential for informed voting. In theory, a voter can be highly knowledgeable about policy issues but ignorant of the names of individual political leaders. However, citizens who paid more than minimal attention to domestic policy issues were likely to run across Reid's name on numerous occasions, and those who pay attention to foreign policy could hardly avoid Cameron's.

In the aftermath of the election, only 46 percent of the public realized that the Republicans had won control of the House of Representatives but not the Senate, and only 38 percent could identify John Boehner as the new speaker of the House of Representatives.

All of the questions above were posed as multiple-choice items. As a result, they likely understate the true degree of ignorance, because some survey respondents prefer to guess on questions when they don't know the right answer rather than admit that they don't know it.[38] Even purely random guessing has a substantial probability of arriving at the right answer on a survey question with only three or four choices.

Political Ignorance and the 2008 Election

Perhaps to an even greater extent than the 2010 midterm election, the 2008 election was an unusually important one. The issues at stake included the conduct of the wars in Afghanistan and Iraq, the future of the health care system, a mortgage default crisis, and the government's developing response to the financial crisis that hit in September 2008—in the middle of the campaign.

As in 2010, a majority of the public did display impressive knowledge about some of the very basic issues at stake in the campaign. For example, by the summer of 2008, some 76 percent of Americans recognized that Democratic nominee Barack Obama supported a timetable for the withdrawal of U.S. troops from Iraq, and 62 percent knew that Republican candidate John McCain opposed it (Table 1.2). By October, some 66 percent knew that Nancy Pelosi was the speaker of the House of Representatives, an increase from several months earlier and an indication that the public was paying some attention to congressional races. Similarly, 61 percent knew that the Democratic Party controlled the House of Representatives before the election.

Public knowledge of even slightly less basic matters was much worse. During the Democratic primaries, health care was a major point of contention in the close race between Barack Obama and Senator Hillary Clinton. Obama forcefully criticized Clinton for proposing a plan requiring all Americans to have health insurance.[39] But only 48 percent of survey respondents realized that *any* presidential candidate had proposed such a plan, and only 42 percent knew that Clinton had done so. Only 35 percent realized that Barack Obama had *not* proposed a plan of this type, while 24 percent wrongly believed that he did. Ironically, Obama later incorporated this aspect of Clinton's plan into his health care bill after he became president. But at the time of the 2008 primaries, this was a major issue of contention between the two candidates.

The Iraq War, the War on Terror, and U.S. relations with the Muslim world were a major focus of debate between the parties. But only 20 percent could identify Sunni Muslims as the largest "group of Muslims worldwide." Conflicts between Sunnis and Shiites had complicated U.S. policy in Iraq and the Middle East as a whole.

TABLE 1.2   *Political ignorance and the 2008 election*

Question (date of survey)	% Correct Answer	% Wrong Answer	% Admit Don't Know
Knew Obama supported a timetable for withdrawal from Iraq (June 18–29, 2008)[a]	76	6	19
Knew Nancy Pelosi was the speaker of the House of Representatives (Oct. 3–6, 2008)[b*]	66	34	
Knew John McCain opposed a timetable for withdrawal from Iraq (June 18–29, 2008)[a]	62	20	18
Know the Democrats controlled the House of Representatives before the election (Oct. 29–31, 2008)[c]	61	22	18
Know Saddam Hussein was not "directly involved" in the September 11 attacks[d]	56	34	10
Knew that at least one presidential candidate had proposed a health care plan requiring all Americans to have health insurance (Feb. 14–24, 2008)[e]	48	23	28
Knew that Hillary Clinton had proposed a plan requiring all Americans to have health insurance (Feb. 14–24, 2008)[e**]	42	31	27
Knew that Condoleeza Rice was the secretary of state (April 30–June 1, 2008)[a*]	42	3	55
Knew that Nancy Pelosi was the speaker of the House of Representatives (June 18–19, 2008)[f*]	39	3	58
Knew that Ben Bernanke was chairman of the Federal Reserve Board (June 18–19, 2008)[f]	36	29	35
Knew that Henry (Hank) Paulson was secretary of the treasury (Oct. 3–6, 2008)[g*]	36	64	
Knew that Gordon Brown was the prime minister of Great Britain (April 30–June 1, 2008)	28	14	58

When the financial crisis hit in September 2008, the TARP bill and other elements of the federal response were headed by Secretary of the Treasury Henry "Hank" Paulson. A September 29 *Newsweek* cover even dubbed Paulson "King Henry" because of his dominant role in the crisis.[40] But an October poll found that only 36 percent of the public knew that Paulson was secretary of the treasury. Paulson, the financial crisis, and the TARP bill became major campaign issues.

TABLE 1.2   *(continued)*

Question (date of survey)	% Correct Answer	% Wrong Answer	% Admit Don't Know
Knew that the Sunnis are the largest "group of Muslims worldwide" (June 18–19, 2008)[f]	20	41	39
Knew that John Roberts is the chief justice of the Supreme Court (June 18–19, 2008)[f*]	15	7	78
Knew Obama did not propose the plan requiring all Americans to have health insurance (Feb. 14–24, 2008)[e***]	35	24	41
Knew that U.S. defense spending is between $400 billion and $599 billion per year (June 17–26, 2008)[h]	7	48	45

NOTE: In a few cases, this table counts some respondents who refused to answer in the same category as those who said that they did not know. Research suggests that it is very rare for respondents who know the correct answer to a question to refuse to give it.

* Indicates not a multiple-choice question.

** The figures in the table count as giving "wrong" answers those who said they did not believe any candidate had proposed such a plan. In the Kaiser survey, only those respondents who said they thought at least one candidate had proposed it were asked specific questions about individual candidates' positions.

*** The figures in the table count as correct answers for Obama the 23 percent of respondents who stated that no presidential candidate had proposed such a plan, as well as the 12 percent who correctly recognized that at least one candidate had, but also knew that Obama had not.

a. Pew Research Center survey.

b. *Time* survey, Oct. 3–6, 2008.

c. CBS News poll, Oct. 29–31, 2008.

d. Newsweek/Princeton Survey Research Associates poll.

e. Henry Kaiser Foundation/Harvard School of Public Health poll.

f. *Newsweek*/Princeton Survey Research Associates poll.

g. *Time* survey, Oct. 3–6, 2008. Both "Henry" and "Hank" Paulson were counted as correct answers.

h. Public Interest Project/Greenberg Quinlan Rosner Research poll, June 17–26, 2008.

A June survey found that only 36 percent could identify Ben Bernanke as the chairman of the Federal Reserve Board. Admittedly, this was before the financial crisis hit and before Bernanke emerged as a key policymaker in forging the federal government's response to it. However, the Federal Reserve's policies were already controversial as possible causes of the ongoing mortgage default crisis and for supposedly failing to stem America's slide into recession.

In view of the ongoing debate over the economy, spending, and the federal budget deficit, it is perhaps noteworthy that only 7 percent could correctly place federal defense spending—the largest single item in the federal budget—within the correct $200 billion range ($400 to $599 billion). While few would argue that voters need to know the precise amount of defense spending, approximate knowledge could still be useful. Only an additional 11 percent could place the level of defense spending within the two closest $200 billion ranges ($200 to $399 billion or $600 to $799 billion).[41] Thus only 18 percent could place defense spending within the correct *$600 billion range* in a survey where three of the six available options would count as correct by that standard.

Political Ignorance and the 2004 Election

The 2004 election campaign was a crucial contest involving important issues including terrorism, the Iraq War, and the future of key questions in economic and social policy. However, Table 1.3 presents evidence from a number of surveys that showed evidence of extensive political ignorance on major issues in the current campaign.

The data cover a number of basic questions related to widely discussed issues that were prominent in both press coverage and political debate. Perhaps the most disturbing result was that large majorities were unaware of the passage of some of the most important and controversial items on the Bush administration's domestic policy agenda: almost 70 percent did not know of the passage of the massive Medicare prescription drug benefit, and nearly 65 percent did not know of the recent passage of a ban on "partial birth" abortion. Similarly, 58 percent admitted they had heard "very little" or "nothing" about the USA PATRIOT Act, the much-debated 2001 legislation that increased law enforcement powers for the claimed purpose of fighting terrorism. This result probably actually understated the number of respondents who knew little or nothing about the Act.[42]

The survey evidence also indicates considerable ignorance about various hot-button domestic and foreign policy issues. Despite widespread press coverage of large job gains in the months prior to the election,[43] the majority of respondents in a June 2004 poll mistakenly believed that there had been a net loss of jobs in 2004. With regard to the most important foreign policy issue in the campaign, a majority mistakenly believed that the Bush administration claimed a link between Saddam

TABLE 1.3   *Political ignorance and the 2004 election*

Question (date of survey)	% Correct Answer	% Wrong Answer	% Don't Know
Knew that defense spending is one of the two largest expenditure areas in the federal budget (Mar. 15–May 11, 2004)[a]	51	43	6
Knew the approximate number of U.S. troops killed in Iraq (April 23–25, 2004)[b]	40 (within 200)	34	26
Knew that increased spending on domestic programs has contributed at least "some" to the current federal budget deficit (Feb. 11–16, 2004)[c]	39	57	4
Claimed to have heard or read at least "some" information about the USA PATRIOT Act (Apr. 28, 2004)b	39 ("some" (27) or "a lot" (12))	58 ("not much" (28) or "nothing" (30))	3
Knew that there had been a net increase in jobs during 2004 (June 7–9)[d]	36	61	3
Knew that Congress had recently passed a bill banning "partial birth" abortions (Dec. 7–9, 2003)[a]	36	17	48
Knew that Congress had recently passed a Medicare prescription drug benefit (Apr. 15, 2004)[a]	31	16	54
Knew that Social Security spending is one of the two largest expenditure areas in the federal budget (Mar. 15– May 11, 2004)[a]	32	62	6
Knew that the Bush administration did not believe that Saddam Hussein was involved in the 9/11 attacks (Dec. 14–15, 2003)[b]	25	58	17
Knew that the current unemployment rate was lower than the average rate for the past thirty years (Mar. 23, 2004)[e]	22	63	15
Claimed to know at least a "fair amount" about the European Union (May 21–23, 2004)[f]	22 ("great deal" (3) or "fair amount" (19))	77 ("very little" (37) or "nothing" (40))	1

a. Princeton Survey Research Associates survey.

b. *New York Times*/CBS survey.

c. Pew Research Center survey, Feb. 11–16, 2004.

d. AP/IPSOS Public Affairs poll, June 7–9, 2004.

e. Fox News/Opinion Dynamics survey, March 23–24, 2004.

f. Gallup survey, May 21–23, 2004.

Hussein and the September 11 attacks (despite the administration's own repeated disclaimers of any such connection), and most did not know approximately how many American lives had been lost in the Iraq War. Similarly, despite the ongoing debate over America's troubled relationship with Europe in the wake of the Iraq War, 77 percent admitted that they knew "little" or "nothing" about the European Union. Knowing the number of Americans killed in Iraq was not absolutely essential to developing an informed opinion on the war. But it was certainly relevant information for voters seeking to balance the war's possible benefits against its costs.

On many issues, the majority were not only ignorant of the truth but actively misinformed. For example, 61 percent believed that there has been a net loss of jobs in 2004, 58 percent believed that the administration saw a link between Saddam Hussein and 9/11, and 57 percent believed that increases in domestic spending had *not* contributed significantly to the current federal budget deficit.

The data in Table 1.3 should not be taken as proof that the public was universally ignorant on every issue. Some basic facts about current public policy *were* well known. For example, 82 percent knew that there was a federal budget deficit,[44] and 79 percent knew that the deficit had increased during the previous four years.[45] Nonetheless the evidence compiled in 1.3 does show that majorities were ignorant of numerous basic facts on some of the most important and most widely debated issues at stake in the election. This result is particularly striking in view of the extremely close and controversial nature of the contest, and the high level of press coverage many of these issues received.

Political Ignorance Evidence from the 2000 ANES Study

Undertaken during every election year since 1948, the survey by American National Election Studies (ANES) is generally considered the most thorough social scientific survey of the U.S. electorate.

The 2000 ANES survey contained a total of thirty political knowledge-relevant questions,[46] more than any other recent ANES survey.[47] These are listed in Table 1.4 along with the percentage of respondents giving correct answers.

TABLE I.4 *Political knowledge questions from the 2000 American National Election Studies survey*

Item	% Giving Correct Answer
Could identify Texas as the home state of George W. Bush*	90
Knew Bill Clinton was moderate or liberal	81
Knew Al Gore favored a higher level of government spending on services than George W. Bush	73
Knew Democratic vice-presidential candidate Joe Lieberman is Jewish	70
Could identify Tennessee as the home state of Al Gore*	68
Knew the Federal budget deficit decreased, 1992–2000	58
Knew Gore is more liberal than Bush	57
Knew Democrats favored a higher level of government spending on services than Republicans	57
Could identify the post held by Attorney General Janet Reno*	55
Knew Republicans controlled the House of Representatives before the election	55
Knew Gore was more supportive of gun control than Bush	51
Knew Republicans controlled the Senate before the election	50
Knew Democrats were more supportive of government guarantee of jobs and standard of living than Republicans	49
Knew George W. Bush was conservative	47 (30 Chose Moderate)
Knew Gore was more supportive of abortion rights than Bush	46
Knew Gore was more supportive of government guarantee of jobs and standard of living than Bush	46
Knew Democrats favored a higher level of government aid to blacks than Republicans	45
Knew Gore was more supportive of environmental regulation than Bush	44
Knew Bush was more likely to favor jobs over the environment than Gore	41
Knew presidential candidate Pat Buchanan was conservative	40
Knew Gore favored a higher level of government aid to blacks than Bush	40
Knew Al Gore was liberal	38 (36 Chose Moderate)

TABLE 1.4 *(continued)*

Item	% Giving Correct Answer
Knew federal spending on the poor increased, 1992–2000	37
Knew the crime rate decreased, 1992–2000	37
Could identify the post held by British prime minister Tony Blair*	35
Could identify Connecticut as the home state of Democratic vice presidential candidate Joe Lieberman*	30
Could identify Wyoming as the home state of Republican vice-presidential candidate Dick Cheney*	19
Could correctly name at least one candidate for the House of Representatives in the respondent's district*	15
Could identify the post held by Senate Majority Leader Trent Lott*	9
Could correctly name a second candidate for the House of Representatives in the respondent's district.*	4

NOTES: All percentages are rounded to whole numbers. N = 1,545 respondents. The exact wording of questions is available from the author or can be found in the 2000 ANES codebook available for downloading at the ICPSR website: http://www.icpsr.umich.edu/index-medium. html. A list of coding changes is available from the author upon request.
*Not a multiple-choice question.

The vast majority of the thirty survey items identified in Table 1.4 are relatively basic in nature and would have been well known to political elites and activists at the time.[48] Many addressed issues that were widely debated during the 2000 campaign, including environmental policy, government spending on public services, abortion, and others. Several questions related to factual matters relevant to the record of the Clinton administration, for which presidential candidate Al Gore and the Democratic Party more generally attempted to claim a share of the credit.[49]

While the thirty questions do not cover all possible relevant issues and facts, they do include a wide range of topics and therefore are a good representative sampling of Americans' political knowledge. Moreover, previous studies have found that political knowledge in one area is usually highly correlated with knowledge in others.[50] Thus we can be reasonably confident that individuals who scored well on the thirty items in the 2000 ANES survey on average possessed greater political knowledge on other matters than those who scored low. Ignorance of one or a few factual details on this or other surveys may not indicate much about the respondent's overall level of political knowledge. But broad ignorance across a wide range of survey items is more telling.

A Glass Half-Empty or Half-Full: How Low Is the Knowledge Level Revealed in the ANES Data?

The average knowledge level in the 2000 ANES survey was generally low. On average, respondents answered only 14.3 questions correctly out of 30.[51] The data seem to confirm Stephen Bennett's earlier findings that about one-third of respondents are "know-nothings" possessing little or no politically relevant knowledge.[52] About 25 percent of respondents got 8.5 correct answers or fewer.[53] Since 17 of the 30 questions had only three possible answers,[54] two had only two possible answers,[55] one more had two correct answers out of a possible three,[56] and several others could also potentially be guessed with lower probabilities of success,[57] a score of 8.5[58] is roughly equal to the score that could be expected as the result of random guessing.[59] My finding of 25 percent "know-nothings" is similar to Bennett's finding of 29 percent.[60]

Nonetheless, it is possible to argue that the average knowledge level revealed in the 2000 ANES study is not too low because the average respondent did achieve correct answers on almost half the questions (48 percent). This claim is flawed for two reasons. First, with a few exceptions, the items in the survey represent very basic political knowledge. Knowledgeable political activists and even citizens who follow politics reasonably closely would probably be able to answer all but a tiny handful of the questions correctly.

The second reason for pessimism regarding the 2000 ANES study results is that they may actually overestimate political knowledge levels. This overestimation is the result of two factors. First, as already noted, multiple choice surveys in general somewhat overestimate the amount of political information possessed by the public because of the possibility of guessing by respondents and because more knowledgeable citizens may be overrepresented among those surveyed.[61] The average respondent in the 2000 ANES study got only about six more correct answers out of thirty than would be expected as a result of random guessing.[62] Although ANES respondents had the option of giving "don't know" answers to questions, past research shows that survey respondents often express opinions about issues they know nothing about to avoid seeming ignorant.[63] Thus it seems likely that many respondents who did not know the answer to various knowledge questions attempted to guess, especially on those items that had only two or three possible answers.

Second, three of the five items with the highest percentage of correct answers represent personal information about candidates in the 2000 election that had little or no value for understanding politics more generally.[64] These three items are the home states of George W. Bush and Al Gore (90 percent and 68 percent correct answers respectively), and Joe Lieberman's religion (70 percent). Bill Clinton's ideology, the second-highest scoring item (81 percent correct answers), is an artifact of generous coding on my part, under which both "liberal" and "moderate" answers were deemed correct. Eliminating the three high-scoring low-value items and two other similar questions which produced much lower percentages of correct answers,[65] produces an average score of 11.5 correct answers out of 25 questions.[66] Much more significantly, the elimination of the five low-value questions (while retaining the Clinton ideology question) increases the proportion of "know-nothings" to about 34 percent.[67] Table 1.5 summarizes the aggregate results of three knowledge scales from the 2000 ANES survey.

TABLE 1.5   *Aggregate knowledge scales from the 2000 American National Election Studies survey*

Scale	Average Number of Correct Answers	% "Know-Nothing" Respondents
30-Question Scale	14.3 (48%)	25
25-Question Scale (Excluding 5 low-value questions)	11.6 (46%)	34
24-Question Scale (Excluding 5 low-value questions and the Clinton ideology question)	0.8 (45%)	35*

*"Know-nothings" include those who scored 7.5 or fewer correct answers out of 24. The calculation is identical to that used for the 25-question scale, except that I subtracted .67 from the expected score based on random guessing to account for the absence of the Clinton item.

As Table 1.5 shows, the already low average knowledge scores on the 2000 ANES survey conceal the existence of a large political knowledge underclass of "know-nothings" who possess very little if any basic political knowledge at all. Depending on which scale is used, this group constitutes from 25 percent to 35 percent of the American public.

Overall, considering the very basic nature of the questions asked, the possibility of guessing, and the high percentage of "know-nothing" respondents, it is difficult to avoid the conclusion that the 2000 ANES survey, like most research using earlier evidence, reveals a low level of political knowledge.

Open-Ended Questions Versus Multiple-Choice Questions

Some scholars claim that open-ended questions severely underestimate the true level of public knowledge because multiple-choice questions often produce better results. For example, a much higher percentage of respondents can identify the chief justice of the Supreme Court in a multiple-choice survey than an open-ended one.[68] A recent study by political scientists Robert Luskin and John Bullock provides evidence suggesting that many of the criticisms of open-ended questions are overstated.[69] In addition, multiple-choice surveys have their own flaws. They overestimate political knowledge because respondents can get the right answer by guessing, and many will do so rather than admit that they don't know the correct answer to a survey question.[70] Moreover, a person who can give the right answer to an open-ended question is likely to know more about the subject in question than one who can only do so if prompted by a multiple-choice format.

The reasonable solution is to make use of both kinds of questions, while keeping in mind their limitations. The vast majority of the questions cited in this chapter are multiple choice, thereby ensuring that they tend to overestimate knowledge levels rather than underestimate them. I have clearly marked the few questions in the tables that are not multiple choice. In my analysis of the 2000 ANES survey, I have chosen not to include an open-ended question about the identity of the chief justice of the Supreme Court that has been the object of particularly detailed criticism.[71]

Finally, we should keep in mind that the vast majority of survey questions posed to the general public by pollsters are fairly simple compared to the full universe of available information on politics and public policy.[72] The questions analyzed in this chapter are overwhelmingly both multiple choice and addressed to comparatively simple factual issues.

Voters and Nonvoters

It is probable that the true knowledge level of the electorate is higher than surveys of the general public suggest, because relatively ignorant people who are eligible to vote are less likely to vote than those who are more knowledgeable. Surveys suggest that the least knowledgeable citizens are less likely to vote and engage in other forms of political participation.[73] However, the differences in voting rates between the knowledgeable and the ignorant are smaller than most surveys suggest, because more knowledgeable citizens are far more likely to falsely report voting than less knowledgeable ones.[74] Age, income, interest in politics, and degree of commitment to an ideology are strongly correlated with misreporting voting,[75] and also with political knowledge.[76] People who are knowledgeable and interested in politics but still choose not to vote are more likely to feel guilty for doing so, and therefore less willing to admit their nonvoting to pollsters. As a result, the voting population is probably much closer in knowledge level to the general public than might be supposed.

Moreover, even if nonvoters are disproportionately ignorant, their lack of political knowledge may not be completely harmless. If they knew more, they could potentially cast better-informed ballots, thereby improving the knowledge level of the electorate.

IMPLICATIONS

Extensive evidence suggests that most Americans have little political knowledge. That ignorance covers knowledge of specific issues, knowledge of political leaders and parties, and knowledge of political institutions. The evidence extends to many of the crucial issues at stake in recent elections in 2004, 2008, and 2010. The latter two campaigns were especially important for shaping policy on major issues, such as the economy, health care, and the wars in Iraq and Afghanistan. Moreover, most of the evidence of ignorance relates to fairly basic issues about the politicians, parties, issues, and the structure of politics.

These results do not by themselves prove that voter knowledge levels are inadequate. Perhaps a little knowledge goes a long way. Nonetheless, the extent of public ignorance is great enough to suggest that voter knowledge optimists at least have their work cut out for them.

Still, we cannot really know whether current levels of political knowledge are adequate until we have a standard to measure them by. The next chapter explains how public knowledge levels fall short of the standards demanded by several prominent theories of democratic participation.

CHAPTER TWO

Do Voters Know Enough?

The typical citizen drops down to a lower level of mental performance
as soon as he enters the political field. He argues and analyzes in
a way which he would readily recognize as infantile within the
sphere of his real interests. He becomes a primitive again.

—JOSEPH A. SCHUMPETER[1]

HOW MUCH SHOULD VOTERS KNOW? Is it enough if they know only
a few basic facts about politics? Or should they understand far more
than that, perhaps even become amateur policy wonks? Is mere factual
knowledge enough, or do voters also need to know some political philosophy? It all depends on what kind of democracy we want to have.
Different theories of democratic participation give divergent answers to
these questions. Some demand far more of voters than others. Unfortunately, voter knowledge often falls short of the requirements of even the
less demanding theories.

To demonstrate this point, we must compare the actual level of
political knowledge to that demanded by four prominent theories of
representation. In ascending order of their knowledge requirements,
the four are retrospective voting,[2] Burkean trusteeship,[3] representation
of popular preferences on specific issues,[4] and deliberative democracy.[5]
All four theories require substantial levels of political knowledge in the
electorate to ensure majoritarian control of the legislative process. This
conclusion is particularly important in the case of the first two, which
are often thought to require very little of voters. For the most part, the
various theories all require not only that voters have opinions on various
issues but that those opinions be at least minimally informed. Otherwise,
there is no reason to believe that, even if the voters are able to get their
way, the resulting policies will actually serve their underlying objectives.[6]

No theory requires voters to have anything approaching a complete knowledge of all the issues. But all require knowledge of at least some crucial basic facts. Unfortunately, the public falls short relative to all four. It is not possible here to consider every conceivable theory of democratic political participation. But these four are extremely well-known and represent a wide range of potential knowledge prerequisites. If public knowledge is insufficient to meet the requirements of even the least demanding of them, it is likely that political ignorance is a serious problem indeed.

Later in the chapter, we take up a question that has largely been neglected by democratic theory: Is it possible for voters to know *too much*?[7] If it is common for political knowledge to cause more harm than good, then we need not be as concerned about political ignorance. It turns out that scenarios in which ignorance is beneficial can indeed occur. But most such cases are situations where knowledge in one area is harmful because of ignorance about another. Overall, beneficial political ignorance is the exception rather than the rule.

This chapter only assesses individual political knowledge. It does not consider arguments suggesting that voters can use "information shortcuts" to make up for low knowledge levels. Perhaps information shortcuts make voters a lot better informed than they seem. And even if individual voters aren't up to the standards demanded by democratic theory, perhaps the electorate as a whole is more knowledgeable than the sum of its parts. These crucial questions are dealt with in a later chapter.[8] But they would not have to be addressed at all if individual voters' knowledge were adequate on its own.

DO KNOWLEDGE LEVELS MEET THE DEMANDS OF DEMOCRATIC THEORY?

Since ancient times, political philosophers have debated the extent of knowledge voters need to have to make democracy work.[9] In modern political thought, retrospective voting, issue representation, Burkean trusteeship, and deliberative democracy are probably the most widely accepted theories of participation. Each has implicit knowledge prerequisites that voters must meet.

Retrospective Voting

Retrospective voting is often considered the least demanding theory of participation. It holds that when voters have the ability to remove leaders whose performance they deem unsatisfactory, they can achieve adequate majoritarian control of government. According to economist Joseph Schumpeter, the most famous modern exponent of the theory, "electorates normally do not control their political leaders in any way except by refusing to reelect them" when dissatisfied with their efforts.[10] Advocates of retrospective voting hope that "the replacement of officials" by popular vote will discipline political leaders because "the electorate can change officials if many people are dissatisfied or hope for better performance."[11]

The theory assumes that citizens can assess the performance of incumbent office-holders and vote to remove those who perform badly or those likely to be inferior to their competitors, from whom we can expect "better performance."[12] Thus, at the very least, retrospective voting requires that the electorate possess sufficient knowledge to determine how well political leaders are performing their assigned duties.

Political scientist Morris Fiorina famously argued that this task is easily accomplished because "[i]n order to ascertain whether the incumbents have performed poorly or well, citizens need only calculate the changes in their own welfare."[13] Unfortunately, such a formulation underestimates the knowledge burden that the theory of retrospective voting requires of citizens.

To assess the impact of incumbent office-holders on "their own welfare," citizens must first know which parts of their "welfare" government can affect. For example, they may need to determine whether a recession has been caused by political leaders' mistakes or by a business cycle downturn that those leaders had no ability to control. If the incumbents' policies were the best available given the circumstances, then it would be counterproductive for retrospective voters to punish them at the ballot box, even if a painful recession still occurred.

In addition to understanding whether government in general can affect a particular problem, citizens need to know which particular officials are responsible for a given issue area. Thus they need to know whether to blame federal, state, or local officeholders for a particular problem, or perhaps all three. In addition, citizens must know how a given problem or issue area has fared during the incumbent's term in office, something which cannot always be determined by looking merely at changes in one's own personal "welfare."

Finally, effective retrospective voting requires citizens to make some determination as to whether or not "better performance" can be expected with alternative policies.[14] Voting incumbents out of office can only succeed in forcing political leaders to attend to the needs of the electorate if the new leaders are likely to do better than their predecessors. If the incumbents' policies were the best that could be had under the circumstances, effective retrospective voters should retain them in office even if they remain unsatisfied with political or economic conditions.

It may be easy to determine that the opposition cannot be worse than the incumbents in those cases where the latter have presided over a massive, highly visible disaster such as the Great Depression of the 1930s. In most elections, however, there is no such vast disaster present; the relative performance of the incumbents is far more difficult to assess.

Thus retrospective voting has four major knowledge prerequisites. Voters must

1. Have some understanding of which problems are caused by government policies or can be alleviated by them
2. Know which incumbent office-holders are responsible for which issue areas
3. Know at least the basic facts about what happened with respect to those issues during the incumbent's term
4. Be able to determine, at least to some extent, whether the incumbents' policies were the best available under the circumstances, or whether their opponents' ideas might have fared better

It may be true that "retrospective voting requires far less of the voter than prospective voting," under which voters must assess the likely impact of opposing candidates' policies in advance.[15] Certainly, effective retrospective voting does not require anything approaching expert knowledge of issues. Nonetheless, it does call for a much greater level of political knowledge than the theory's more enthusiastic advocates acknowledge.[16]

The evidence suggests that voters often fall short of the knowledge prerequisites of retrospective voting. During the 2010 election, the state of the economy was by far the most important issue on the public agenda. Despite that fact, two-thirds of the public did not know that the economy had grown during the previous year, and 61 percent believed that it had actually shrunk.[17]

The 2000 American National Election Studies (ANES) survey also shed some light on the question of whether citizens possess basic knowledge about what has happened with respect to major issues during an incumbent's term. Only 37 percent of citizens knew that the crime rate had gone down during the term of the incumbent President Clinton, 37 percent knew that federal spending on the poor had gone up, and a more impressive 58 percent knew that the federal budget deficit had gone down.[18] Since crime, the deficit, and welfare reform were three of the most important political issues of the 1990s, and all three were stressed by both major parties, the low knowledge levels revealed in the 2000 ANES survey create room for serious doubt that the knowledge prerequisites of retrospective voting had been met for most citizens. Even the 58 percent figure for deficit reduction is not very substantial given the prominence of the issue in political discourse of the 1990s. Furthermore, for all three questions, the respondent got "credit" for a correct answer as long as he or she got the trend line correct; it could not catch mistakes such as underestimation or overestimation of the *degree* of change.[19] These results are consonant with research conducted by others, which shows that voters are often ignorant of very basic issue trends, such as inflation and unemployment.[20]

Given that majorities are often ignorant of basic information regarding trends in issues, it is hard to avoid the conclusion that most citizens fail to meet the knowledge prerequisites of the retrospective voting theory. Simply put, they often do not know what is going on. Even if they manage to surmount this particular hurdle, the low knowledge levels observed in surveys over the decades make it unlikely that the majority can achieve the more difficult tasks of (1) determining which problems can be affected by government policy and (2) understanding which officials are responsible for what issues. On the latter point, studies have repeatedly found that citizens have, at best, a very limited knowledge of how authority over issue areas is distributed in our complex political system.[21]

In addition to being a normative theory of political participation, retrospective voting is also the name of a commonly used information shortcut that voters often resort to. I discuss the shortcut in Chapter 4.

Burkean Trusteeship

The trustee theory of representation associated with eighteenth-century politician and political theorist Edmund Burke is another model that at first glance seems to require very little voter knowledge. Instead of deciding specific policy issues or even assessing the job performance of political leaders, Burke claimed that voters should choose representatives of superior judgment and virtue—a "natural aristocracy"—and then leave actual policy decisions to them.[22] Explicitly factoring voter ignorance into his theory, Burke argued that leaving political decisions to the discretion of an elected elite is the best option because most ordinary citizens lack sufficient sophistication to "think or act without direction."[23]

Superficially, it may seem that trusteeship theory places very little knowledge burden on voters. Instead of being forced to evaluate complex public policy options or even retrospectively assess the performance of incumbent office-holders, voters need only determine which candidate has the greatest ability and virtue—in other words, which would be the best trustee.

Unfortunately, however, the amount of knowledge necessary to make this decision is far from trivial. At the most basic level, voters acting on a trusteeship theory need to know who the candidates are and something about their backgrounds and qualifications. To determine who is most qualified to serve as a trustee office-holder, citizens surely also need to know something about the responsibilities of the office—that is, to know what the would-be political leader is to be a trustee over. For this reason, the trusteeship voter may need to have at least some knowledge of policy after all.

Furthermore, as modern critics of Burke have pointed out, there may well be disagreement over the question of which skills and virtues are most important in a good trustee-leader. Voters with differing ideologies and interests may reach divergent conclusions on this question.[24] The bitter debate over the impeachment of President Bill Clinton in 1998–99 was in part a result of deeply rooted disagreements between liberals and conservatives as to the importance of personal virtue in political leaders.[25]

For voters to be able to choose Burkean trustees, they must have an understanding of the connection between different personal qualities of candidates and their ability to make good public policy. To the extent that opposing ideologies posit divergent answers to these questions, voters must have some ability to assess those ideologies as well.

Like retrospective voting, Burkean trusteeship turns out to require greater political knowledge in the electorate than may initially seem to be the case. At the very least, voters must know (1) the responsibilities of a given office and (2) the connection between the skills and virtues of opposing candidates and their ability to fulfill those duties. In addition, they may also need to have some understanding of the differing answers that opposing ideologies give to question 2.[26]

Trusteeship theory is concerned more with the personal qualities of political leaders than with their policies or issue positions. The most basic knowledge requirement is that voters at least know who the leaders are, a prerequisite that is often not met, except in the case of those aspiring to the presidency. Immediately after the 2010 election, only 38 percent of Americans knew the name of John Boehner, the newly chosen speaker of the House of Representatives.[27]

Early in the same year, the same percentage could identify Harry Reid as the leader of the Democratic majority in the Senate and a key mover of the Party's legislative agenda.[28] In the 2000 ANES study, only 15 percent of respondents could name even one candidate running for the House of Representatives in their district.[29] An earlier study found that only 30 percent could name both their state's U.S. senators.[30] The 2000 ANES study also revealed that only a mere 9 percent could name the post held by Senate Majority Leader Trent Lott, then the federal government's most powerful and prominent Republican elected official.[31] The president and vice president do generally enjoy a high level of name recognition. But most other elected leaders do not.

In cases when voters do know something about the candidate in question, the personal attributes they focus on may be irrelevant to job performance. For example, several recent studies find that a candidate's perceived physical attractiveness significantly affects his or her share of the vote.[32]

Given that the majority of citizens often do not even know who their political leaders are, it is unlikely that they can know enough about their qualifications and personal virtue to meet the demands of the trusteeship theory. In many cases, voters seeking to apply the trusteeship approach may also be stymied by their ignorance of the responsibilities of the office involved, which makes it difficult to decide what skills those who hold the office should possess.[33]

Representing Majority Preferences on Specific Issues

The representation of majority views on particular issues is probably the most intuitive concept of representation. The basic idea is that democratic control ensures that the government pursues policy objectives chosen by the public, or at least a majority thereof.[34] Unfortunately, it requires that voters possess substantial political knowledge. In the classic 1960 formulation of Angus Campbell and his colleagues, majoritarian control of policy outcomes on a particular issue requires that voters (1) know of the issue's existence, (2) have a position on the issue, and (3) know the positions of opposing candidates on the issue.[35] These three prerequisites—formidable in themselves—are in fact insufficient. Voters must also have some understanding of how the opposing candidates' policy proposals relate to the advancement of their ultimate goals.[36]

Merely knowing that Candidate X supports Policy Y is not enough to determine whether electing him will advance the voters' goals on that issue. Assume that voters have the goal of reducing crime and that one candidate in an election proposes to accomplish this objective by expanding prison space, while his or her opponent opposes that approach.[37] Clearly, it is not enough for voters to know that they wish to reduce crime and that one side in an election seeks to do so by building more prisons. They also need to have sufficient knowledge to make some judgment as to whether building new prisons really will help to control crime or not. In rare instances, voters might value the existence of a policy for its own sake, without regard to consequences. This may be true of policies on purely "symbolic" issues, such as the design of the state or national flag. In most cases, however, voters want results as well as symbols.

Meeting all four of these knowledge prerequisites is often very difficult, especially with regard to issues that are complex or not transparent to the public. The size and scope of modern government make it virtually impossible for most ordinary citizens to even be aware of much of what the government does, much less have an informed opinion on it.[38]

Voter knowledge of individual issues has been the focus of extensive social science research over many years, with consistent findings showing that voters have little knowledge of many key policy issues.[39] As noted earlier, during the 2010 election, when the state of the economy was by far the most important issue on voters' minds, the majority of the public was unaware that the economy had actually grown in the year prior to the election.[40] Most of the public was also unaware that tax cuts were included in the Obama administration's stimulus legislation, probably the most important policy enacted to try to improve the condition of the economy.[41]

During the 2008 presidential election, the majority of voters were unaware of basic facts related to the War on Terror, the rival candidates' health care plans, and other major issues in contention between the two parties.[42]

Surveys conducted in 2004 showed that most citizens were ignorant of basic facts about several important policy issues at stake in that election. These included key antiterrorism policies such as the Patriot Act, the Bush administration's massive new prescription drug entitlement, and the state of the economy.[43] Strikingly, 70 percent of voters were unaware of even the very existence of the prescription drug plan, even though it was the largest new government program enacted in decades.

Ignorance is often a problem even with respect to relatively simple, emotionally salient issues. For example, *Kelo v. City of New London*,[44] the Supreme Court's 2005 decision upholding the condemnation of private property, including homes, for "economic development" drew a broader political backlash than any other legal decision in decades.[45] According to surveys, over 80 percent of the public said they opposed the decision, including 63 percent "strongly" opposed.[46] A record forty-four states and the federal government enacted legislation purporting to forbid the types of takings upheld by the Court.[47] Yet a 2007 Saint Index survey found that only 21 percent of respondents knew whether their states had enacted reform laws in the aftermath of the decision, and only 13 percent could correctly answer a follow-up question asking whether the laws adopted by their state would be "effective in preventing the condemnation of private property for economic development."[48] Such widespread ignorance was a key factor behind the enactment of "reform" legislation that in most states allowed economic development takings to continue under other names while purporting to ban them.[49]

In numerous states, the new laws banned "economic development" condemnations that transferred property to private parties, while allowing virtually identical takings to continue under the guise of eliminating "blight." Many states defined "blight" so broadly that virtually any area could be declared blighted and condemned if a local government wanted to take it; in recent years, courts have declared such unlikely areas as downtown Las Vegas and Times Square in New York City to be "blighted" and therefore permissible sites for blight condemnations.[50] Unfortunately, relatively ignorant voters probably could not tell the difference between new laws that genuinely abolished economic development takings and those that only pretended to do so.

The 2000 ANES survey data contained ten questions asking respondents to compare George W. Bush's and Al Gore's or Democratic and Republican Party positions on major policy issues. Table 2.1 summarizes the results.

TABLE 2.1 *Political knowledge survey items on specific policy issues: 2000 American National Election Studies survey*

Item	% Giving Correct Answer
Al Gore favors a higher level of government spending on services than George W. Bush	73
Democrats favor a higher level of government spending on services than Republicans	57
Gore is more supportive of gun control than Bush	51
Democrats are more supportive of government guarantee of jobs and standard of living than Republicans	49
Gore is more supportive of abortion rights than Bush	46
Gore is more supportive of government guarantee of jobs and standard of living than Bush	46
Democrats favor a higher level of government aid to blacks than Republicans	45
Gore is more supportive of environmental regulation than Bush	44
Bush is more likely to favor jobs over the environment than Gore	41
Gore favors a higher level of government aid to blacks than Bush	40

NOTES: All questions are taken from Table 1.4. All percentages are rounded to whole numbers. N = 1,545 respondents.

A majority of respondents correctly placed the two parties or candidates' relative positions on only three of ten questions, and on two of these the percentage giving the correct answer was only slightly over 50 percent.[51] This data may overestimate the true level of respondent knowledge because full credit for a correct response was given for any answer that placed Democrats to the ideological left of Republicans or Gore to the left of Bush on the issue in question. The coding did not consider the correctness of the absolute placement of the parties or candidates on the survey's scale, nor did it measure the accuracy of the size of the gap the respondent perceived between their positions.

Consideration of these factors, if it had been possible, would almost certainly have led to an even bleaker portrayal of voter knowledge of the issues addressed in the comparison items. In any event, it seems clear that on a wide range of basic public policy issues, a majority of citizens failed to meet a basic knowledge prerequisite of the issue representation model: knowing where the opposing candidates and parties stand on the issue in question.

Public understanding of some issue differences was much higher in 2004 than in 2000.[52] Often, knowledge of a candidates' party identification helps voters figure out what his or her likely issue positions will be.[53] But knowledge of opposing parties' stances is just one of the four prerequisites of issue-based voting.

The evidence presented here shows that citizens often lack information on the easiest of the knowledge prerequisites for effective issue voting: knowing about the very existence of key issues and policies, what the basic facts about particular policy issues are, and where the parties stand relative to each other. It does not directly assess whether voters possess sufficient knowledge to accomplish the much more difficult task of predicting the likely consequences of the opposing parties' policies for their own values and interests. Unfortunately, survey evidence on this point is relatively sparse. But it seems unlikely that those ignorant of basic knowledge of public policy would often possess much more complex knowledge.[54]

Deliberative Democracy

Over the past three decades, numerous political theorists and legal scholars have advocated deliberative democracy as an alternative to less demanding conceptions of democratic government.[55] Deliberative democracy advocates contend that it is not enough for voters to be able to force political leaders to follow their "naked preferences" on particular issues.[56] Instead, citizens should be able to engage in fairly sophisticated deliberation about public policy, and to base their advocacy of particular policies on the right "type of reasons."[57]

Deliberative democracy as a normative theory of political participation is distinct from the use of deliberation for the purely instrumental purpose of trying to increase political knowledge. Some scholars defend the latter without necessarily subscribing to the broader agenda of those who argue for deliberative democracy as an intrinsically valuable ideal. The instrumental case for deliberation as a tool for increasing political knowledge is considered in Chapter 7.[58]

Advocates of normative deliberative democracy disagree among themselves as to what criteria citizen deliberation should meet.[59] For example, Amy Gutmann and Dennis Thompson claim that citizens must "appeal to reasons that are recognizably moral in form and mutually acceptable in content" and that, if they rely on empirical claims, those assertions must be "consistent with relatively reliable methods of inquiry."[60] Many deliberative democrats believe that their "ideal . . . requires citizens to express their impartial judgments of what conduces to the common good of all citizens, and not their personal preferences based on judgments of how measures affect their individual or group interests."[61] Many advocates also believe that voter judgments about what advances the common good must be based on deliberation or "informed" preferences.[62] Other scholars, such as the late John Rawls and Ronald Dworkin—neither of whom qualified as a full-blown advocate of deliberative democracy— would require citizens engaged in political deliberation to restrict or abjure claims based on religion or—in the case of Rawls—those that rely on any "comprehensive moral doctrine."[63] Rawls would have citizens limit appeals to such doctrines to cases in which the citizen's overall set of views is "reasonable, and one that can be seen to be reasonable by all other citizens."[64]

Jürgen Habermas, one of the most influential deliberative democrats, urges that the deliberative process only take account of citizen arguments that are based on "impartiality" and incorporate the "mutual recognition of competent subjects."[65] Even a less-ambitious version of deliberative theory would still judge deliberation by whether or not it produces results similar to those of an ideal deliberative structure in which "everyone recognizes (or tends to recognize) a good reason when they see one," and whether participants in deliberation give "serious" consideration to all opposing views.[66]

Despite their other differences, deliberative democrats are generally critical of "aggregative" theories of democracy that merely seek to match public policy to voter preferences.[67] Instead, they insist that voters must actively discuss policy issues and do so in an intellectually rigorous and morally legitimate way. As Joshua Cohen puts it, "the deliberative conception emphasizes that collective choices *should be made in a deliberative way*, and not only that those choices should have a desirable fit with the preferences of citizens."[68]

Most theories of deliberative democracy therefore impose at least two types of knowledge requirements on voters. First, citizens must have empirical knowledge of the policy issues before them and the likely results of adopting alternative proposals. They must "sincerely weight the merits of competing arguments in discussions together" and ideally do so on the basis of "reasonably accurate information."[69] For example, voters considering whether or not to adopt free trade or protectionism need to have some knowledge of the economics of comparative advantage and the likely consequences of trade restrictions for consumers and producers.[70] In this respect, the knowledge burden of deliberative democracy focuses on some of the same kinds of information as the retrospective voting and policy representation theories. But deliberative democracy probably requires greater factual knowledge of this kind, because the voters are expected to engage in serious deliberation on policy alternatives.

Second, under deliberative democracy the voters must also have moral and philosophical knowledge that enables them to determine whether various arguments advanced in the deliberative process meet the normative demands of deliberative democratic theory or not. For example, Gutmann and Thompson[71] and Habermas[72] insist that deliberators should make only arguments that treat all citizens as equals. Thus supporters and opponents of free trade or any other policy could not justify their positions merely by arguing that their preferred policy would benefit one group at the expense of another to whose welfare they are indifferent. This implicit requirement of moral and philosophical sophistication is unique to deliberative democracy, differentiating it sharply from other theories of participation. If voters are required to have not only factual but philosophical knowledge, the information burden on them becomes correspondingly greater.

Overall, deliberative democracy imposes even greater knowledge burdens on citizens than those demanded by other theories of participation. In addition to knowing the details of a given policy issue, citizens of a deliberative democracy must have sufficient reasoning ability and philosophical knowledge to be able to analyze and debate the issue in the way that the theory demands. Whatever the other strengths and weaknesses of deliberative democracy, it is important to recognize that it places an enormous knowledge burden on the electorate.

Since the knowledge demands of deliberative democracy are much greater than those of the other three theories considered, it is even more clear that most citizens fail to meet the exacting knowledge prerequisites of this theory of participation. Because voters often lack even very basic knowledge of major public policy issues, they will rarely if ever have sufficient knowledge to deliberate about policy alternatives in a sophisticated way. There is far less survey data available on citizens' knowledge of philosophical and moral issues. Still, it seems unlikely that more than a small fraction of the population has sufficient knowledge of these matters to satisfy most deliberative democracy advocates.[73]

Deliberative democracy is undermined not only by ignorance but also by voters' lack of incentive to rationally evaluate the information they do possess.[74] Deliberative democrats advocate rational, systematic, and unbiased deliberation over public policy issues. They want deliberators to consider each other's opinions "on the merits."[75] This ideal is difficult or impossible to realize if most citizens are highly biased and irrational in assessing the political information that comes their way.[76] If they tend to be closed-minded and unwilling to accept opposing evidence, it seems unlikely that many of them can engage in the sort of unbiased dialogue deliberative democrats champion.

Some advocates of deliberative democracy recognize that the electorate falls short of its demanding knowledge requirements and have proposed various mechanisms for increasing knowledge.[77] It is possible that the process of deliberation itself can improve voters' knowledge and understanding of issues.[78] But it is difficult to see what incentive voters would have to acquire more than minimal knowledge and understanding unless they were somehow forced to participate in deliberative processes that increased their knowledge, or stimulated by positive incentives to do so. Similar problems arise with other types of efforts to raise knowledge to the level demanded by deliberative democracy. Whether negative or positive, any such incentives would have to be substantial in order to achieve the large increases in knowledge that would be necessary.[79]

As an extensive literature review concludes, most "people tend to prefer nondeliberative forms of reasoning" and are particularly unwilling to deliberate "for very long."[80]

Given the popularity of the deliberative democracy model among political philosophers and legal scholars, much work remains to be done to show that this theory can somehow be made workable in a world of widespread political ignorance.

Pure Proceduralist Theories of Democracy

Some versions of normative democratic theory are purely "proceduralist." They defend democracy on the ground that its decision-making procedures are procedurally just, completely independent of their outcomes.[81] In theory, a pure proceduralist theory of democratic participation might be completely indifferent to political knowledge. Even if voters are utterly ignorant, the demands of the pure proceduralist theory could potentially be met so long as proper democratic procedures were followed.

In practice, however, proceduralist theories of democracy usually build some degree of deliberation and voter knowledge into their definitions of proper procedure.[82] A pure proceduralist theory that has *no* knowledge prerequisites at all seems extremely unattractive. For example, it would have to endorse a democratic process in which voters decide major policy issues in complete ignorance of the likely consequences of their actions. It would even have to endorse an electoral process where citizens decide who to vote for at random, or by flipping a coin. Such pure proceduralism would also have difficulty justifying the exclusion of small children and the mentally insane from the ballot.[83] To avoid these problems, a pure proceduralist must accept the need for voter knowledge prerequisites of some kind.[84] And it seems likely these would have to be at least as stringent as those of the less-demanding theories discussed earlier, such as retrospective voting.

CAN VOTERS KNOW TOO MUCH?

Democratic theory includes a great deal of consideration of the possibility that voters might know too little. Much less thought has been given to the possibility that voters might sometimes know *too much*. This possibility deserves serious consideration. If political knowledge often causes more harm than good, then we should worry less about political ignorance. If knowledge turns out to be a net harm most of the time, we might even celebrate ignorance instead of decrying it.

It turns out that there are several scenarios in which voter knowledge can actually cause harm. On rare occasions, ignorance really *can* lead to bliss! But most such cases are situations where knowledge in one area becomes dangerous only because of ignorance in another.

Good Knowledge Combined with "Bad" Values

The most obvious situation in which political knowledge might cause harm is one where voters use their knowledge to promote policies that implement "bad" values. As used here, the term *values* refers to a person's ultimate goals, as opposed to the means used to achieve those objectives. For example, a person might want to maximize her happiness and seek to increase her income as a means to pursue that end, believing that she will be happier if she has more material wealth. In that case, happiness is the ultimate value, while wealth is merely a means to an end.

Why might political knowledge exacerbate the harm caused by an electorate with bad values? Consider an electoral majority that is highly racist and wants to inflict as much harm as possible on a despised racial minority. If such racist voters become more knowledgeable about the effects of various government policies, they might be able to force elected officials to implement policies that increase the minority group's suffering even more.

If the racist majority increases its knowledge of the activities of government officials, it can more effectively identify and punish any who are "slacking off" in their persecution of the despised minority. This, in turn, gives office-holders a stronger incentive to adopt harsh discriminatory policies than they would have if the electorate was less well informed.

This scenario isn't just hypothetical. In the Jim Crow–era South, political leaders sometimes adopted more discriminatory policies against African Americans than they personally favored in order to satisfy racist public opinion.[85] Alabama governor George Wallace became one of the most notorious defenders of racial segregation in the 1960s, when he famously "stood in the schoolhouse door" to prevent African-American students from integrating the formerly all-white University of Alabama. But Wallace ran his first campaign for governor in 1958 as a relative racial moderate. As a result, he was defeated because of what the voters perceived as his insufficient commitment to white supremacy.[86] A chastened Wallace decided that he would never allow a political opponent to "out-nigger me again" and duly adopted a more segregationist line in future campaigns, which were more successful.[87] Had Alabama voters been less well informed about Wallace's moderation in 1958 or less aware of the possibility of more harshly segregationist alternative policies, Wallace might have acted differently.

The same analysis can be extended to cover other situations in which increased political knowledge might enable voters with "bad" values to implement those values more fully. Consider the case of anti-Semitic German voters in the Weimar Republic, or radical Islamist voters in newly democratizing countries in the Muslim world. Increasing knowledge might cause the former to support the Nazis or other ultranationalist parties, and cause the latter to vote for radical Islamist parties that plan to repress liberals, religious minorities, and women.

This book does not provide a defense of any particular vision of political morality. But unless we adopt the view that all values are equally good—including those of racists and Nazis—we must admit that good political knowledge might sometimes be put in the service of "bad" values.

Yet what looks to us like bad values is often just another form of factual political ignorance. For example, some Jim Crow–era white racists probably hated African Americans without any ulterior purpose, and supported segregation for that reason. But many others supported it because of factually mistaken beliefs about the consequences of allowing integration and giving blacks equal legal rights. Many believed that this would result in a massive increase in violent black crime against whites or in a harmful "degeneration" of the white race caused by interracial marriage.[88] Greater public knowledge of the actual effects of segregation and integration might not have eliminated racism entirely. But it would surely have diminished white support for harsh segregationist policies.

Similarly, some of the hostility of the Nazis and other early twenti-eth-century German nationalists toward Jews and support for military expansionism was based on an inherent hatred of Jews and foreigners. But a key factor in Nazi thinking was the belief that Jews were harming the German economy and that the world economic system was a zero-sum game in which, in the long run, one nation could improve its wel-fare only at the expense of others.[89] If most German voters in the 1920s had understood that the Jews were a net benefit to the German economy and that Germany could prosper without conquering its neighbors, that would not have completely eliminated either anti-Semitism or support for military expansionism. But it would likely have greatly diminished public support for both.

More recently, public hostility to homosexuality has been motivated in large part by the false belief that homosexual orientation is caused by upbringing and environment rather than genetic factors. A 2007 Gallup poll found that 35 percent of Americans believed that homosexuality is caused by "upbringing and environment," while 42 percent answered (correctly) that it is a condition "a person is born with."[90] People who believe that homosexuality is caused by upbringing or environment are far more likely to believe that it is morally unacceptable and that homo-sexual sex should be illegal.[91]

Overall, one cannot deny the possibility that good knowledge will sometimes help voters to act more effectively on bad values. But it is equally true that much of what looks to us like bad values is at least in large part the result of factual ignorance.

High Knowledge Levels Combined with Voting Based on Narrow Self-Interest

Another possible mechanism by which increased political knowledge could cause harm is if voters use accurate knowledge to cast votes on the basis of narrow self-interest. For individual voters to use the political system to pursue their narrow self-interest may not be morally reprehen-sible in and of itself. But if all or most voters act this way, it could have negative systematic effects that leave everyone worse off.

For example, some economists contend that in a situation in which all voters have perfect information and use it to advance their narrow self-interest at the ballot box, the end result will be highly inefficient "rent seeking": redistribution that damages the economy and leaves most of the population worse off.[92] Self-interested voters could cast their ballots in favor of candidates who promise to transfer wealth to them at the expense of other groups in society, thereby triggering a dangerous political cycle in which incentives for economic production are undermined because wealth-producers know that anything they make will just be a target for redistribution to rival interest groups.

The more political knowledge self-interested voters have, the greater their ability to identify opportunities to transfer wealth to themselves at the expense of other groups, and the greater the potential extent of rent-seeking. It could therefore be argued that high voter knowledge and self-interested voters are a dangerous combination.

In reality, this problem is more theoretical than real. The overwhelming consensus of studies of voter motivation concludes that the vast majority do *not* choose their political views based on narrow self-interest. Instead, they usually vote "sociotropically" on the basis of what they see as the interests of society as a whole.[93] This is particularly true in the area of economic policy, where voters generally focus on the state of the economy as a whole rather than their own individual pocketbooks.[94] On most issues, therefore, we need not worry about the possibility that increases in political knowledge will enable self-interested voters to engage in destructive rent-seeking.

But even a highly knowledgeable but narrowly self-interested electorate might be better than one that is equally self-interested yet much more ignorant. With the knowledgeable electorate, politicians will at least have strong incentives to pursue policies that benefit the majority of voters in order to stay in power. If the knowledgeable majority would be better off under a different set of policies, it can use its knowledge to remove the incumbents and vote in supporters of policies that benefit them more.

To the extent that interest group rent-seeking is a problem, the highly knowledgeable majority can even vote in leaders who will impose constitutional or other structural constraints on the power of government to benefit some interest groups at the expense of others.[95] The framers of the U.S. Constitution sought to achieve this goal by establishing constitutional protection for property rights.[96]

The more knowledgeable the electorate is, the better their understanding of the dangers of rent-seeking is likely to be and the better they will be able to determine which measures are needed to control it. Even voters with perfect information might not be able to suppress harmful rent-seeking entirely. But they are likely to achieve greater success the more knowledge they have.

A highly knowledgeable but narrowly self-interested majority could potentially cause more harm than good if they support policies that create small benefits for the majority while inflicting much higher costs on the minority. Consider a policy that creates $100 of benefit each for 51 percent of the population at the expense of imposing $200 in costs on each of the other 49 percent. In this case, the harm imposed on the minority is almost twice as great as the benefit to the majority. Yet a self-interested majority is likely to adopt the policy if they know about it and understand its effects.

However, highly knowledgeable voters could reduce the incidence of such inefficiency through logrolling.[97] In this example, the 49 percent minority could agree to accept a program that transfers say $125 to each member of the majority group in exchange for the latter agreeing not to vote for the less efficient program that would give them only $100 each at the expense of inflicting much higher costs on the minority. The minority need not persuade every member of the majority group to accept the deal; they would only have to win over enough of the former majority to form a new majority themselves. Through this trade, both the majority and the minority would be better off than they would be if the majority group simply forced the minority to accept the original lopsided proposal. The more knowledgeable the electorate, the more easily it can identify and understand opportunities for mutually beneficial logrolling that can potentially make everyone better off.

By contrast, an electorate composed of voters who are narrowly self-interested but generally ignorant about the effects of policy is more likely to adopt policies that actually make the majority worse off rather than better. They are more likely to mistakenly conclude that a harmful policy actually advances their interests. Even with narrowly self-interested voters, therefore, high levels of political knowledge are likely to be better than low ones. Whether or not narrowly self-interested voters are preferable to more altruistic ones, knowledgeable self-interested voters are generally preferable to equally selfish ignorant ones.

Ignorance That Offsets the Negative Effects of Other Ignorance

Sometimes, voter ignorance in one field can offset the negative impact of ignorance in others. The public might wrongly believe that Policy X has beneficial effects even though it actually causes more harm than good. If incumbent officials fail to adopt X and the public finds about it, the voters could replace the incumbents in the next election, choosing opposing candidates who will now have strong incentives to implement X.

For example, voters tend to support protectionism despite the consensus of economists across the ideological spectrum that free trade is the better policy for improving the economy and helping the poor.[98] Perhaps for this reason, President Obama promised to renegotiate the North American Free Trade Agreement and other free trade treaties during the 2008 campaign.[99] Once he became president, however, Obama backed away from this commitment, possibly because he and his advisers feared that heightened protectionism would further damage an already weak economy.[100] During a February 2009 visit to Canada, the president warned that "[n]ow is a time where we've got to be very careful about any signals of protectionism, because as the economy of the world contracts, I think there's going to be a strong impulse, on the part of constituencies in all countries, to see if they can engage in beggar-thy-neighbor policies."[101] As of 2012, the president has suffered little political damage for this reversal, even though public support for protectionism remains high.[102]

One possible reason for the president's ability to avoid a political backlash on this issue is that most voters may simply be unaware that he reneged on this particular campaign promise. If so, and if economists are right to believe that free trade is superior to protectionism, public ignorance about trade policy might have offset the potential harm that could have been caused by public ignorance about the effects of trade. If the public was knowledgeable about Obama's policy but remained ignorant about the effects of free trade and protectionism, the president might have been forced to adopt a more harmful policy.

Whatever one thinks about the specific case of trade policy, we cannot dismiss the general possibility that ignorance in one area can sometimes offset ignorance in another. However, such a happy accident can only occur in cases when three conditions hold:

1. The majority of the public support a harmful policy because of ignorance about its true effects.
2. Political leaders, if left to their own devices, will adopt a different, better policy.
3. Public ignorance about policy enables officials to follow their own preferences.

If any of the three conditions is absent, then ignorance is likely to make things worse rather than better. If the public actually supports a more beneficial policy than elites do, public ignorance about the true state of policy increases the likelihood that bad policies will be adopted. If the public is knowledgeable about the policy choices made by leaders, but ignorant about policy effects, leaders will be incentivized to adopt bad policies.

In addition, policy outcomes are still likely to be best if the public is relatively well informed about *both* policy decisions and policy effects. In that scenario, voters have the greatest likelihood of pushing policy-makers in beneficial directions.

FALLING SHORT OF THE KNOWLEDGE MARK

Public knowledge levels fall well short of the requirements of normative theories of political participation. This is probably not surprising in the case of highly demanding theories such as deliberative democracy. It is more noteworthy that the majority of the public do not even meet the requirements of relatively simple theories such as Schumpeterian retrospective voting.

There are situations when voters can have too *much* knowledge. In such cases, political ignorance might actually improve the performance of the democratic process rather than make things worse. But these cases are unlikely to be the norm. Moreover, in most of them, ignorance in one area has beneficial effects only because it partially mitigates the negative impact of other types of ignorance. Rare cases of beneficial ignorance are a small silver lining in our generally bleak political knowledge cloud. Overall, however, the sky is still mostly dark.

Although current knowledge levels fall short of the demands of democratic theory, it is possible that this result is merely accidental and easy to change. The next chapter suggests that ignorance will not be easy to alleviate by explaining why much of it is the result of rational behavior rooted in the basic structure of democracy.

CHAPTER THREE

The Rationality of Political Ignorance

The single hardest thing for a practising politician to understand is
that most people, most of the time, don't give politics a first thought
all day long. Or if they do, it is with a sigh, . . . before going back
to worrying about the kids, the parents, the mortgage, the boss,
their friends, their weight, their health, sex and rock 'n' roll. . . .

For most normal people, politics is a distant,
occasionally irritating fog.

—TONY BLAIR[1]

MANY PEOPLE CONFLATE political ignorance with sheer "stupidity."[2]
But often, ignorance is actually smart. Even highly intelligent voters
can rationally choose to devote little or no effort to acquiring political
knowledge. Indeed, political knowledge levels have stagnated over the
past several decades, despite the fact that IQ scores have risen enormously
during the same period.[3]

Most political ignorance is actually rational. For most people, the
benefits of devoting more than minimal time and effort to learning
about politics are greatly outweighed by the costs. As former British
prime minister Tony Blair puts it, they understandably prefer to spend
their time attending to "the kids, the parents, the mortgage, the boss,
their friends, their weight, their health, sex and rock 'n' roll."[4] Similarly,
President Barack Obama once wrote that most of the ordinary citizens
he encountered "were too busy with work or their kids to pay much
attention to politics."[5]

To say that most voters are ignorant because they are rational is not
to suggest that their political behavior is completely rational in every
way or that they perfectly calculate the costs and benefits of acquiring

information. It merely suggests, as Blair and Obama recognized, that most citizens have a rough general sense that devoting more than minimal time and effort acquiring political information is rarely worth the trouble.

The rationality of most political ignorance has profound implications for democratic theory. A particularly crucial one is that rationally ignorant voters will often also find it rational to do a poor job of analyzing the information they do possess. In addition, it turns out that many people can rationally choose to vote, while at the same time remaining ignorant of basic political information. Rational ignorance also makes voters more vulnerable to political deception and misinformation.

Widespread political ignorance is problematic regardless of whether it is rational. Irrational or purely accidental ignorance can still be dangerous. But, as we shall see, the rationality of ignorance makes it an even more difficult challenge to democracy than it might be otherwise.

In many ways, political ignorance is no different from widespread ignorance on many other matters where it is rational for individuals to invest little or no time to acquiring information. Even the smartest and best-educated people have the time, energy, and mental capacity to assimilate only a tiny fraction of all the information potentially available to them.

As discussed further on, widespread ignorance is also common on a wide variety of nonpolitical subjects, including basic science. The challenge posed by political ignorance, however, is that behavior which is individually rational may have major negative effects on society as a whole. Most other examples of rational ignorance do not pose as blatant a conflict between individual rationality and collective goals.

WHY POLITICAL IGNORANCE IS RATIONAL

Political ignorance is rational because an individual voter has virtually no chance of influencing the outcome of an election—possibly less than one in one hundred million in the case of a modern U.S. presidential election.[6] A recent analysis concluded that in the 2008 presidential election, American voters had a roughly one in sixty million chance of casting a decisive vote, varying from one in ten million in a few small states to as low as one in one billion in some large states such as California.[7] The chances of influencing the outcome of a state or local election are greater, but still extremely low. As a result of such daunting odds, the incentive to accumulate political knowledge is vanishingly small, so long as the only reason for doing so is to cast a "better" vote.

Since one vote almost certainly will not be decisive, even a voter who cares greatly about the outcome has almost no incentive to invest heavily in acquiring sufficient knowledge to make an informed choice. An informed electorate is a typical example of a "public good" that consumers have little incentive to help pay for because they can enjoy its benefits even if they choose not to contribute to its production.[8] Moreover, individuals have little incentive to contribute to the production of public goods because they know that their individual contributions are unlikely to make a difference to the final result.

The classic example of a public good is clean air. An individual citizen can enjoy the benefits of clean air in his city even if he drives a gas-guzzling car that generates an unusually high amount of pollution. If other residents of the city restrict their output of air pollution, the individual driver can enjoy clean air even without changing his habits. If the other residents continue to pollute, the individual driver also has no incentive to change his own behavior. Even if he buys a cleaner car or starts taking the bus, that will not have any noticeable effect on the overall level of pollution. The effect of any one car on pollution levels is infinitesimally small. For this reason, most economists conclude that air pollution is unlikely to be effectively controlled unless some external power, such as the government, forces individuals and firms to reduce their emissions of harmful pollutants.

In the same way, an individual voter has little incentive to become well-informed about politics. If other voters become well informed, she can reap the benefits of a more knowledgeable electorate even if she remains completely ignorant. If the rest of the electorate has a low level of knowledge, the individual voter cannot improve electoral outcomes merely by becoming better informed herself. The likelihood that her knowledge will make a difference to electoral outcomes is not significantly greater than the likelihood that the removal of one gas-guzzling car will have a decisive impact on the level of air pollution in a big city. In this way, political ignorance is a kind of "pollution" of the democratic process.

Even highly intelligent and perfectly rational citizens can therefore choose to devote little or no effort to the acquisition of political knowledge. Only those who value political knowledge for reasons other than voting have an incentive to learn significant amounts of it. Acquiring extensive political knowledge for the purpose of becoming a more informed voter is, in most situations, simply irrational. This point applies even in cases when political information is available for free through the media, the Internet, or other sources. So long as learning the information and analyzing its significance requires time and effort, the process is still costly for citizens. Time and energy are valuable resources in and of themselves.

The logic of rational ignorance applies just as readily to highly altruistic and civic-minded citizens as to narrowly self-interested ones.[9] Even a 100 percent altruistic person—someone who always chooses to prioritize the welfare of others over his own whenever the two conflict—would not rationally devote much of his time to acquiring political information for the sake of casting an informed vote. No matter how great the benefits to others of a "correct" electoral outcome, the altruist's ballot has almost no chance of bringing it about; in a large electorate the chance that his vote will be decisive is vanishingly small.

The rational altruist would therefore seek to serve others in ways where a marginal individual contribution has a real chance of making a difference to their welfare, such as donating time or money to charitable organizations. By spending time and effort on becoming an educated voter, the altruist might actually *diminish* others' welfare by depriving them of the services he might have conferred on them through alternative uses of the same resources.

The applicability of the collective action argument to altruistic voters obviates—at least in this case—one of the standard criticisms of economic models of politics: that they rest on unwarranted assumptions of self-interested behavior.[10] The prediction of rational voter ignorance rests on no such assumption. As discussed further on, an altruist might rationally choose to vote despite the very low probability of casting a decisive ballot. The cost of going to the polls is also extremely low. But the time and effort needed to acquire more than minimal political knowledge is much greater.

We cannot know for certain that the rational ignorance hypothesis is correct. But the available evidence strongly supports it. Otherwise, it is difficult to explain the fact that political knowledge levels have remained roughly stable at low levels for decades, despite massive increases in education levels and in the availability of information through the and now the Internet.[11] With rationally ignorant voters, however, the main constraint on political knowledge is not the availability of information but the willingness to take the time to study and learn it.

None of this suggests that *all* political ignorance is the result of rational decision-making. And it certainly does not imply that most citizens make careful, detailed calculations of the costs and benefits of acquiring political knowledge. More likely, the average person simply has a rough intuitive sense that devoting more than minimal effort to acquiring political information isn't worth the effort because it is unlikely to make any difference to political outcomes.

Rational Ignorance and the Paradox of Voting

If the rational choice explanation of voter ignorance is sound, why do people bother to vote at all? Rational choice models of politics appear to predict that all or most voters should not even show up at the ballot box, given the infinitesimal likelihood of affecting the electoral outcome. More precisely, they predict nonvoting unless the voter has some reason for casting a ballot that is unrelated to the likelihood of changing the result. For example, he or she might vote out of a sense of duty or out of a desire to express his or her political views.[12]

If people vote for such reasons, however, it is possible that the same motives will also lead them to become informed. Critics therefore resist the rational ignorance hypothesis on the ground that it allegedly also predicts that citizens should choose not to vote.[13] After all, if people can decide not to acquire political information because of the insignificance of their individual vote, why shouldn't they also decide not to vote at all, for the exact same reason? As Russell Hardin puts it:

> Suppose we conclude that it is plausibly rational for a person not to master the logic of collective action, and that they therefore vote despite the lack of objective interest in doing so. *Then why do they seem to follow the logic in not investing in the knowledge they would need to vote intelligently?*[14]

However, it turns out that the decision to vote is rational so long as the voter perceives a significant difference between candidates and cares even slightly about the welfare of fellow citizens, as well as his or her own.[15] A simple calculation suggests why this is true.[16]

Assume that Uv equals the expected utility of voting, Cv equals the cost of voting, and D equals the expected difference in welfare per person if the voter's preferred candidate defeats her opponent. Let us further assume that this is a presidential election in a nation with three hundred million people, that the voter's ballot has only a one in one hundred million chance of being decisive, and that the voter values the welfare of his fellow citizens an average of a thousand times less than his own.[17]

The figure of one in one hundred million is used for ease of exposition. Adopting the slightly more accurate figure of one in sixty million—the average odds of decisiveness in the 2008 presidential election—would not significantly alter the result.[18]

Thus, we get the following equation:

EQUATION 3.1:

The Utility of Voting

$$D*(300 \text{ million}/1000) / (100 \text{ million}) - Cv = Uv$$

If we assume that Cv is $10 (a reasonable proxy for the cost of voting) and that D is $5,000, then Uv equals $5, a small but real positive expected utility.

In this simplified example, the benefits that the voter expects her fellow citizens to get from the victory of the "better" candidate are expressed in monetary terms. But they could just as easily be nonfinancial benefits, such as a better foreign policy or a cleaner environment. So long as the voter believes that these benefits, discounted by the likelihood that her vote will be decisive, outweigh the costs of voting, it is rational for her to vote. While it is extremely rare for elections to be decided by one vote, such events do occur, as in the case of two Georgia mayoral elections in 2009.[19] The low probability of a one-vote margin of victory may be offset by the large expected benefits and the low cost of the act of voting itself.

Actual voters are unlikely to calculate the costs and benefits of voting this precisely. But they might make an intuitive judgment incorporating very rough estimates of D and C. Furthermore, the fact that voting is a low-cost, low-benefit activity ensures that there is little benefit to engaging in precise calculations such as these. So voters might rationally choose to go with a default option of voting and forego any detailed analysis.[20] The cost of making a precise calculation could itself easily outweigh the benefit of saving time and money on voting.[21]

It would therefore be rational to make do with a very rough intuitive estimate—as people routinely do for many decisions in everyday life. That people do in fact make such rough calculations about the utility of voting is confirmed by the finding that people who believe there is a great difference between the opposing candidates are more likely to turn out than those who believe that the difference is small, as well as by the fact that turnout is higher in elections that are expected to be close.[22] It is also reinforced by the sensitivity of turnout to relatively small poll taxes, which greatly reduced turnout in states that had them until the federal government banned them in the 1960s.[23]

By contrast, the acquisition of political information in any significant quantity is a vastly more difficult and time-consuming enterprise than voting itself.

Equation 3.2 illustrates this point. Assume that Upi equals the utility of acquiring sufficient political information to make a "correct" decision and Cpi equals the cost of acquiring political information. Thus:

EQUATION 3.2:

The Utility of Acquiring Political Information For Voting Purposes

$$D^*(300 \text{ million}/1000) / (100 \text{ million}) - Cpi = Upi$$

If we conservatively estimate Cpi at $100 by assuming that the voter need only expend ten hours to acquire and learn the necessary information while suffering opportunity costs of just $10 per hour, then the magnitude of D would have to be nearly seven times greater—$33,333 per citizen—in order for the voter to choose to make the necessary expenditure on information acquisition. It is unlikely that many otherwise ignorant voters will perceive such an enormous potential difference between the opposing candidates as to invest even the equivalent of $100 in information acquisition. This theoretical prediction is consistent with the empirical observation that most citizens in fact know very little about politics and public policy, but do vote.

The analysis changes only slightly if the voter does not care about the welfare of the entire nation but only about that of a subset, such as his racial or ethnic group. Alternatively, he may care about everyone in the nation to at least some extent, but value the utility of some groups more than others. Similarly, it may be that the voter believes that his preferred candidates' policies will benefit some groups more than others.

In each case, we can still calculate the utility increase to whatever groups a voter does care about and discount it by the extent to which she cares about them less than about herself, and by the likelihood of her vote being decisive. As long as the resulting number is greater than the cost of voting, it will still be rational to go to the polls. At the same time, the cost of acquiring information is still likely to make being well informed irrational.

Sometimes, of course, voters may value different groups' welfare unequally. For example, ethnocentrism leads some Americans to place greater emphasis on the welfare of members of their own racial or ethnic groups than others.[24]

Equation 3.3 demonstrates the result that obtains if Equation 3.1 is modified to assume a voter who cares far more about the welfare of a subgroup of the population numbering fifty million than about the rest of the public, valuing members of that group five times as much as the rest.

EQUATION 3.3:

The Utility of Voting, Assuming Unequal
Valuation of Different Groups' Welfare

$$D*((250 \text{ million}/1000) + (50 \text{ million}/200)) / (100 \text{ million}) - Cv = Uv$$

In this example, Uv will turn out to be $8.33, a slightly higher figure than in Equation 3.1. At the same time, it would still be irrational for the voter to pay the costs of becoming adequately informed. Plugging the new estimates into Equation 3.2, the per-person difference in welfare would have to be over $20,000 in order to justify a decision to pay the price of becoming informed.

As with the decision to vote itself, we need not assume that individual voters make a detailed and precise calculation about the costs and benefits of information acquisition, or those of voting. They probably instead simply have an intuitive sense that there is little or no benefit to making a major effort to increase their knowledge about politics. Most people similarly assume without precise calculation that there is little benefit to acquiring information about such subjects as theoretical physics or cell biology, though these bodies of knowledge also have great value to society as a whole. Indeed, the costs of the time and effort needed to make a truly precise calculation probably exceed the benefit for the vast majority of people.

Some scholars argue that the odds of a single vote being decisive are much lower than the equation used here.[25] If their calculations are correct, the incentive to acquire political knowledge is even lower than I suggest. It would also be irrational to vote unless the voter perceives an unimaginably large difference between the opposing candidates.

In my view, the formula used here—largely adapted from the work of statistician Andrew Gelman and his colleagues—is more accurate than those that assign vastly lower probabilities of decisiveness.[26] But very little in my argument hinges on the difference between the two. Both lead to the conclusion that it is rational for voters to be ignorant about politics.

Lower odds of decisiveness suggest that it is also irrational for most voters to cast a ballot. However, given the existence of disagreement among respected scholars, a rational voter might still choose to vote if he thought that Gelman's model had some substantial chance of being correct. If he believes that it has a 50 percent chance of being right, then he would assume that he has a 1 in 120 million chance of casting a decisive vote, as opposed to the 1 in 60 million estimated by Gelman. The latter figure is, of course, very similar to the 1 in 100 million used in equations 3.1 and 3.2.

More realistically, the average citizen probably lacks the time and expertise to study either the Gelman model or the alternatives. Unless he or she finds the reading interesting or has an extensive background in statistics, the costs of doing the reading and analyzing the models would be far greater than the expected benefits.[27] Thus the rational citizen could reasonably base his or her decisions on voting and acquiring political information on a rough intuitive sense that the chance of decisiveness is extremely low, but still higher than zero. And that is exactly what most people actually seem to do.

Why a Rationally Ignorant Voter Can Still Have Political Opinions

A important objection to this attempt to reconcile rational ignorance with the paradox of voting is that a rationally ignorant voter who realizes that she has little political knowledge should not be confident about the validity of her judgment as to which candidate is better. She should assume that her estimate of the benefits of her preferred candidate's victory might also be inaccurate. Perhaps the rationally ignorant voter should be agnostic about the relative merits of the two candidates, a position that would once again make voting irrational.

But this critique ignores the fact that the voter in question does not know in which direction her estimate is wrong, or by how much. She could potentially overestimate the benefits of her preferred candidate's victory. But in the absence of contrary evidence, she should assume that there is at least an equal chance that she has *underestimated* those benefits.

Assume that the best evidence known to the would-be voter suggests that the victory of Candidate A will give each citizen an average of $5,000 in benefits more than would a win for Candidate B. If the person in question has no reason to believe that she is more likely to overestimate than underestimate the relative merits of A and B, she must still assume that the expected benefit of the "right" candidate winning is $5,000 multiplied by the number of citizens. Thus even an ignorant voter fully aware that her ignorance might cause her to estimate erroneously might still rationally choose to cast a ballot.

Perhaps the mere recognition that many people disagree with her should lead the would-be voter to be less confident in her views. If she doesn't know much about a subject, but does know enough to realize that there is a lot of opposition to her conclusions, maybe she should worry more about the possibility that she might be wrong. Perhaps those other people are on to something, possibly even because they have relevant knowledge that she does not.

Knowledge of such disagreement should not, however, lead the rational but ill-informed voter to become agnostic about her views. If the fact that many people disagree with her should give her pause, the fact that many others hold similar views should, with equal logic, reinforce her confidence. If you believe that the Democratic Party's platform is, overall, better for the country than that of the Republican Party, the fact that millions of Republicans disagree is a relevant consideration, but one balanced by the fact that millions of Democrats feel the same way as you do. It is possible that some of those Republicans know of flaws in the Democratic platform that you are unaware of. But by the same token, it's possible that some of the Democrats have information unknown to you proving that the Democratic platform is even *better* than you think it is. Maybe they also know of evidence showing that Republican policies are even worse than you previously believed.

In sum, the rational but relatively ignorant voter can still have opinions on political issues. Agnosticism is not the only rational stance to take in the face of ignorance.

The argument here does not assume that most real-world voters are perfectly rational in their evaluation of the information they possess.

Indeed, I conclude the opposite.[28] The point is that even an ignorant voter who *did* rationally evaluate his limited stock of information might still conclude that one party is superior to the other and cast his ballot accordingly.

This conclusion undercuts claims that rational ignorance would be harmless if voters did not also engage in irrational evaluation of the information they have—a theory that rests on the assumption that a person who knows he has little information about political issues would rationally remain agnostic about them.[29] If the voter knows he has little information but still believes that the evidence he does have comes down on one side of an issue, he would be rational to hold to that belief in the absence of further information, given that he does not know whether he erred by agreeing with that side too much or too little.[30]

What If Voters Care About the Size of the Winner's "Mandate"?

The analysis described in the previous section does not change if voters value the margin of victory for their preferred candidate as well as the victory itself.[31] For example, a voter might want her preferred candidate to win by a large margin rather than a small one in order to be able to claim a more impressive "mandate" for her party's platform. Conversely, if the voter supports the losing candidate in an election, she might prefer the winner's margin of victory to be as *small* as possible. In reality, the electorate rarely conveys a clear "mandate" for extensive policy change for the winners, and political elites rarely come to the conclusion that one exists.[32] Still, a voter might overestimate the likelihood that any given election will be perceived as creating a mandate, or might believe that the current election is an exceptional case.

Either way, it is still far less costly to cast a ballot than to become informed about issues. Moreover, the chances of an individual vote being decisive to the size of a "mandate" are still likely to be infinitesimally small, just as are those of winning. After all, it is highly unlikely that any significant number of voters value the difference between their preferred candidate getting 58 percent of the vote and getting 58.0000001 percent. Rather, what matters to some is something like the difference between a "small" mandate and a medium-size or "big" one. Perhaps, for example, public opinion sees a 58–42 margin as a decisive "landslide," while a 57–43 margin is considered merely a "normal" victory. The chance that any one vote will make the decisive difference between a small mandate and a medium or big one is no greater than the likelihood that it will make the difference between winning and losing, and may even be smaller.[33]

There are several other important reasons to believe that the paradox of voting does not invalidate a collective action problem explanation of voter ignorance.[34] First, it is possible that the unexpectedly high incidence of voting is simply the result of people overestimating the potential impact of their vote.[35] Survey data suggest that over 70 percent of voters believe that their individual votes "really matter."[36]

Such overestimation may in fact be *rational* to the extent that acquiring an accurate knowledge of the impact of voting may for many be more expensive than the relatively modest effort required to vote in major elections. If so, it is plausible to hypothesize that the degree of overestimation is great enough to stimulate voting, but far too small to stimulate the much greater investment of time and effort necessary to acquire a substantial amount of political information. Voters who don't take the time to calculate the numbers could readily conclude that their chance of influencing the outcome of a presidential election is, say, one in ten million, rather than one in sixty million or one in one hundred million. But it seems highly unlikely that they would conclude that the true probability is one in ten or one in twenty.

Second, even if the paradox of voting really is explainable by the "expressive utility" of voting or by "irrational" conceptions of duty,[37] it is still possible that such motives are not powerful enough to induce voters to pay the heavy costs of becoming well informed. Indeed, if voters cast ballots out of a sense of duty, that is a reason why they would go to the polls even without being well informed. The same point applies if voters go to the polls in order to be able to tell others they did so, as suggested by one recent study.[38] Similarly, if the voter simply wants to express his or her views regardless of whether they are backed by adequate knowledge, that too can lead to ill-informed voting. The empirical evidence showing that voter knowledge levels are very low is of course consistent with such scenarios.

However, the "expressive utility" explanation of voting has various weaknesses. If the voter's sole objective is simply to express his views in a public way,[39] it is not clear why the same objective couldn't be more easily achieved simply by staying home and telling people who you support in conversation or in a phone call. Better still, in the age of the Internet, the would-be voter could instead send an e-mail announcing his electoral preference to as many people as he can. This would be a more clear expression of preference than casting a vote in a secret ballot election in which no one can see what the voter decides.

If, on the other hand, the voter merely desires to express her views on the election without necessarily revealing them to others, she has the option of simply stating them aloud while no one else is present or writing them down in a document that she never shows to anyone. All of these options are likely to be easier and less time-consuming than going to the polls. Yet few if any voters view such activities as a substitute for casting a ballot.

The duty-based explanation for voting is likely true, at least for many voters.[40] However, it is complementary to the rational choice explanation rather than a competitor with it. After all, it is not clear why voters would feel a duty to undertake an action that makes no difference. The reason why a voter who cares about the welfare of his or her fellow citizens is likely to feel a duty to vote is because of the perception that doing so could make a difference. A similar analysis applies if the voter chooses to vote merely because others might ask about it, and think less of him if he says he did not cast a ballot.[41] Presumably, the reason why the nonvoter's reputation would suffer is that the questioners believe that he violated a civic duty, and they believe in the existence of that civic duty because his vote can make a meaningful contribution to society.

Rational Ignorance or Just Plain Simple Ignorance?

A possible alternative to the theory of rational ignorance is the idea that widespread political ignorance is just an honest mistake. Given the complexity of the political world, it is possible that voters are "inadvertently" ignorant, simply unaware that there is a body of information out there that might improve the quality of their political decisions if they learned it.[42] Instead of rational ignorance, low levels of political knowledge could be the result of just plain simple ignorance.

The biggest difficulty with the inadvertent ignorance theory is that it fails to explain why so many people are ignorant even of very basic facts about politics. Simple intuition suggests that, to be an adequately informed voter, it might help to know the names of the opposing candidates, the major policies adopted by the government in recent years, and which officials are responsible for which issues. If one is planning to cast a vote based on the state of the economy, it should not be hard to figure out that it might help to check the data on whether the economy has grown or shrunk recently.

Such basic information is readily available in the media and, now, on the Internet. Yet a large percentage of the public, often a majority, fails to learn it. If you are planning to purchase a TV, it's not difficult to figure out that you will make a better decision if you acquire some basic information about the price, reliability, and picture quality of competing brands. Even a person with little knowledge of the TV market can readily grasp that much. The TV consumer who fails to get that basic information is unlikely to do so simply through mere "inadvertence." If he remains ignorant on such points, it is likely because he doesn't care very much about the choice of a TV or because he prefers to devote the time and effort needed to acquire that information to other pursuits that he considers more important. The same point applies to voters' failure to acquire basic political information.

Moreover, if political ignorance is inadvertent, one would expect knowledge levels to increase substantially over time as education levels have risen and political information becomes more widely available at lower cost, thanks to modern technology. The more education one has and the more political information is readily available, the higher the likelihood that individuals will be exposed to the idea that there are bodies of knowledge available that could help them inform their voting decisions. Yet, as previously noted, political knowledge levels have risen little if at all over the past several decades, despite major increases in education and the availability of information.[43]

The fact that voters are often unaware of even very basic political information and that this ignorance has persisted in the face of rising education levels and the information technology revolution is hard to reconcile with the idea that ignorance is merely inadvertent "simple" ignorance. On the other hand, it is clearly consistent with rational ignorance. Demand for information, not supply, is the main constraint on political learning in a world where most people are rationally ignorant about politics.

Other Examples of Rational Ignorance

Political ignorance is hardly unique. Public ignorance is also common on a wide range of other issues, including basic science, geography, and history. For example, over 20 percent of the population in both the United States and Europe does not know that the earth revolves around the sun rather than vice versa.[44] A 2009 Gallup poll found that only 39 percent of Americans say they "believe in the theory of evolution," with 25 percent rejecting evolution and 36 percent saying they have no opinion.[45] A 2006 National Geographic Foundation study found widespread ignorance of basic geography among young adults, with 63 percent unable to find Iraq on a map (despite extensive news coverage accorded to the country due to the Iraq War), 88 percent unable to find Afghanistan, and majorities also unable to find major states such as New York on a map of the United States.[46]

Similarly, there is widespread public ignorance about the extent to which various environmental and chemical hazards do or do not pose a threat to public health.[47] A 1997 CNN/*Time* poll found that 80 percent of Americans believe that the U.S. government is hiding knowledge of the existence of extraterrestrial life and that 50 percent even believe that extraterrestrials have abducted humans.[48]

What these examples have in common with political ignorance is that there is little incentive for most people to seek out accurate knowledge about them. Most Americans can live their lives just as happily as they would otherwise even if they have wildly inaccurate perceptions about evolution, astronomy, geography, or UFOs. Ignorance about these subjects is therefore rational in much the same way as political ignorance. Ignorance about environmental risks is a more complicated case, since some such risks can be avoided or mitigated through individual action. But in the case of risks that can be addressed only through public policy or that, conversely, lead to wasteful public expenditures because we overestimate their significance, it is rational for individuals to do little to acquire accurate knowledge about them.

The existence of widespread rational ignorance beyond the political realm makes the theory of rational ignorance more plausible within it. Political ignorance is not an unusual special case. It is just one of many examples of rational ignorance, albeit an unusually dangerous one.

THE RATIONALITY OF ILLOGICAL INFORMATION USE

Contrary to some misunderstandings,[49] the theory of rational ignorance does *not* predict that voters will choose not to acquire any information at all. Rather it predicts that they will acquire very little or no information *for purposes of voting*. But some voters will acquire information for other reasons. Scholars, politicians, political activists, journalists, and others have professional reasons for being informed about political developments. Yet such professional users of political information are only a tiny fraction of the population. Far more common are those who acquire political knowledge because they find it interesting.[50] There are not enough such people to eliminate widespread political ignorance. But they do nonetheless form by far the largest bloc of relatively well-informed voters.

A helpful analogy is the case of sports fans. Fans who acquire extensive knowledge of their favorite teams and players do not do so because they can thereby influence the outcome of games. They do it because it increases the enjoyment they get from watching the game and rooting for their favorite teams. Similarly, "political fans" derive enjoyment from rooting for their preferred parties, candidates, ideologies, and interest groups, while deriding the opposition. They may also derive satisfaction from having their preexisting views validated, and from a sense of affiliation with a group of like-minded people.[51] But if many of the citizens who acquire significant amounts of political knowledge do so primarily for reasons other than becoming a better voter, it is possible that they will acquire knowledge that is of little use for voting, or will fail to use the knowledge they do have in the right way.

Most people realize that the outcome of an election matters more than the result of a game. If an individual voter knew that her decision would determine the winner of a presidential election, she would almost certainly consider the matter more carefully than if she were given a similar opportunity to unilaterally determine the winner of the next Super Bowl or World Cup. But when individuals know that they in fact have only an infinitesimal chance of influencing either result, they might still evaluate political information and sports information in the same highly biased manner.

Dedicated sports fans routinely play up evidence that makes their team look good and its rivals look bad, while downplaying anything that cuts the other way. Committed Boston Red Sox fans who passionately root against the New York Yankees are unlikely to evaluate the evidence about these teams objectively.[52] Many Yankees fans no doubt feel the same way about the Red Sox. Similarly, Republican partisans who reflexively despise President Barack Obama, and Democrats who reflexively support him against criticism, might well want to acquire information in order to augment the experience of cheering on their preferred political "team." If this is indeed their goal, neither group is likely to evaluate Obama's performance in office objectively or accurately.

This intuition is confirmed by studies showing that people tend to use new information to reinforce their preexisting views on political issues while discounting evidence that runs counter to them.[53] For example, experimental evidence shows that political partisans not only reject new information casting doubt on their beliefs but sometimes actually respond by believing in them even more fervently.[54] One study shows that conservatives presented with evidence showing that U.S. forces failed to find weapons of mass destruction in Iraq were actually strengthened in their preexisting view that WMDs *were* found.[55] Similarly, liberals confronted with evidence that 2004 Democratic presidential candidate

John Kerry had incorrectly claimed that the Bush Administration had "banned" stem cell research persisted in their preexisting belief that the charge against Bush was correct.[56] Although some scholars view such bias as irrational behavior,[57] it is perfectly rational if the goal is not to get at the "truth" of a given issue in order to be a better voter but to enjoy the psychic benefits of being a political "fan."

Economist Bryan Caplan calls this "rational irrationality."[58] As he puts it, rationally ignorant voters may limit not only the amount of information they acquire but also "how rationally they process the information they do have."[59] To put it a different way, such citizens' mode of processing information may be rational for purposes of psychic gratification but irrational for purposes of improving the quality of their votes. The latter will rarely be the main goal of information acquisition, because there is too little chance that achieving it will have any impact on electoral outcomes. As George Akerlof explains:

> [I]nformation is interpreted in a biased way which weights two . . . goals: agents' desire to feel good about themselves, their activities, and the society they live in, on the one hand, and the need for an accurate view of the world for correct decision-making, on the other hand. . . . [B]ecause any individual's influence on the public choice outcome is close to zero, each individual has an incentive to choose a model of the world which maximizes his private happiness without any consideration of the consequences for social policy.[60]

The conjecture that political fans may be pursuing "private happiness" at the expense of truth is supported by a 2006 study showing that the most knowledgeable voters tend to be more biased in their evaluation of new evidence than those with less prior political information.[61] If those who acquire political knowledge do so in order to cast "better" votes, such a result would be difficult to explain. But if the main goal is to enjoy psychic benefits similar to those available to sports fans, the greater bias of the more politically knowledgeable is perfectly rational. The fact that they acquired more knowledge in the past suggests that they value the "fan" experience more than those who acquired less. Thus it is not at all surprising that they tend to be more close-minded in their evaluation of new information, because acknowledging that the other side may have a good argument would diminish their psychic gratification.

Similarly, most citizens tend to discuss political issues only with those who agree with them,[62] and that tendency is most pronounced among "those most knowledgeable about and interested in politics."[63] The same goes for selection of media sources, with committed Republicans and Democrats both preferring media that align with their partisan proclivities;[64] though it is also true that many people watch very little partisan media because they watch little political news of any kind.[65]

In an important recent book, political psychologist Jonathan Haidt describes experimental evidence showing that people tend to reason more carefully and logically when they know in advance that they will have to explain their conclusions to well-informed people who do not necessarily share their preexisting views.[66] Limiting political conversations to people who agree with us undermines this form of accountability and incentivizes what Haidt describes as "laziness" and irrationality in decision-making.[67]

Such avoidance of opposing views would be difficult to explain if the goal of political knowledge acquisition were truth-seeking. A truth-seeker would search out opportunities to hear opposing points of view in order to test the validity of his or her own. As John Stuart Mill famously argued, the truth is best attained through consideration of alternative viewpoints: "He who knows only his own side of the case knows little of that. His reasons may be good, and no one may have been able to refute them. But if he is equally unable to refute the reasons on the opposite side, if he does not so much as know what they are, he has no ground for preferring either opinion."[68] Haidt's analysis of the experimental data provides support for Mill's argument. Nonetheless, limiting discussion to those one agrees with and media use to ideologically congenial sources is perfectly rational if the objective is *not* truth-seeking. Such constraints help achieve the competing purpose of taking part in a political "fan" group.

Critics of Caplan's rational irrationality theory sometimes claim that it requires voters to "*know* that their opinions are wrong."[69] Otherwise, they would not rationally be choosing to indulge irrationality, but simply falling into "inadvertent" error.[70] However, rational irrationality does not require an actual belief that one is endorsing incorrect views, merely a decision not to make an effort to carefully evaluate one's views in an unbiased way.

A person can believe that his views are correct while also realizing that he has not made an effort to investigate the subject in question more than superficially, or to think rigorously about it. Almost everyone holds views of this type on at least some matters. For example, I believe that Harrison Ford is one of the best actors in the world, despite the fact that I lack any expertise in the study of film. I also have not investigated the views of expert film critics on the subject, rigorously compared his performances with those of his peers, or even seen all of his movies. Although I recognize that I might change my mind if I studied the issue in more detail, I think the cost of doing so would outweigh the benefit, and I will likely hold on to my admittedly ill-informed view.[71]

RATIONAL IGNORANCE AND THE
ROLE OF INTEREST IN POLITICS

The theories of rational ignorance and rational irrationality do not predict that citizens will avoid acquiring political knowledge entirely. Rather, they imply that little or no knowledge will be acquired for the purpose of voting. Accordingly, the most powerful determinant of political knowledge is expected to be entertainment value or some other reason not clearly related to voting.

This prediction is confirmed by studies showing that by far the most powerful determinant of political knowledge is a survey respondent's level of interest in politics.[72] When controlling for other variables likely to affect political knowledge, such as race, gender,[73] education, income, and exposure to various forms of media, interest in politics has a far greater effect on political knowledge than virtually any other variable.[74] Table 3.1 dramatically illustrates this contrast.[75]

Holding all other variables constant, a change in interest in politics from the lowest to the highest level on the scale increases political knowledge almost 50 percent more than the expected difference in knowledge between a middle school dropout and a holder of graduate

TABLE 3.1   *Relative impact of changes in variables on political knowledge: 2000 American National Election Studies survey*

Variable	Expected Increase in Political Knowledge Score (30-point scale)
Interest in Politics: Moving from Lowest to Highest Level	11.1
Education: Dropout in Middle School or Earlier to Graduate Degree	7.7
Media Exposure: Lowest to Highest Level of Media Exposure*	3.8
Income: Under $5000 Annual Household Income to Over $125,000	3.4
Political Activity Beyond Voting: Lowest (Zero acts in past year) to Highest Level of Political Activity (Eight or more acts)**	2.8

NOTE: The impact of change in each variable was measured while holding fifteen other control variables constant. The control variables are those listed in the Appendix.

* This variable combines the effects of the TV, newspaper, talk radio, and Internet variables in the Appendix.

** This scale measures whether the respondent has engaged in eight different types of political activity within the past year: trying to influence others' votes, putting up a campaign sign or button, going to political meetings, contributing money to a candidate, contributing money to a party, contacting a public official on an issue, and attending protest marches.

degree. Moreover, this analysis probably understates the true impact of interest in politics because it controls for media exposure to political news, which may itself be in part a function of interest in politics.

The overwhelming dominance of political interest over other variables provides some confirmation to the rational ignorance theory.[76] Citizens who acquire political information seem to do so primarily because it is a personal consumption good rather than for the purpose of contributing to the public good of a well-informed electorate. The only variable that seems to have an even remotely comparable effect is level of education. Shifting from a middle school dropout level of education to a graduate degree level, not surprisingly, leads to a predicted knowledge increase of almost eight points on the thirty-point scale.

Unfortunately, however, the failure of the past several decades' rise in education levels to produce even modest increases in political knowledge casts serious doubt on the likelihood that we can expect future increases in knowledge from this source.[77] Moreover, even if future improvements in education levels have a greater impact on political knowledge than past ones did, we can hardly expect education levels to rise by as much as our stylized middle-school-dropout-to-graduate-degree comparison implies. A more realistic rise in education, say from high school graduate to college graduate, would increase political knowledge by an average of roughly 1.3 points on the 30-point scale for those individuals enabled to go to college under this scenario.[78] While such an increase would be desirable, it seems unlikely that it would have a marked effect on overall political knowledge levels in the electorate.

We cannot, of course, categorically rule out the possibility that some future change in American politics and society will drastically increase aggregate levels of political knowledge. The possibility of such developments is considered in Chapter 7. Even so, the persistence of rational political ignorance suggests that it is likely to be with us for the foreseeable future.

The dominance of interest in politics as a predictor of political knowledge also highlights the dangers of rational irrationality. If most citizens who acquire political information do so primarily for reasons other than truth-seeking, there is little reason to expect them to analyze it in a rational or unbiased way.

IGNORANCE, IRRATIONALITY, AND SUSCEPTIBILITY TO DECEPTION AND MISINFORMATION

The combination of rational ignorance and rational irrationality makes citizens more susceptible to political misinformation and deception. An ignorant voter may believe outlandish claims that she would reject if she had the benefit of greater knowledge. Similarly, a person who analyzes political information in a highly biased way is more likely to accept falsehoods that reinforce his preconceived views.

A variety of conspiracy theories and other highly dubious misinformation is believed by large portions of the American public. A survey conducted by economist Neil Malhotra and political scientist Yotam Margalit in early 2009 showed that some 25 percent of non-Jewish Americans believed that "the Jews" deserved at least "a moderate amount" or "a great deal" of blame for the financial crisis of 2008.[79] Some 32 percent of self-identified Democrats and 18 percent of Republicans endorsed that view.[80] A March 2010 Harris Poll survey found that 25 percent of Americans agreed with the "birther" claim that President Barack Obama "was not born in the United States and so is not eligible to be president."[81] About 45 percent of self-described Republicans, 24 percent of independents, and 8 percent of Democrats endorsed "birtherism."

One can find comparable examples of misinformation on the political left. A 2007 poll of likely voters found that 35 percent of Democrats believed that President George W. Bush "kn[e]w about the 9/11 attacks in advance," while 26 percent were not sure.[82] By comparison, only about 12 percent of Republicans and 18 percent of independents took the same view.[83]

Belief in many other political conspiracy theories is common as well, including claims that the government is hiding evidence of visitation by alien civilizations, claims that the AIDS virus was deliberately manufactured to target African Americans, and assertions that government agencies planned the assassinations of President John F. Kennedy and other prominent political leaders.[84]

Rational ignorance is surely a contributing factor to belief in this kind of misinformation. Political knowledge tends to be highly correlated with education, and less-educated survey respondents were more likely to endorse birtherism, 9/11 conspiracy theories, and the claim that "the Jews" are to blame for the financial crisis.[85] People who are unfamiliar with the normal functioning of the political system and economy are more likely to find dubious disinformation plausible than are those with greater knowledge.

For example, one of the factors that makes birtherism implausible to more knowledgeable voters is that, if Barack Obama were genuinely constitutionally ineligible to become president, his political opponents would have had strong incentives to uncover this fact and use it to force him to withdraw from the race. Both Obama's 2008 Democratic primary opponent, Hillary Clinton, and his Republican general election opponent, John McCain, had highly professional, well-funded campaigns. If there was any real evidence proving that Obama was not born in the United States, they would likely have uncovered it. Reasonably well-informed voters would have understood this and discounted birtherism accordingly.

9/11 conspiracy theories are implausible for similar reasons. For the Bush administration to have deliberately chosen to let the attacks happen despite knowing about them in advance, the president would have had to organize a conspiracy involving numerous officials in the White House, intelligence agencies, the Department of Defense, and elsewhere. Given the highly leak-prone nature of American government, the overwhelming likelihood is that any such conspiracy would be leaked, especially given its morally outrageous nature. Some official in the know would surely have revealed the information, whether for moral reasons or a desire to avoid criminal prosecution for complicity in the plot if its existence were later revealed by others.

In addition, the revelation that high-ranking officials deliberately chose to allow a terrorist attack that killed thousands of Americans would have destroyed the administration politically and severely damaged the Republican Party as a whole. Even if the president and his advisers were sufficiently amoral to consider such a conspiracy, they would quickly realize that the political risks far outweighed any possible gain.

Finally, the claim that "the Jews" caused the financial crisis is implausible to objective observers with even a passing knowledge of the standard economic explanations for the crash. Moreover, it is not clear why Jews would want to cause a financial collapse in which Jewish investors and financiers suffered no less than gentiles.[86]

In all these cases, basic political and economic knowledge could greatly reduce the likelihood of belief in such implausible falsehoods. Rationally ignorant voters who lack such knowledge, however, are more susceptible to believing them.

Rational irrationality also deserves some of the blame. It is probably no accident that Republicans are disproportionately susceptible to birtherism, while Democrats are far more likely to endorse 9/11 conspiracy theories. It is no secret that partisan Republicans tend to be hostile to Obama, while most partisan Democrats felt similarly about Bush. These predispositions make partisans more willing to believe any claim that reflects poorly on their political enemies—often without carefully considering whether the claim is true or even plausible.

Such bias seems irrational if the partisans' only goal is to get at the truth, to determine whether the allegations against Bush or Obama are accurate. But it is perfectly rational if their objective is at least partly to enjoy the emotional satisfaction of being confirmed in their preexisting views. After all, the partisan voter who mistakenly embraces birtherism or 9/11 conspiracy theories suffers no personal harm as a result, while deriving at least some psychological benefit.

This emphasis on ignorance and irrationality focuses on the demand for misinformation: voters come to believe dubious theories such as birtherism because of a combination of their own ignorance and psychological proclivities. But what of the supply side?

It is common to blame widespread belief in political misinformation on distortions peddled by politicians, activists, and the media.[87] During the 2008 presidential campaign, widely respected political columnist Stuart Taylor denounced both candidates for promoting numerous "distortions" about their opponents, and the media for failing to "provide consistently accurate and fair reporting and analysis of all the charges and countercharges."[88] There is little doubt that politicians and activists often do exploit falsehoods about their opponents, or that the media sometimes fail to effectively counter the distortions.

But these factors do not explain why so many voters believe charges such as birtherism or 9/11 conspiracy theories, which are easily refuted by knowledge of basic background facts about the political system. Voter ignorance and unwillingness to take the time to seek out accurate information must share the blame for the spread of such ideas.

As Taylor himself recognized, "one reason that candidates get away with dishonest campaign ads and speeches may be that it is so hard for undecided voters like me to discern which charges are true, which are exaggerated, and which are false. Most people can't spend hours every day cross-checking diverse sources of information to verify the accuracy of slanted stories and broadcasts."[89] In other words, voters' unwillingness to devote time and effort to acquiring political information is part of the reason why dubious charges are often believed.

However, Taylor was wrong to assume that voters need to spend "hours" each day in order to avoid falling for crude political deceptions. With many of them, as with birtherism, basic knowledge of the politics should lead voters to be extremely skeptical even without having to do additional background research.

Even in the case of less implausible distortions, a reasonably knowledgeable voter could choose to be skeptical based on his or her understanding that politicians and activists often have incentives to make bogus charges against their opponents. Indeed, a 2010 poll found that 68 percent of Americans name politicians as the least trustworthy profession, with salespeople (9 percent) and lawyers (7 percent) a distant second and third.[90]

The fact that so many citizens are willing to believe outlandish charges by politicians, despite their recognition that politicians are often untrustworthy, is a further symptom of rational irrationality. When the charge in question conforms to the voters' preexisting biases, they often check commonsense skepticism at the door.[91]

Stuart Taylor and other observers wonder why the media do not do more to correct such distortions, lamenting that the media often fail to provide unbiased and accurate coverage of the charges and countercharges. But the media largely respond to market incentives. If voters wanted unbiased coverage, media outlets would have strong incentives to provide it. Those that succeeded in doing so would get increased audience shares and advertising profits as a result.

In reality, however, those citizens most interested in politics and in following political news tend to seek out information sources that confirm their preexisting opinions rather than present competing points of view objectively.[92] In behaving as they do, politicians and the media are catering to public demand.

Moreover, it is significant that political misinformation is often widely believed even when it does not get endorsed by respectable media sources. Few if any major media outlets have endorsed either birtherism or 9/11 conspiracy theories. But that has not prevented these ideas from attracting significant support among the public, especially among partisans predisposed to believe the worst about their political opponents.

A SMART BUT IGNORANT PUBLIC

For most voters, ignorance about politics turns out to be rational. It is not simply a consequence of stupidity or inadequate learning skills. Smart people can be ignorant too. Moreover, contrary to some interpretations of rational choice theory, rational ignorance is compatible with choosing to vote. Because the cost of voting is so much lower than that of becoming informed, moderately altruistic citizens could rationally choose to vote while also choosing to devote very little time and effort to becoming informed about politics. For similar reasons, most voters also make little effort to engage in unbiased evaluation of the information they do learn.

Obviously, rational ignorance theory is only an imperfect representation of reality. Yet it is generally supported by the available evidence. It sets strict limits to the amount of knowledge most ordinary voters are likely to be willing to acquire. Efforts to alleviate the problem of voter ignorance will have to work within that constraint.

The rational nature of political ignorance still leaves open the possibility that voters can offset their ignorance through information short-cuts. If these shortcuts are easy and cheap enough to use, even rationally ignorant voters might successfully avail themselves of them. The next chapter considers the extent to which shortcuts can offset rational ignorance and irrationality. Unfortunately, it turns out that the shortcomings of shortcuts often outweigh their benefits.

CHAPTER FOUR

The Shortcomings of Shortcuts

[D]emocratic theory . . . was forced by lack of the
instruments of knowledge for reporting its environment, to
fall back upon the wisdom and experience which happened
to have accumulated in the voter. . . . The community
could take its supply of information for granted.

—WALTER LIPPMAN, *PUBLIC OPINION*[1]

WE RARELY HAVE PERFECT INFORMATION about anything in life.
Much of the time, we cope with our ignorance by using information
shortcuts. You may not know much about particular TVs. But if you
know that Sony products generally have a good reputation, that can
help you decide which TV to buy. Perhaps voters with generally low
knowledge levels can make up for it by using similar shortcuts. At least
until recently, this was the dominant view among political scientists and
economists.[2] If it is correct, political ignorance need not be a major concern for democratic theory. As it turns out, some shortcuts are genuinely
useful. Unfortunately, however, most are not nearly as effective as their
more enthusiastic advocates believe.

Many shortcuts to informed voting have been proposed in the literature on the subject: information from daily life, political parties, cues
from opinion leaders, retrospective voting, and the so-called "miracle
of aggregation" are among the most important.[3] Although several of
these shortcuts have genuine merit, they fall short of offsetting the
dangers of political ignorance. Some of them might even lead to worse
decision-making by poorly informed voters who possess little preexisting information.[4]

Shortcut theories also implicitly assume that the person using the shortcut chooses it because of its likelihood of increasing his or her chances of

getting at the truth. If, however, information shortcuts are chosen for other reasons unrelated to their truth value, voters could systematically rely on biased shortcuts that make their perceptions of political reality less accurate than before. Unfortunately, the "rational irrationality" discussed in Chapter 3 makes it perfectly logical for individual voters to choose shortcuts on the basis of their entertainment value, conformity with preexisting views, or other psychological gratification, rather than truth value.

Questioning the effectiveness of information shortcuts used by ordinary citizens can be criticized as "elitist."[5] However, there is nothing inherently elitist about a critique that holds that voters are engaging in perfectly rational behavior, given the insignificance of individual votes. The problem is not that voters who use inadequate shortcuts are necessarily dumber or less virtuous than more knowledgeable "elites." Rather, it is that citizens lack sufficient incentive to acquire adequate knowledge or evaluate the information they do learn in an unbiased way.

INFORMATION FROM DAILY LIFE

Some scholars[6] argue that rational voters will make use of information acquired through ordinary daily-life interactions.[7] Such information is virtually "free" since the activities that produce it would, by definition, be undertaken even in the absence of any political purpose. Some advocates of this shortcut argue not only that it will be utilized, but that it goes a long way toward meeting voters' informational needs.[8] For example, voters allegedly can obtain "a good deal of information" about the economy from personal financial transactions such as managing a checking account or seeking employment.[9]

Personal Experience and Rational Ignorance

While it would be foolish to deny that *some* helpful information can be derived from ordinary life, its usefulness to otherwise ill-informed voters is often greatly overestimated. Three major limitations of such information are particularly important. First, by definition, this approach is of no help in dealing with the many political issues that the vast majority of voters do not encounter in daily life. For example, information from daily life isn't relevant to most foreign policy issues.

Second, even if the voter has carefully calculated the changes in his welfare and developed a judgment about an incumbent's policies, he cannot readily determine whether his welfare will be improved by electing the opposing candidate. Even if things have gotten worse under President X, perhaps the opposing Candidate Y's program is even more harmful. This possibility cannot be ruled out without substantive issue knowledge going beyond personal experience.

Most important of all, substantive knowledge is required to determine whether or not a particular personal experience really is the result of public policy and, if so, which political actors are responsible. Ill-informed voters attempting to make political judgments on the basis of personal experience may fall into egregious errors.

Even with respect to unemployment and inflation, basic economic issues with which most people have substantial personal experience, ill-informed voters tend to make spectacular mistakes. In a survey taken during the 1992 election, during which economic issues were a particular focus of publicity, the vast majority of respondents could not estimate the inflation or unemployment rate within 5 percentage points of the actual level.[10] The electorate's mean estimates of both rates were approximately twice as high as the real level.[11] Such misperception apparently played a major role in swinging the 1992 election against incumbent president George H. W. Bush.[12] Poorly informed voters are more likely than well-informed ones to make sweeping generalizations from personal experience with unemployment, yet less likely to make *accurate* connections between experience and policy.[13]

If errors of this magnitude occur in the cases of inflation and unemployment, even more serious mistakes can be expected with other, more remote, issues. And even a correct estimate of unemployment and inflation is only a minimal prerequisite to determining which side's policy on these issues will better serve the voter's interests. One still needs to know to what extent incumbents are responsible for current rates and whether or not their opponents are likely to do better. Information from daily life is unlikely to be of more than minimal help in making such decisions.

Personal Experience and Rational Irrationality

So far, we have assumed that voters drawing political inferences from personal experience do so for the sole purpose of using them as an information shortcut to understand public policy better. However, the phenomenon of rational irrationality suggests that political inferences drawn from personal experience might instead serve other psychological objectives, including some that may be in conflict with the search for truth. For example, psychological literature shows that people often prefer to blame others for their own mistakes.[14]

The same tendency may well affect their evaluation of the political significance of their experiences. Survey respondents have a strong "anti-foreign bias" that leads them to blame immigrants and foreign competitors for economic problems suffered by their own country.[15] If one loses a job or has to take a pay cut, it will be psychologically easier to blame malevolent foreigners than one's fellow Americans, and easier to blame the policies of the government than to blame yourself.

Obviously, such irrationality is far from unique to *political* interpretations of personal experience. But it is likely to be especially prevalent there, because the incentives to evaluate one's experience more objectively are so weak. If I mistakenly blame a co-worker for my own failures on the job, the result could be loss of the opportunity to get a promotion or even getting fired. If, on the other hand, I mistakenly blame Congress or the president for inflation, I suffer little if any penalty for my error.

POLITICAL PARTIES

The idea that political parties can help voters economize on information costs has a long and venerable lineage, dating back to Democratic Party leader and later president Martin Van Buren, founder of the first modern mass-based party.[16] The basic argument is that voters can infer candidates' policy stances from their partisan affiliations rather than undertaking the much more difficult task of inquiring into the views of each individual aspirant to office.[17]

This claim has considerable merit. Voters are often able to tell where one major party stands relative to the other.[18] For example, in 2004, 92 percent of voters knew that John Kerry was to the left of George Bush on government aid to blacks, 66 percent on gun control, and 64 percent on environmental policy.[19] At the same time, voters are sometimes ignorant even of these kinds of basic differences between the parties. Just four years earlier, in 2000, only 46 percent of American National Election Studies respondents knew that Bush was less supportive of abortion rights than Al Gore, and only 40 percent knew that Gore supported higher levels of government assistance for blacks.[20]

Appealing as it is, the political party shortcut often obscures almost as much as it reveals. At best, a candidate's party affiliation is a clue to his or her policy stances, but it tells the voter little about the likely *effects* of those policies. In principle, the notion of a "running tally" may help a voter to determine the merits as well as the content of a party's policies. But it is difficult to do so without significant substantive knowledge.[21]

If conditions are good under the rule of Party X, how does the voter know that this is due to the success of the party's policies rather than to factors beyond the government's control, preexisting favorable trends resulting from decisions made by the party's predecessors in power, personal characteristics of the party's officeholders that are not representative of the party as a whole (and thus might be misleading as predictors of future behavior), or crafty manipulation of public policy by the party's leadership as a result of which temporary success is achieved at the price of long-term harm?

The voter cannot get around this dilemma simply by aggregating large amounts of experience, since it is unlikely that a given voter has been following politics long enough to experience more than two or three governments headed by any one party.[22]

The party identification shortcut can be actively misleading in situations when parties at the state or local level differ from their national counterparts. For example, many local elections in the United States are highly noncompetitive in part because voters vote for local offices based on their perceptions of the national party—perceptions that are often misleading if the local party differs substantially from the national organization, as is often the case.[23] As a result, local governments often can get away with poor performance so long as the incumbents' national party remains the preferred choice of most voters in the area.[24]

Party shortcuts might also be more difficult to use when there are more than two parties, and voters have to do more than make a simple binary choice. For example, voters found it far more difficult to figure out which presidential candidate most closely matched their policy preferences in the 1992 and 1996 presidential elections, when there were three major candidates rather than the usual two.[25] This problem is of only limited relevance to the United States, which has long had a stable two-party system in which competitive third-party candidates are rare. But it matters more in some other democracies where there are multiple parties.[26] Even in the United States, it matters greatly in primary elections, when voters choosing between multiple presidential candidates of the same parties succeed in "correctly" picking the one with the policy views closest to their own only about 31 percent of the time.[27]

It is also important to recognize that political ignorance might itself reduce the value of the party identification shortcut by weakening the ideological constraints on parties themselves. A party faced with a well-informed electorate may have to hew closely to the voters' preferences or face defeat. With a relatively ignorant electorate, however, party leaders can exploit the electorate's "blind spot" and exercise a great deal of discretion in adjusting their positions on issues in order to pursue objectives of their own or win the support of narrow interest groups.[28] This makes it more difficult to predict a candidate's policy views on the basis of his or her partisan affiliation, even for relatively well-informed voters.

While real, the informational benefits of parties are likely exaggerated by conventional wisdom. Party affiliation often gives voters useful insight on the likely policy positions of candidates. But that type of knowledge is often insufficient for informed voting.

Parties and Rational Irrationality

As with personal experience shortcuts, the effectiveness of party identification shortcuts is also undercut by rational irrationality. Ideally, voters should evaluate what they know about each party's record in an unbiased way, seeking only to determine how well it measures up to its rivals. In reality, however, voters with a strong sense of identification with one party tend to discount any evidence that it is performing poorly and overvalue evidence indicating that it is doing well.[29] They even fall prey to factual errors that make their preferred party's record look better and the opposition's worse.[30] For example, Republicans are more likely than Democrats to know the correct answer to questions about whether the federal budget deficit has increased since President Barack Obama took office, because the correct answer reflects poorly on his record.[31]

This makes little sense from the standpoint of casting an informed ballot. But it is perfectly rational if one recognizes that voters might form an emotional attachment to their preferred party and its ideology, and prefer to avoid the psychological discomfort of seeing their cherished beliefs undermined. As in other cases, the low probability of casting a decisive ballot undercuts the incentive to make any effort to combat this bias.

The biases of committed partisans might be insignificant if independent swing voters could evaluate party records' effectively. However, as discussed further on,[32] swing voters with no strong commitment to either party tend to have the lowest levels of political knowledge and therefore the least likelihood of being able to assess the incumbent party's performance accurately.

The Binary Choice Fallacy

An implicit assumption of the party identification shortcut literature is that voters need only have sufficient political knowledge to choose between the two options available to them in an election: the Democratic and Republican candidates, for example. If the voter knows enough to determine which of the two available parties is more likely to achieve his or her policy objectives, that is enough.

This binary choice model does not take account of primary campaigns, in which all the candidates are from the same party; "nonpartisan" elections in which candidates are not identified by party to the voter;[33] and elections in multiparty systems, when voters must consider numerous different party options, not just two.

But even on its own terms, the binary choice model is incomplete. Political knowledge does not merely affect the outcome of elections with the parties' candidates and platforms taken as given. It can also influence the selection of those candidates and platforms themselves. Especially since the advent of modern public opinion polling made it easier to measure it, parties and candidates have often sought to match their issue positions to majority public preferences.[34] Over time, majority opinion heavily influences the content of government policy.[35]

Even after controlling for a wide range of demographic variables, including race, gender, income, occupation, and others, knowledgeable voters have vastly different policy preferences from less-informed ones.[36] They tend to be more socially liberal, more fiscally conservative, and more supportive of higher taxes, among other examples.[37] They are also less likely to fall for gross political misinformation, and more likely to be able to effectively monitor the performance of government officials.[38] Faced with a much more knowledgeable electorate, politicians and parties would have strong incentives to change their policy platforms, as well as stronger incentives to avoid poor performance in office. The magnitude of the change is likely to depend on the magnitude of the increase in political knowledge.

If the electorate as a whole were significantly more knowledgeable than it is, the result would not only be a greater chance of making the "right" choice among the existing political options. Rather, the options themselves would be very different.

CUES FROM OPINION LEADERS

If the vast bulk of the electorate is generally ignorant, perhaps it can follow the lead of the knowledgeable minority of political activists— "opinion leaders." This line of argument is one of the most common in the literature on shortcuts.[39] Instead of keeping close track of issues themselves, voters can respond to "cues" issued by political activists of value orientations similar to their own:

> What is important is that there are perhaps five percent [of voters] who are activists and news junkies who do play close attention. If they see that something is seriously wrong in the country, they sound the alarm and then ordinary people start paying attention.[40]

Voters can also rely on cues from endorsements by trusted organizations and well-liked celebrities.[41]

Opinion Leaders and Rational Ignorance

Unfortunately, the strategy of following cues from opinion leaders often creates at least as many difficulties for ignorant voters as it solves. Because of the immense asymmetry of information between leaders and followers and the low incentive of the latter to monitor the leaders' performance effectively, serious principal-agent problems surely will arise. Principal-agent problems occur in situations where the person who delegates authority—the "principal"—has difficulty monitoring the performance of the person he delegates to—the "agent." From the perspective of the principal it is difficult to conceive of a more difficult principal-agent relationship than that between ignorant voters and highly knowledgeable, well-organized political activists.

When voter interests and activist interests coincide closely, the difficulties of monitoring need not be so acute. But this state of affairs is far from being common. Political activists differ greatly from the general population on a wide range of demographic and socioeconomic characteristics;[42] they also tend to be more extreme in their views.[43]

Most important of all, opinion leaders acquire interests that diverge sharply from those of voters *simply by virtue of becoming opinion leaders.* As political activists, their power, prestige, social status, and opportunities for pecuniary gain will tend to rise with the perceived importance of their issue positions to the public; they thus have strong incentives to exaggerate the importance of political problems and to push for political solutions (or at least solutions with a prominent role for activists) in preference to private sector ones. Even when voters are aware of these incentives for exaggeration and attempt to discount activist claims as a result, they have no way of knowing how *much* discounting is required.

Even if there exists a subset of opinion leaders whose interests do coincide with those of a given voter, that voter still faces an extraordinarily difficult problem in determining which ones they are. Since the whole point of relying on opinion leaders is to economize on information costs, the voter is unlikely to invest heavily in researching the leaders' qualifications. And unlike in the case of most private sector specialist professionals, the voter cannot simply judge the quality of activists' performance by the results of the policies they advocate, since it is not usually possible to determine which social outcomes are the result of public policy without considerable substantive knowledge of the issues.

A successful strategy of following cues from opinion leaders requires voters to first decide *which* leaders' cues to follow and then monitor these leaders in order to avoid a variety of principal-agent problems that are likely to arise.[44] Neither of these is possible without considerable substantive voter knowledge of the issues. Without such knowledge, opinion leaders are as likely to be misleading as they are to be informative.

Opinion Leaders and Rational Irrationality

Rational irrationality further complicates the search for good opinion leaders. Advocates of the opinion leader theory argue that voters choose opinion leaders on the basis of their perceived knowledge and trustworthiness.[45] However, opinion leaders might instead be chosen in large part because of their entertainment value or ability to reinforce citizens' preexisting prejudices. For example, Arthur Lupia and Matthew McCubbins show that experimental test subjects tended to trust statements about the desirability of new prison construction made by talk show hosts Rush Limbaugh and Phil Donahue if they perceived them as knowledgeable and say that they "agree" with their views on other issues.[46]

In reality, however, there is little reason to believe that Limbaugh and Donahue have any significant knowledge about the costs and benefits of prison construction. Survey respondents who perceived them as knowledgeable about the issue were probably wrong to do so.[47] Their willingness to defer to Limbaugh and Donahue's views on a technical policy issue that the talk show hosts likely had little expertise on may well have been driven by a general sense that these opinion leaders' views conformed to their own preexisting opinions; thus the importance of perceived "agreement" between the talk show host and the respondent on other issues.

Such decision-making is probably not conducive to rational electoral choices. But it is perfectly understandable in a situation where most voters have little incentive to maximize the quality of their electoral decisions and instead form political opinions in large part for other reasons.

RETROSPECTIVE VOTING

The retrospective voting shortcut hypothesis holds that voters judge politicians by past performance rather than current promises. A high percentage of voters seem to do just that.[48] Politicians who know that voters will engage in retrospective voting are likely to anticipate the public's future reactions and try to cater to them in advance.[49] Such "auditing" of past performance might well be easier than predicting the future effects of candidates' policies. "[R]etrospective voting," it is said, "requires far less of the voter than prospective voting."[50] But does it?

To avoid misunderstanding, it is important to differentiate the use of *retrospective voting* as a term denoting a particular information shortcut from its use as a normative theory of democratic participation, discussed in Chapter 2.[51] Unfortunately, both theories often go by the same name.

There are several reasons to doubt that the retrospective voting shortcut is as effective as often claimed. In some cases, voters are not even aware of the very existence of major policies. As noted in Chapter 1, some 70 percent of Americans were unaware of the enactment of President George W. Bush's prescription drug benefit plan in 2003, the largest new government program in decades.[52] Similarly, many are routinely unaware of the existence of major government programs structured as tax deductions and payments for services.[53]

Even when voters are aware of the existence of a relevant government policy, ignorance remains an obstacle to effective retrospective voting. As noted earlier, it is often difficult for relatively ignorant voters to determine which social outcomes are the result of public policy and which ones aren't. To take a prominent example in the literature, many models of electoral retrospection are based on "sociotropic" voting, in which voters make their decision on the basis of the condition of the national economy rather than that of their own personal finances.[54] Yet a person ignorant of economics often cannot tell whether economic conditions are the result of (1) the policy of the current government,

(2) delayed effects of its predecessors' policies, or (3) factors completely independent of any government action.

Studies of retrospective voting show that voters often blame and reward incumbents for conditions beyond their control. Incumbents derive great electoral benefit and suffer comparably severe harm as a result of changes in economic conditions that arise from swings in the world economy that national governments cannot influence.[55] At the state level, voters in oil-producing states reward governors for increases in oil prices caused by world market conditions and for improvements in the economy caused by national economic trends.[56] They also punish governors for deterioration in national economic conditions.[57]

Voters also punish incumbents for the impacts of such uncontrollable events as droughts and shark attacks.[58] Even more dubiously, incumbent governors and senators benefit when popular local sports teams win crucial victories close to election day.[59] The record of a city's sports teams has a substantial impact on mayors' prospects for reelection.[60]

When a given condition really is the result of current government policy, the voter may not be able to determine whether current conditions are positive or negative; for example, if temporary economic sacrifice might be a necessary precondition for future progress.

Even in focusing on major issues, such as the state of the economy, retrospective voters generally consider only changes in income and economic growth that occurred in the last few months of an incumbent president's term, ignoring the administration's entire previous record.[61] This myopia prevents voters from accurately assessing incumbents' economic policy performance.

Recent experimental data also confirm that voters tend to overweight the most recent events in making retrospective evaluations of incumbents, and that they are easily distracted by irrelevant events.[62] Overall, modern evidence substantiates nineteenth-century French economist Frederic Bastiat's complaint that the public tends to focus on immediate short-term "effects" of economic policy that are easily "seen," while ignoring more indirect, long-term effects that usually remain "unseen."[63]

Occasionally, voters may assign responsibility for a important policy to the wrong party because they are confused about when that policy was enacted. In 2010, only 34 percent of Americans realized that the massive and controversial $700 billion TARP bailout of the banks was enacted under Republican president George W. Bush, while 47 percent wrongly believed that it had been enacted under the Democratic incumbent Barack Obama.[64]

Finally, ignorance of the structure of government makes it difficult for voters to decide which elected officials deserve the credit or blame.[65] This defect is of particular importance for retrospective voting theory, which emphasizes that the electorate "passes judgment on leaders, not policies"[66] and thus implicitly assumes that voters know which leaders are responsible for what. As mentioned, voters often reward and punish state politicians for national trends. They also systematically underestimate politicians' responsibility for some issues, while overestimating their impact on others.

Compared to a sample of political scientists specializing in American politics, the public substantially underestimates the ability of the president and Congress to control the composition of the federal budget, the influence of the Federal Reserve on the state of the economy, and the impact of state and local governments on public schools.[67] The Federal Reserve Board, of course, is not an elected agency. But its members are selected by the president and confirmed by the Senate, so the board members' performance should be an element in voter assessment of senatorial and presidential performance. On the other hand, the public assigns the president and Congress excessive blame for a wide range of other trends, including crime rates, education, and short-term economic conditions.[68]

Both excessive and insufficient attribution of responsibility are dangerous. If voters assign too little responsibility, officials can more easily get away with poor performance. If they assign too much, the results of an election are more likely to be determined by irrelevant issues and less likely to be controlled by those issues that the leaders in question *do* have the power to affect. Thus a state governor who does an excellent job on issues within her control might be defeated because voters hold her responsible for a national recession that she had no control over.

To sum up, voters seem to lack the knowledge they need to engage in effective retrospective voting on most issues.[69] As political scientists Christopher Achen and Larry Bartels put it:

> Voters operating on the basis of a valid, detailed understanding of cause and effect in the realm of public policy could reward good performance while ridding themselves of leaders who are malevolent or incompetent. But real voters often have only a vague, more or less primitive understanding of the connections (if any) between incumbent politicians' actions and their own pain or pleasure. As a result, rational retrospective voting is harder than it seems, and blind retrospection sometimes produces consistently misguided patterns of electoral rewards and punishments.[70]

When Retrospective Voting Works

The retrospective voting argument does, however, possess an important kernel of truth. It can impose a kind of "rough justice" on political leaders who have failed badly.[71] If a policy failure is large, highly visible, and easily attributable to a particular set of incumbents, it is certainly likely that they will be voted out of office, as the elections of 1932, 1980, and 2006 suggest. Moreover, the bigger the failure, the less likely it is that the opposing party's performance will be even worse.

The ability of voters to punish large and obvious policy failures by incumbents is one of the major advantages of democracy over dictatorship. It probably helps explain the remarkable fact that no mass famine has ever occurred in a modern democracy, no matter how poor.[72] By contrast, famines deliberately engineered by the government have often occurred in dictatorships.[73]

Even generally ignorant and irrational voters can recognize a mass famine when they see one, and are likely to hold political incumbents responsible for it. Similar factors may explain the fact that democratic governments rarely if ever engage in mass murder against their own citizens, while many authoritarian and totalitarian dictatorships do so routinely.[74]

As with a mass famine, even a generally ignorant public is likely to become aware of mass murder carried out by their leaders and punish them at the polls accordingly. For similar reasons, democracies also tend to do better than dictatorships at limiting the damage caused by massive natural disasters such as earthquakes and hurricanes.[75] Even relatively ignorant voters are unlikely to overlook the presence of massive devastation. On the other hand, voters tend to reward disaster relief spending far more than disaster prevention spending, though the latter is much more effective in limiting the loss of life and property.[76] Relief spending is far more visible to poorly informed voters than is prevention spending, especially since the latter must be undertaken *before* a disaster actually happens, at a time when few voters are focused on the issue.

Unfortunately, the preconditions of magnitude, visibility, and easily traceable accountability rarely obtain in real life. And even in the case of a very large policy failure, leaders may escape blame if the full impact of the failure is not felt until after they are out of office.

Retrospective voting may in some ways be easier in democracies that have fewer different levels and branches of government than the United States. For example, New Zealand is a unitary state that has neither federalism nor the tripartite separation of powers present in American government. Most political power is concentrated in the hands of a single national parliament.[77] In such countries, it is easier for voters to know which policymakers are responsible for which decisions. However, neither the United States nor most other democracies are likely to adopt unicameral, nonfederal systems of government similar to New Zealand's in the near future. Separation of powers and federalism often have important advantages of their own.[78] Even when they do not, it is often difficult to radically restructure a long-established political system.

Retrospective Voting and Rational Irrationality

The effectiveness of retrospective voting is also undercut by rational irrationality. Rather than evaluating incumbents' performance in an unbiased way, partisans tend to negatively evaluate the record of their political opponents and to be biased toward a favorable evaluation of their own preferred party.[79] Republican partisans tend to assign credit to Republican office-holders for any positive events that occur, while being reluctant to blame them for negative ones. Democratic partisans, of course, have the opposite bias.[80] Indeed, partisanship affects not only the assignment of praise and blame for current conditions, but even voters' perceptions of the conditions themselves. Democratic partisans claim that unemployment and inflation rates worsen when a Republican president is in office and improve when the incumbent is a Democrat—even if the reality is the exact opposite of these perceptions; Republicans are similarly biased in favor of Republican presidents and against Democratic ones.[81]

In principle, the bias of partisans could be offset by the efforts of independent voters, who might be more objective in their evaluation of incumbents. However, as noted further on, independents without strong ideological and partisan commitments tend to have the lowest levels of political knowledge, and thus are unlikely to be able to accurately assess incumbents' records.[82]

ISSUE PUBLICS

If voters cannot keep track of all the important issues, perhaps they can at least focus on a few that are of particular concern to themselves.[83] For instance, blacks are more likely than whites to be familiar with civil rights issues.[84] In theory, such "issue publics" can make up for ignorance of more general policy issues within the electorate as a whole.

Attempts to confirm the issue public hypothesis empirically show that it has only limited validity. As a general rule, knowledge of different aspects of public policy is highly correlated.[85] Still, some studies do show that voters with a particular interest in a given issue know more about it than their general level of political knowledge would predict.[86] Even when significant differences in knowledge between groups do exist, they do not necessarily demonstrate that the knowledge of the better-informed group is adequate for informed voting, only that members of that group know *more* about an issue than does the rest of the electorate. The difference is crucial, because most studies showing that issue publics are better informed about a particular issue than the rest of the electorate rely on surveys tapping only very basic knowledge. For example, survey respondents with an unusually high level of interest in abortion, labor policy, and defense spending were more likely to be aware that these issues had been raised in a Senate campaign.[87] This, however, does not prove that these voters actually understood the likely effects of opposing policies on these issues.

Even if the voter does have an adequate knowledge of the narrow issue of particular concern to him, informed voting with respect to that issue might still be inhibited by ignorance of the "rules of the game" of government policy. Using political scientist Shanto Iyengar's example,[88] a black voter may have sufficient *specific* knowledge to conclude that current civil rights policy should be changed, but not enough *general* knowledge of the structure of government to determine which elected officials have to be voted out to do it. Even in the land of the blind, the one-eyed person cannot be a true king if kingship requires seeing things that can only be discerned with two eyes.

Voter ignorance also undercuts the utility of issue publics in two further, less obvious ways. First, the rationally ignorant voter cannot readily tell which aspects of public policy really are part of the issue of interest. One of the neglected aspects of issue-public research is the question of how the scope of the relevant "issue" is defined in the first place.

If the connection between two or more matters of public policy is not obvious or is ignored by politicians and the media for their own reasons, voters may fail to pick it up. Social Security reform, for instance, is almost never defined as a racial issue, yet the lower life expectancy of blacks combined with the fact that they pay Social Security payroll taxes at the same rate as whites turned Social Security into a major hidden redistribution from black workers to white retirees.[89] The subtlety of the connection leads the relevant black issue public to ignore it. Such problems might often prevent an issue public from ever forming to begin with. Thanks in part to political ignorance, some potential issue publics are likely to be numbered among Mancur Olson's "forgotten groups who suffer in silence."[90]

Most fundamentally, voter ignorance of general issues may vitiate the benefits of issue publics even in situations where the issue publics have fully adequate information about their more specific concerns. If each specific issue area is controlled by a subset of the electorate with a special interest, while these same subsets remain ignorant of generally applicable issues, the outcome may well be a process of mutually destructive plundering that leaves each group worse off than it would have been had there been no issue publics to begin with.

Within its particular bailiwick, each issue public pushes for its preferred policies without regard to the potential negative effects on other issues. A classic "tragedy of the commons" ensues in which the general interest is routinely neglected in favor of the particular. For these reasons, it is by no means clear that an electorate divided up into issue publics is in a better position to pursue its policy objectives than one that is uniformly ignorant across the board.

As with other information shortcuts, the issue public shortcut may also be weakened by the possibility of rational irrationality. If voters choose which issues to focus on not on the basis of their objective importance to societal well-being but on the basis of their entertainment value or other personal psychological benefits, the resulting issue publics are unlikely to improve voting decisions.

"ONLINE" INFORMATION PROCESSING

In some cases, measures of political knowledge that focus on consciously known information might understate true knowledge levels because we take account of a great deal of information subconsciously. Such "online" information processing might lead to incorrect survey answers about knowledge items that respondents previously "processed" and incorporated into their decision-making.[91] For example, I may have heard at Time A that a politician had a major ethics scandal. By Time B, when I respond to a survey question on the subject, I could have forgotten all about the scandal. But I also may have incorporated the relevant information from the scandal into my judgment of the politician, and ratcheted down my estimate of his trustworthiness. Online processing could, in theory, be an ideal shortcut for rationally ignorant voters because it requires very little time and effort.

Online Processing as a Substitute for Conscious Knowledge

There is little doubt that voters acquire at least some useful political knowledge through online processing. For example, it can sometimes help voters make better judgments of candidates than they could with their consciously known knowledge alone.[92] At the same time, however, online processing has significant limitations, and the available evidence suggests that it does not come close to fully offsetting the impact of political ignorance.

If online processing could fully replace basic political knowledge or come close to it, we would not observe large differences in issue views between survey respondents with high and low levels of knowledge, after controlling for other variables. The low-knowledge respondents could simply use online processing to offset their relative lack of conscious knowledge. Yet differences between high- and low-knowledge respondents are very large on a wide range of issues in both domestic and foreign policy.[93]

Similarly, it is striking that retrospective judgments of incumbents seem to be heavily influenced by knowledge levels, with most survey respondents' opinions only being influenced by the most recent state of the economy, discounting the evidence of the rest of the incumbents' term.[94] If online processing were a generally effective substitute for conscious knowledge, one would expect it to be especially useful with respect to an issue—the state of the economy—that is almost always one of the most important concerns of voters. Even if voters can't remember what the growth rate or the unemployment rate was a year or two before an election, online processing might enable them to subconsciously incorporate that information in their overall assessment of the incumbent leadership. Yet, at least with respect to many voters, online processing fails to do this.

It is also difficult to see how online processing can offset ignorance of basic information about the structure of the political system, such as knowing which officials are responsible for what issues. If a voter does not know that Officeholder X is responsible for Issue Y, she cannot incorporate new information about that issue into her evaluation of X's performance, whether consciously or by online processing. It is hard to imagine how X's responsibility for Y could itself be known only subconsciously and thereby be able to affect the processing of new information about it. But such a possibility cannot be definitively ruled out.

On balance, online processing surely makes political ignorance a less severe problem than it would be without it. But much of the most worrisome evidence of ignorance is unlikely to be overturned by it. In particular, it does not seem to offset the flaws of retrospective voting, make up for lack of very basic structural knowledge, or account for the ways in which the views of the knowledgeable differ from otherwise similar voters who are comparatively ignorant.

Online Processing and Rational Irrationality

If online processing falls short of fully solving the problem of ignorance, it may actually exacerbate the dangers of political irrationality. Evaluating new information rationally and objectively often requires conscious effort.[95] When we do not exert such effort, we are more likely to fall prey to various cognitive biases, including overvaluing information that reinforces our preexisting views and discounting that which cuts against them.[96] Rational irrationality, therefore, is likely to be a more serious danger in situations where we impulsively react to new political information than if we carefully consider it over time.

Almost by definition, online processing involves quick, often almost instantaneous judgments about the significance of new information. Since the individual then forgets or discards the relevant data, he or she has little if any opportunity to reconsider it later. As a result, judgments made on the basis of online processing may be even more susceptible to rational irrationality than are evaluations of consciously remembered information. Initial reactions to new information presented to survey respondents are often heavily influenced by partisan, ideological, and other biases.[97] But if the information is remembered, we at least have the opportunity to reflect on it later and perhaps reduce the impact of our biases. With online processing, that opportunity is largely absent.

Voters with lower levels of preexisting knowledge may be even more likely to make biased snap judgments when engaged in online processing than those with higher levels. This problem may be part of the reason why less-informed voters are more likely to alter their evaluation of candidates on the basis of superficial traits, such as physical appearance.[98]

Overall, online processing certainly helps voters make decisions and can sometimes substitute for conscious knowledge. But it only seems to close a modest part of the knowledge deficit, and in some cases could even make things worse by increasing the impact of irrationality.

THE "MIRACLE OF AGGREGATION" [99]

If the rationally ignorant portion of the electorate commits its errors randomly, the power of aggregation might result in these errors canceling each other out. When mistakes are truly random and the electorate is sufficiently large, every "erroneous" vote for Candidate X should be offset by a similarly errant one for opposing Candidate Y. Only the non-randomly distributed votes of the relatively informed voters will have a real impact on the outcome; that outcome will thereby be decided "as if" the electorate as a whole were informed. [100]

It is ironic that this line of argument should be put forward by writers committed to developing a defense of majoritarian democracy against charges of voter incapacity. [101] Taken seriously, it implies that the votes of the vast majority of the electorate are just "noise" obscuring the "signals" sent by the informed few, as one advocate puts it. [102] If the argument is correct, elections would have the same outcome if the ballots of the well-informed minority were the only ones counted.

Regardless, the magic of aggregation can only work if (1) the errors largely are random, and (2) the informed minority that decides electoral outcomes are representative of the interests of the rest of the population. The evidence suggests that neither precondition holds true.

Nonrandom Distribution of Errors

If the miracle of aggregation works, the best-informed voters might have a distribution of preferences on major political issues that differs little from that of the least informed, whose errors should randomly cancel each other out. However, extensive evidence shows that an increase in political knowledge leads to different views on nearly all issues tested. Scott Althaus' major 2003 study found that increased political information leads voters to become much more socially liberal and economically conservative across a wide range of issues, when controlling for background variables such as race, gender, and income.[103] It also leads to greater support for an interventionist foreign policy, but slightly lesser support for the use of military force.[104] Earlier studies also found major effects on issue opinion resulting from increasing knowledge.[105]

Moreover, increased policy-specific knowledge can lead to major changes in opinion even among survey respondents who already have high general levels of political knowledge, a result that suggests that even the most knowledgeable fraction of the electorate that supposedly determines the true electoral outcome might still lack sufficient information to deal with all the crucial issues on the public agenda.[106]

The impact of knowledge on opinion is not inconsistent with the evidence of rational irrationality that shows people resisting new information that goes against their preexisting views.[107] People can be biased in their evaluation of evidence without being completely impervious to new data. Moreover, the bias is likely to be less among those who don't have strong preexisting commitments.[108]

The existence of such effects partly mitigates the negative impact of rational irrationality. Rationally irrational voters do still sometimes change their minds in the face of new evidence, even if not as often as they would if they were less biased in their assessments of what they learn. But such information effects also suggest that rational ignorance may be even worse than it initially seems to be. What the voters don't know often turns out to be a crucial factor influencing their decisions.

Some studies do find that an increase in information does not change voting decisions on particular issues. For example, poorly informed voters who used simple information shortcuts voted the same way as much better-informed ones on a complex California auto insurance initiative.[109] Overall, however, information seems to have a major impact on opinion across many important issues.

The miracle of aggregation hypothesis might also hold true if poorly informed voters simply choose their views at random or have no views at all. In that scenario, the poorly informed would split 50-50 on each issue, and public opinion would be determined by the views of the well-informed

TABLE 4.1   *Political knowledge by strength of party identification: 2000 American National Election Studies survey*

Self-Described Party Alignment	Average Political Knowledge Score (Mean number of correct answers on 30-point scale)
"Strong Republican"	18.5
"Independent-Republican"	15.6
"Strong Democrat"	15.3
"Independent-Democrat	14.1
"Weak Republican"	14.0
"Weak Democrat"	13.2
"Independent-Independent"	9.5

NOTE: This 30-point knowledge scale is based on the questions used in Table 1.4.

minority. Obviously, however, that scenario is equally implausible, in light of the obvious fact that many of the poorly informed do have views on political issues and do not choose them randomly.

These conclusions should not be surprising. One of the main reasons why errors are nonrandomly distributed is that voters really *do* try to use several of the other information shortcuts discussed earlier. As a result, ill-informed voters often draw misleading inferences about economic conditions and other issues.[110]

Under some conditions, the miracle of aggregation might work even if the distribution of errors is not random.[111] But for this result to hold, the quality of each individual voter's judgment must improve significantly the higher the correlation there is between errors.[112]

The miracle of aggregation could also be salvaged by evidence showing that the members of the well-informed minority are likely to be the swing voters who change electoral results. In reality, as Table 4.1 shows, the most knowledgeable voters tend to be committed partisans, while independent swing voters are the most ignorant. This result is in line with other research showing that independent voters with weak ideological commitments and party identification tend to have the lowest levels of political information.[113]

Representativeness of the Informed Minority

The random distribution hypothesis fares little better in meeting the second precondition, that of representativeness of the informed. The small minority of well-informed voters differ systematically from the rest in gender, income, race, age, religion, ideology, and a host of other politically relevant attributes.[114] It would be remarkable if the interests of this small, unrepresentative subset of the population coincided more than very roughly with those of the population at large.

The problem of lack of representativeness is partly mitigated by the fact that voters tend not to vote on the basis of personal material self-interest but rather "sociotropically," on the basis of their view of the welfare of society as a whole.[115] This fact would probably mitigate the control of electoral outcomes by the knowledgeable minority in a world in which the miracle of aggregation holds true.[116] The knowledgeable would be trustworthy guardians of their fellow citizens' welfare.

To some extent, this conclusion is valid. However, it is important to recognize two key caveats. First, self-interest does influence opinion on at least some issues, including policy toward smoking[117] and gun control.[118] Self-interest might also affect the priority that people place on one issue relative to others.

Second, non-self-interested voting does *not* necessarily mean that the voter weights the interests of all members of society equally. For example, racial prejudice might lead voters to undervalue the welfare of groups they dislike, or even actively value the infliction of harm on them. Although such prejudice has declined, it still sometimes influences public opinion on key issues.[119] A major recent study finds that "ethnocentrism"—the tendency to value one's own racial or ethnic group above others—influences American public opinion on a wide range of issues in both domestic and foreign policy.[120]

In any event, speculation about a world in which well-informed minorities determine the outcome of elections is of limited interest, given the reality that poorly informed voters neither choose their opinions at random nor abstain from voting or having views altogether.

Aggregation and Diversity

Some scholars argue that aggregation can work especially well if participants have diverse views and abilities.[121] When a large and diverse group seeks a solution to a problem, it can often make better decisions than a smaller, more expert group because it can pool its diverse collective knowledge which, in the aggregate, is greater than that of the smaller group.

There is little doubt that diversity can sometimes improve the quality of group decision-making. To take a highly simplified example, a group of one hundred people that each has one unit of relevant knowledge might outperform a group of ten each of whom has five units. Even though the average member of the second group has five times more knowledge than the average member of the larger one, the total knowledge of the larger group is twice as great as that of the smaller one (one hundred versus fifty).

Voting, however, is a poor way to take advantage of such diversity. Much of the evidence supporting the idea that diversity leads to better decisions involves experiments or simulations in which diverse participants work together and learn from each other's mistakes by building on each other's work.[122] For example, Lu Hong and Scott Page developed a model in which each of numerous diverse agents seeks a solution to a problem, and then the next participant is able to take advantage of the information produced by the searches of those who came before.[123]

Hélène Landemore, another leading academic advocate of the diversity theory of aggregation, analogizes the benefits of diversity for voting decisions in the classic movie *Twelve Angry Men*, in which a group of diverse jurors, all but one of whom are initially persuaded that a murder defendant is guilty, deliberate until they reach the correct conclusion that there is reasonable doubt.[124]

There is, however, a crucial difference between voting in elections and the jury deliberations in *Twelve Angry Men*. The jurors spent a great deal of time and effort "collectively brainstorming the available information and arguments and putting them through the many filters and lenses of the group."[125] They listened carefully to opposing points of view, and most tried hard to consider them objectively. By contrast, most voters either spend little or no time collecting political knowledge, or focus primarily on conversation partners and media that reinforce their preexisting biases.[126] Few make much effort to seek out opposing views or to evaluate them in an unbiased way. Had the jurors in the movie cast their final votes after briefly considering their own preexisting biases, paying little or no attention to alternative views, all but one of them (the original dissenter famously played by Henry Fonda), would have voted to convict. Yet that is precisely how most voters in elections tend to act.

Jurors deliberate carefully and take their responsibilities seriously in part because they realize that their votes are likely to have a major impact on the outcome. It usually takes all twelve jurors to convict in a criminal case, so even one dissenter can change the result. By contrast, voters in an election have only an infinitesimally small chance of having a decisive effect,[127] with the result that they have little incentive to seek out information or deliberate carefully. If we apply this point to the electorate of one hundred voters with one hundred total units of knowledge, this group is less likely to outperform the smaller, more expert group if each of the one hundred voters simply makes a decision based on his or her own stock of knowledge, without accessing that of the others. In that event, each member of the large group is still utilizing only his or her original one unit of knowledge rather than the one hundred possessed by the group as a whole.

Even if members of a diverse group vote without careful thought and deliberation, they might still outperform a smaller, more expert group if their biases are more likely to randomly cancel each other out. In a diverse group, one subgroup's views are likely to be "negatively correlated" with those of other groups.[128] When one group makes a mistake in one direction, the other makes a mistake in the other.

Unfortunately, however, this dynamic is not enough to counter ignorance-induced errors that affect a majority of the total group. And, as we have seen, increasing knowledge has major aggregate effects on collective opinion.[129] If diversity within the electorate were enough to offset the effects of ignorance or make them random, the effects of knowledge should be random as well. As Landemore recognizes, diversity is only likely to "trump" individual knowledge if the participants in the diverse group are "relatively smart (or not too dumb)."[130] An electorate where most voters often lack very basic political knowledge and regularly do a poor job of evaluating what they do know, is likely to fall short of that ideal in many cases.

Even when a mistake is not common enough to effect the majority of the group, a diverse but ignorant group can still easily make mistakes. Consider an electorate of 1,000,000 voters each with one unit of knowledge, similar to the electorate of 100 voters described earlier. We will also assume that they are voting in an election between Candidate A and Candidate B, and that A is likely to be the better choice, given the group's objectives. Assume, further, that 990,000 of them vote essentially randomly, with the result that any errors they make cancel each other out. If, among, the remaining 10,000, 6,000 are on average more prone to making an error in favor of B, then the group as a whole will almost certainly reach a wrong decision, even though the net bias in favor of B is very small. In a large group that makes decisions by majority voting, if the prevalence of ignorance-induced error in one direction is only slightly more common than error in another, then diversity will not be able to offset the effects of ignorance.[131]

The Condorcet Jury Theorem

Closely related to the idea of the "miracle of aggregation" is the use of the Condorcet Jury Theorem as a defense of democratic competence. First described by the Marquis de Condorcet in the eighteenth century, the Condorcet Jury Theorem shows that the probability of a majority vote reaching the "correct" outcome increases statistically as the number of voters increases, so long as each individual is at least slightly more likely to vote the "right" way than the "wrong" way.[132] If the group is large enough, it is more likely to choose the correct option than a small group in which each individual has a much greater chance of being right than each individual within the large group.

For example, it turns out that a majority vote in an electorate with one million voters each of whom has only a 51 percent chance of voting for the best of two available options is more likely to reach a correct decision than an electorate with one hundred voters each of whom chooses the right option 90 percent of the time.[133] This result suggests a possible defense of democratic decision-making in a large electorate where most voters are only moderately informed. The large size of the electorate could make up for the lower knowledge levels of each individual voter.[134]

Unfortunately, this argument has several serious weaknesses. One is that it usually works only if voters are, on average, more likely to choose the correct option than the "wrong" one. If instead of being 51 percent likely to choose the right answer, each voter is actually 51 percent likely to choose the wrong one, the Jury Theorem shows that a large electorate will choose the wrong option with virtual certainty, indeed with slightly greater certainty than a small electorate in which each individual voter has a 90 percent chance of being wrong. Given the fact that a majority of voters are systematically misinformed on many issues, there is probably a large number of cases in which the average voter is likely to err in this way.

The theorem also assumes that voters make their decisions independently of each other. If they do not, the mistakes of one can affect others, making a correct decision less likely.[135] In real life, of course, voter decisions are usually not independent, and voters are often greatly influenced by the views of others.[136]

Moreover, the traditional version of the Condorcet Jury Theorem implicitly assumes that voters will not reduce their efforts at information acquisition as the size of the electorate grows and the chance of casting a decisive vote declines. Once rational ignorance is introduced into the equation, it turns out that increasing the size of the electorate often *reduces* the chance of getting a correct answer, because voters acquire less information than they would in a smaller group.[137] For this reason, it would be undesirable to have juries with hundreds or thousands of members render verdicts on trials by majority vote, as was the practice in ancient Athenian courts.[138] Individual jurors would pay less attention to the evidence and consider it less carefully because they would realize that their votes had little chance of affecting the outcome. Large-scale democratic electorates face similar perverse incentives.

SHORTCUTS FALLING SHORT

Overall, the shortcuts to informed voting discussed in the literature are far less helpful to voters than their advocates suggest. In many instances, they may be actively misleading. No currently known shortcut fully substitutes for basic political knowledge, or comes close to doing so.

This is not to say that shortcuts are completely useless. Far from it. Some of them are helpful in particular instances, especially in dealing with relatively simple political issues. Most notably, retrospective voting enables voters to punish incumbents who are responsible for large and visible disasters, such as mass famines. This is a great advantage of democracy over rival political systems, and we owe it at least in part to the availability of information shortcuts. The problem is that shortcuts are far less effective in dealing with the less visible and more complicated issues that constitute the vast bulk of modern government policy.

If shortcuts fall short, what can be done to manage the problem of political ignorance? Chapter 5 begins the task of answering this question by arguing that the dangers of ignorance can be reduced by limiting and decentralizing government power.

Foot Voting vs. Ballot Box Voting

Immigration is the sincerest form of flattery.

—JACK PAAR, COMEDIAN AND TV TALK SHOW HOST[1]

THE STRENGTHS AND WEAKNESSES of constitutional federalism have been debated for centuries. We have also had centuries of debate over the extent to which there should be constitutional constraints on the scope of government power more generally.[2] But one major possible advantage of decentralization and limited government has often been ignored in the debate so far: its potential for reducing the costs of widespread political ignorance.[3]

The argument here is simple: federalism enables citizens to "vote with their feet," and foot voters have much stronger incentives to make well-informed decisions than conventional ballot box voters. The same goes for limits on the power of government that enable citizens to vote with their feet in the private sector.[4] Restricting the size and complexity of government can further alleviate the problems of political ignorance by reducing the knowledge burden imposed on voters.

The informational advantages of foot voting over ballot box voting suggest that decentralized federalism can increase both citizen welfare and democratic accountability relative to policymaking in a centralized unitary state. Since at least the pioneering work of Charles Tiebout,[5] scholars have analyzed foot voting extensively.[6] But its informational advantages over ballot box voting have often been ignored. Incentives for knowledge acquisition are much stronger when citizens have the option of voting with their feet rather than just at the ballot box. The same holds true for incentives to make rational use of the information that is acquired.

This chapter also considers some empirical evidence indicating the informational superiority of foot voting over ballot box voting. It turns out that even a severely oppressed and often poorly educated group can acquire sufficient information to engage in effective foot voting.

Finally, we will see how limits on the scope of government have some of the same informational advantages as political decentralization. Indeed, those advantages may be even greater in light of the fact that exit costs are usually lower in private sector markets than in the case of interjurisdictional migration. Limited government also helps alleviate the problem of political ignorance by reducing the knowledge burden on voters imposed by the size and complexity of the modern state. The informational benefits of foot voting strengthen the case for constitutional limits on central governments in order to facilitate decentralization. They also strengthen the case for limits on the power of government relative to the private sector.

The argument presented here is comparative. It holds that foot voting has significant informational advantages over ballot box voting, not that foot voting overcomes all information problems completely. But such comparative analysis is important because foot voting and ballot box voting are the most important realistic alternatives facing many societies across a wide range of issues.

Foot voting and political decentralization do have some genuine shortcomings. Among the most important ones are moving costs, the possibility of destructive "races to the bottom" in which competition between regions enables harmful policies to prevail, and the danger that federalism might lead to the oppression of minority groups. Each of these is sometimes a genuine problem. But these dangers are not as severe as sometimes claimed, and do not negate the informational advantages of foot voting.

Political ignorance is just one of many factors that have to be weighed in deciding how centralized a political system should be. But it does make the case for decentralization stronger than it otherwise would be.

INFORMATIONAL ADVANTAGES OF FOOT VOTING

As discussed in Chapter 3, rational ignorance creates two serious problems of political knowledge. First, voters have little incentive to acquire political knowledge for the purpose of making better electoral decisions.

Second, they have incentives to be irrational in the way they analyze whatever information they do learn. Foot voting provides much stronger incentives than ballot box voting for both information acquisition and rational information use. People voting with their feet are largely free of the collective action problems that lead to rational ignorance in the political process.

Information Acquisition

As we have seen, one of the main causes of political ignorance is the fact that it is "rational." Because even an extremely well-informed voter has virtually no chance of actually influencing electoral outcomes, he or she has little incentive to become informed in the first place, at least if the only purpose of doing so is to cast a "correct" vote. By contrast, people "voting with their feet" by choosing the state or locality in which to live are in a wholly different situation from the ballot box voter. If a "foot voter" can acquire information about superior economic conditions, public policies, or other advantages in another jurisdiction, he or she can move there and take advantage of them even if all other citizens do nothing. This creates a much stronger incentive for foot voters to acquire relevant information about conditions in different jurisdictions than for ballot box voters to acquire information about public policy.

The same goes for foot voting in the private sector. Most people probably spend far more time and effort acquiring information about the purchase of a car or a TV than determining which presidential candidate to vote for. This is surely not because a TV is more important or more complicated than the issues decided by the president. It is because the individual's decision on which car or TV to buy is far more likely to make a real difference to the outcome than is a single vote in any election.

Adam Przeworski, one of the world's leading scholars of democratic decision-making, laments that "[n]o rule of collective decision-making other than unanimity can render causal efficacy to equal individual participation."[7] But foot voting comes close. It is an option that can be made available to most, if not all, of the population, and individuals' choices are causally effective in a way that ballot box votes are not. Moving costs and other constraints limit the extent to which participation in foot voting is completely equal. But, as we shall see, these constraints are not nearly as severe as conventionally thought. And, obviously, individual influence over government policy in ballot box voting systems is also far from fully equal.

Some evidence suggests that public knowledge of local government may be even lower than national political knowledge.[8] Political knowledge of different levels of government is difficult to compare, given the divergent nature of the issues addressed by national as opposed to local government, and the different structures of the two. But if it is true that knowledge of local government is lower than knowledge of national politics, that finding might cut against the theory that foot voters are better-informed than ballot box voters.

However, the most recent in-depth comparison of local and national political knowledge concludes that the two are roughly comparable, with 39 percent of a sample of Philadelphia adults qualifying as "know-nothings" with respect to local politics, and 38 percent with respect to national politics.[9] Women and African Americans, groups that score relatively poorly on measures of national political knowledge, tend to do much better relative to whites and men on measures of local political knowledge.[10] There is also some evidence showing that political knowledge and civic engagement are higher in smaller localities,[11] where foot voting is easier than in larger ones where exit entails greater moving costs. Admittedly, it is not clear whether this knowledge advantage is due to greater exit opportunities or to the greater likelihood of an individual vote being decisive in a smaller electorate. Quite possibly, both factors play a role.

This rough parity between local and national political knowledge is impressive in light of the facts that media coverage focuses more on national politics, local politics addresses lower-stakes issues, and local elections are often more difficult for voters to understand than national ones because candidates often have less clear connections to political parties.[12] Most localities are also relatively ideologically homogenous compared to national politics,[13] which reduces the need to acquire political information in order to make voting decisions, since the differences between candidates with a realistic chance of winning are likely to be smaller.

In most cases, foot voters also do not need to acquire as much information as ballot box voters in order to be adequately informed. Unlike a ballot box voter, a foot voter need not connect his judgment of relative conditions in various states to specific elected officials and their policies.[14]

If ballot box voters do not realize which officials are responsible for which issues or don't separate out the impact of public policy from that of other social conditions, they may end up punishing or rewarding incumbent office-holders for outcomes they have no control over.[15] The office-holders themselves can try to take credit for positive developments that were not really caused by their policies. Presidents, for example, try to take credit for any economic prosperity that occurs during their term in office, even if they did little or nothing to cause it.

By contrast, foot voters don't need comparably detailed knowledge. It is often enough for them to know that conditions are better in one state or locality than another, and then be able to act on this knowledge by moving. Not only does foot voting create a stronger incentive to acquire knowledge than ballot box voting, it also usually requires less knowledge to implement effectively. From a foot-voting perspective, it may not matter much that many Philadelphians are unaware of the names of top city officials or their positions on key issues,[16] even though this information is of greater significance for ballot box voters. The relative homogeneity of local politics also makes detailed political information less important at the local level.[17] If a foot voter knows a locality's general political orientation, she can have a good sense of its politics even if she knows little about particular officials, though it would be wrong to conclude that variation between individual officials is totally unimportant.

To be sure, foot voting decisions do involve some informational complexities. For example, better conditions in one state relative to another could be the result of luck or other temporary random factors that could quickly change. If wages are higher in one state than another, that might be the result of having higher-skilled labor rather than superior economic policy or better opportunity. A low-skilled worker moving to such a state would not necessarily be better off than before. Potential migrants may need to give consideration to such issues before deciding where to move.

In addition, the existence of multiple jurisdictions might lead to confusion as to which jurisdictions are responsible for which issues. Leaders of one jurisdiction might take credit for their neighbors' successes and slough off the blame for their own failures.[18] Would-be migrants also might have difficulty evaluating the many different kinds of public services provided by competing local governments.[19]

However, these difficulties are not as great as those that face ballot box voters. If conditions have been better in one jurisdiction than another for a long time, that suggests it probably is not merely the result of temporary luck. Similarly, individuals can focus on the opportunities and living conditions available to people in the destination state with skills similar to their own.

Evaluating public services and determining which officials are responsible for what issues is also a serious problem for ballot box voters in a unitary, centralized state.[20] If that state provides a variety of public services, it will be hard for rationally ignorant voters to evaluate it, and especially to compare those services to potential alternatives. In a unitary state, there may not be any real-world examples where those alternatives have actually been tried, so voters will find it harder to evaluate them than would foot voters in a decentralized system where at least some of the alternatives have been tried in another jurisdiction.

The mere existence of federalism does create one information problem that may be absent in a unitary state: under federalism, ballot box voters may find it difficult to determine which level of government is responsible for a given issue.[21] But given that the United States and other nations with well-established federal systems are unlikely to abolish federalism, transferring more authority to lower-level governments would not make this problem any worse than it would be otherwise. A federal system in which the central government has 50 percent of the policymaking power is no less potentially confusing than one where it has 40 percent.

Moreover, the enormous size and complexity of modern government ensure a great deal of potential confusion even in a unitary state. The additional complexity introduced by federalism may be partially offset by the fact that, if state and local governments bear responsibility for more issues, voters in one area need no longer consider the handling of those policies in other parts of the country, including those with very different conditions. New York voters, for example, need not consider the impact of federal education policy on Texas schools if education policy were left to states or localities. This reduces the information burden faced by the electorate.[22]

Overall, foot voters have much stronger incentives than ballot box voters to overcome whatever information problems they face. Evaluating the quality of public services is often difficult, and both ballot box voters and foot voters will sometimes fail at the task. But the latter have stronger incentives to succeed at acquiring and analyzing the necessary information. Whether or not immigration is the "sincerest form of flattery," as Jack Paar put it, it is usually the best-informed.[23]

Information Use

In addition to providing superior incentives for information acquisition relative to ballot box voting, foot voting also improves incentives for rational information use. Part of the reason for this is the same as that which underlies foot voters' superior incentive to acquire information: the absence of a collective action problem. But there are also other reasons to expect foot voters to make better use of the information that they acquire than ballot box voters do.

As we have seen,[24] people have a strong tendency to process political information in a highly biased way that tends to confirm their preexisting ideologies and prejudices. This is true of both ordinary voters and political activists and experts. By contrast, most modern Americans lack the same kind of commitment to their states that many have to their ideologies and partisan affiliations. Over the past hundred years, citizen identification with state and local governments has greatly diminished in most parts of the country, replaced by a sense of national identity as Americans.[25] For that reason, people are likely to be more objective in analyzing information bearing on their decisions about where to live than their decisions about whom to vote for. The latter implicate strong partisan and ideological commitments, and sometimes also ethnic or religious ones. The former—at least in the modern United States—usually do not.

Some scholars claim that the decline of identification with state governments is an argument *against* federalism,[26] because citizens no longer have a sense of community that is linked to their states. However, citizens' diminished commitment to states and localities facilitates effective foot voting, and to that extent actually strengthens the case for devolution of power away from the center.

This point applies with much lesser force to countries where the regional governments are the focus of ethnic or ideological loyalties. For example, French Canadian nationalists may be strongly attached to Quebec and reluctant to move to other provinces even if the latter have better policies.

The concern here is not that ethnic, religious, or regional attachments are irrational in and of themselves. For present purposes, they are no more so than any other value a person might have. Rather, the point is that a strong emotional commitment to a particular location might make it more difficult for a person to avoid bias in evaluating factual information about its strengths and weaknesses relative to those of alternative areas.

Even in federal systems where there are strong associations between ethnicities and jurisdictions, however, foot voters may still be more rational in their evaluation of information than ballot box voters if their ethnic group is in the majority in more than one jurisdiction. Moreover, even in the relatively rare cases when foot voters' biases in favor of their home jurisdiction are as powerful as those of ballot box voters in favor of their ideology or party, the former will still have stronger incentives to try to overcome their biases because their choices are more likely to be decisive.

The Role of Interjurisdictional Competition

Interjurisdictional competition also improves the acquisition of information by foot voters. States and localities seek to attract new residents and businesses as sources of tax revenue. Therefore, state and local governments have strong incentives to establish policies that will appeal to potential immigrants and convince current residents to stay.[27] The power of the competitive pressure comes from governments' constant need to attract additional revenue to finance expenditures that can pay off key interest groups and increase political leaders' reelection chances. Interstate and interlocality competition for residents facilitates the creation of public policies that advance the interests of the majority, even in the absence of informed ballot box voting.[28]

Competition also gives both state governments and private organizations incentives to disseminate information about the advantages of living in one jurisdiction as opposed to others. While the same is true of competitors for political office, information disseminated by competitors in the foot-voting market is arguably less likely to be inaccurate or misleading than political advertising. Since foot voters have strong incentives to examine information more closely than ballot box voters, competitors in the former market are less likely to get away with deceptive or overly simplistic claims than those in the latter. Political rhetoric and advertising routinely employ misleading or deceptive rhetoric and claims,[29] some of which are quite effective. By contrast, as discussed later in this chapter, evidence suggests that competitors in the market for foot voters generally disseminate relatively accurate information to their "consumers" even in cases when the latter are extremely poor and ill-educated.

Competition also enables foot voters to take advantage of the information acquisition efforts of knowledgeable minorities to a greater extent than ballot box voters can. "Marginal" consumers most likely to move for the purpose of obtaining a given service also tend to have higher knowledge levels.[30] Competition for these marginal movers can improve the quality of services even for those who are less well informed. By contrast, knowledgeable minorities are less helpful for ballot box voters, because candidates can more easily win elections by appealing to a much larger number of ignorant voters, and because marginal swing voters in elections tend to be among the most ignorant.[31]

Implications for Group Migration

The informational advantages of foot voting over ballot box voting potentially extend to group migration, as well as migration by individuals and families. Historically, religious and ideological groups have sometimes chosen to migrate together in order to establish a community where they could live in accordance with their principles. Well-known examples from American history include the Pilgrims' migration from Europe to establish their colony at Plymouth and the migration of the Mormons to Utah.[32] Such group migration differs from moving decisions by individuals or families because it requires coordination across a larger number of people, and is often undertaken for the purposes of establishing a community based on a specific religion or ideology. Obviously, individuals can move for religious or ideological reasons as well. But they cannot establish a whole new community based on those principles.

Group migration within a federal system need not involve the establishment of an entirely new state or city, as happened with the Mormons. It could simply mean moving from one existing state to another whose policies are more hospitable to the group's purposes. For example, Mennonite religious groups in Canada and the United States migrated west without any intention of establishing their own state or province.[33]

Some aspects of group governance may raise informational problems similar to those that arise from ballot box voting. In a large group with a democratic governance structure, individual members might have little incentive to acquire information to base their votes on. They could be rationally ignorant for much the same reasons as most voters are. However, group migration does generally include an individually decisive choice on the part of each member to join the group in the first place, and often an additional decision to choose to migrate along with the other members instead of stay behind. For these reasons, participants in group migrations probably have stronger incentives to acquire and rationally evaluate relevant information than do ballot box voters.

THE POWER OF FOOT VOTING UNDER ADVERSE CONDITIONS: AFRICAN AMERICANS IN THE JIM CROW–ERA SOUTH

There has not yet been a definitive study that empirically documents the informational advantages of voting with your feet over ballot box voting under controlled conditions. But there is telling historical evidence of impressive information acquisition by foot voters even under extremely adverse circumstances. The case of African Americans in the

Jim Crow–era South, roughly 1880 to 1960, is a particularly noteworthy example. During that time, southern state governments adopted a wide variety of laws discriminating against and oppressing their black populations; this extensive system of racial oppression was collectively known as "Jim Crow."

If information acquisition for foot voting could be effective under the severely adverse conditions endured by southern blacks in the Jim Crow era, it is likely to be at least equally so in other, less extreme circumstances. Moreover, the limited available evidence suggests that black southern foot voters were better-informed than the on average wealthier and more educated southern white ballot box voters of the same era.

Obviously, foot voting could not and did not completely alleviate the suffering endured by early twentieth-century African Americans. In a society as racist as the United States at that time, there probably wasn't any politically feasible comprehensive solution to their problems. But their experience does show that foot voters can obtain adequate information to make good decisions, even under very difficult circumstances.

Southern Black Migration During the Jim Crow Era

African Americans in the Jim Crow–era South, most of them poorly educated and many illiterate, were able to learn enough information about the existence of relatively better conditions in other states to set off a massive migration to the North and also to parts of the South that were relatively less oppressive than others.[34] Between about 1880 and 1920, over 1 million southern-born African Americans migrated to the North or the West.[35] By 1920, these migrants accounted for some 10 percent of the total black population of the United States, which then stood at 10.4 million.[36] There was an even larger black migration from South to North in the years immediately following World War II.[37] The earlier migration, however, is of special interest for present purposes because during this period southern blacks were even more severely disadvantaged than during the later one and would have found it more difficult to acquire information about migration opportunities.

In addition to migration from the South to other parts of the country, there was also extensive African-American population movement within the South itself.[38] Intra-regional migration was often driven simply by the search for economic opportunity, but also by differences between southern political jurisdictions in the degree to which they oppressed the local black population.[39]

Southern blacks in the early twentieth century labored under severe disadvantages that one might expect to prevent effective foot voting. Most were extremely ill-educated, in part as a deliberate result of state government policy. As late as 1940, only 5.4 percent of southern blacks over the age of twenty-five were high school graduates, compared to 24.6 percent of contemporary southern whites.[40] Even those southern blacks who did have access to education nearly always attended inferior segregated schools that were deliberately structured to provide only very limited education for black students.[41] In light of these problems, the success of so many African-American migrants in acquiring the knowledge they needed is strong evidence in support of the informational advantages of foot voting.

Information Acquisition by Southern Black Migrants

Southern black workers relied on a variety of information sources to facilitate migration decisions. One important resource was the information provided by relatives and acquaintances already living in the North or in more tolerant southern jurisdictions.[42] Many black migrants were "armed with firsthand reports from trusted friends and relatives" about conditions in the North.[43] Ballot box voters cannot easily rely on comparably knowledgeable and trustworthy information sources.[44]

Other information was provided by the contemporary black media, which actively encouraged migration.[45] But some scholars put special emphasis on the information-spreading activities of "emigrant agents" employed by businesses seeking to recruit African-American workers.[46] The agents provided valuable information to African Americans considering moving to the North, and sometimes also helped arrange transportation for them. While agents had obvious incentive to exaggerate the benefits of moving,[47] this was to some extent kept in check by information provided by migrants who had already made it to the North,[48] and by the likelihood that workers who were deceived about the opportunities available to them might move back to the South themselves and tell others to disbelieve the agents. These mechanisms provided a check on deception by emigrant agents of a kind that is not usually available in the case of political rhetoric used to persuade ballot box voters.

In addition to acquiring information about job opportunities, many black migrants also chose to move in part because they came to realize that northern state governments and social mores were less hostile to blacks than those in the South. Although economic opportunity was a key factor in motivating migration, the desire to escape racial repression was also important. Migrants themselves often cited lynching, racial discrimination, and other hostile government policies as important factors in their decision to leave the South.[49]

Some contemporary African-American leaders recognized the potential of foot voting as a tool for mitigating their people's oppression, and urged southern blacks to consider migrating to the North. As early as 1886, Frederick Douglass—the most prominent African-American leader of the nineteenth century—argued that "*diffusion* is the true policy for the colored people of the South," that as many blacks as possible should be encouraged to move to "parts of the country where their civil and political rights are better protected than at present they can be at the South," and that "[a] million of dollars devoted to this purpose [of assisting black migration out of the South] would do more for the colored people of the South than the same amount expended in any other way."[50] A 1917 NAACP publication claimed that migration north was "the most effective protest against Southern lynching, lawlessness, and general deviltry."[51]

Effective Use of Knowledge

Most scholars agree that black migration to the North during the Jim Crow era was generally effective in achieving the migrants' goals. Although the North was far from free of racism, most migrants were able to better their lot significantly, both economically and from the standpoint of protecting their civil and political rights.[52] These results suggest that the migrants made effective use of the knowledge that they acquired, and generally chose their destinations wisely.

As the theory of foot voting under competitive federalism would predict,[53] the resulting migration not only benefited the migrants themselves but also forced racist southern state governments to "grant . . . African-Americans greater educational opportunities and greater protection in their property and person" in an effort to get them to stay and continue to provide labor for southern white-owned farms and businesses.[54] For example, fear of losing black labor was one of the motives that led southern state governments to finally make some belated efforts to crack down on the lynching of African Americans in the 1920s.[55] Lynching was cited as an important cause of their decision to move by many migrants.[56] In a related dramatic example, interjurisidictional competition for the labor of migrating black coal miners led to successful lobbying by coal companies for a reduction in school segregation in early 1900s West Virginia.[57] As Douglass had predicted back in 1886, "the condition of those [southern blacks] who must remain will be better because of those who go."[58]

Obviously, the ability of southern blacks to vote with their feet did not come close to fully mitigating the baneful effects of Jim Crow.[59] Foot voting was an improvement over preexisting conditions, not a panacea. It did, however, provide important informational benefits and a measure of political empowerment to a widely despised and poorly educated minority.

Although exact comparisons are difficult, it seems likely that potential southern black migrants of the Jim Crow era were able to learn considerably more about relative conditions in different jurisdictions than most modern voters have learned about the basics of our political system. At the very least, large numbers of poor and ill-educated southern blacks learned enough to understand that relatively more favorable employment opportunities and public policies awaited them in other jurisdictions, a realization that contrasts with the inability of most modern citizens to acquire sufficient knowledge to engage in effective retrospective voting.[60]

If foot voting could provide powerful informational advantages in the exceptionally adverse conditions of the Jim Crow–era South, there is strong reason to expect that it is more effective under modern conditions, in which education levels are much higher, information costs are lower, and no large group is as thoroughly oppressed as were poor southern blacks a century ago. People in less dire circumstances than early twentieth-century southern blacks can acquire information more easily.

Comparison with Contemporary
Southern White Ballot Box Voters

In considering Jim Crow–era black migration as a case of foot voting, it is difficult to make a direct comparison to ballot box voting. Most southern blacks during that period were, of course, denied the right to vote, so they did not have the opportunity to address through ballot box voting the same issues that many sought to resolve through foot voting. However, southern whites of the same period did address racial issues at the ballot box, and it is worth comparing their apparent knowledge levels with those of black foot voters.

White southerners had far higher average income and education levels than African Americans. As of 1940, 24.6 percent of southern white adults over the age of twenty-five had high school diplomas, compared to just 5.4 percent of southern blacks.[61] And this difference in quantity of education was combined with a massive difference in quality.

Despite these comparative disadvantages, southern black foot voters seem to have acquired fairly accurate information about migration opportunities and made effective use of their knowledge of which jurisdictions had policies more favorable to blacks. By contrast, southern white ballot box voters seem to have been ignorant of important basic facts relevant to Jim Crow–era racial policy.

Widespread southern white support for Jim Crow policies in the early twentieth century was in part based on purely normative disagreement with racial egalitarianism. However, white support for many such policies was also in part the result of gross ignorance on factual matters and failure to make rational use of political information.

To take one of the most notorious examples, for decades large proportions of white southern voters seem to have accepted the blatantly false claim that many if not most black men were out to rape white women.[62] This widely accepted myth was the principal rationale justifying the southern states' policy of permitting the lynching of numerous blacks accused (often falsely) of the rape or murder of whites.[63] Although scholars and civil rights advocates demonstrated the falsity of such claims as early as the 1890s,[64] most of the white southern electorate apparently remained unaware of this fact, or unwilling to consider it.[65]

Southern white voters were also, for decades, unable to recognize that the exclusion of the region's large African-American population from much of the educational and economic system was an important contributing factor to the region's underdevelopment—a point obvious to most economists. Although the relative economic backwardness of the South was a major issue in regional politics throughout the late nineteenth and early twentieth centuries, few white southerners urged desegregation as a method for promoting economic development until well after World War II, and even then such views were mostly advanced by business leaders and other elites rather than by ordinary voters.[66]

In the absence of suitable survey data from the period, it is difficult to say whether these white southern views on racial issues were driven by ignorance per se, or by failure to rationally evaluate the information voters did know. Most likely, a combination of both was at work. Either way, the result is consistent with the rational ignorance hypothesis, and also contrasts with the more effective acquisition and use of information on racial issues by black foot voters.

There are, of course, some important distinctions between Jim Crow–Era white ballot box voting on racial issues and black foot voting. Racial issues were obviously of greater importance to African Americans than to whites, and the former therefore probably had stronger incentives to be informed about them. Moreover, the knowledge necessary for effective foot voting is in some respects simpler than that necessary for ballot box voting.[67]

However, the similarities between the two cases are still strong enough to make the comparison meaningful, even if imperfect. Race and its associated economic underdevelopment were among the most important political issues in the Jim Crow–era South, and whites had almost as great a political stake in them as did blacks. The one-party system and other political institutions of the pre–Civil Rights Movement South were organized around the objective of maintaining white supremacy.[68] Moreover, to the extent that whites did have less interest in racial issues than blacks, this factor is at least partially offset by their higher income and education levels.

FOOT VOTING IN THE PRIVATE SECTOR

The informational benefits of foot voting make the case not only for federalism as an alternative to centralization, but for the market and civil society as an alternative to government. The private sector may, in many situations, be an even better mechanism for foot voting than is federalism. Voting with your feet against a product in the market usually has much lower moving costs than doing so against a regional or local government. One can switch to a different product or firm without changing one's residence. The same point holds true for most civil society organizations. In this respect, the informational argument for foot voting has implications for the balance between the government and the private sector, as well as for the relationship of one level of government to another.

It is undeniable that citizens acting in the private sector also make mistakes due to ignorance or irrationality.[69] But some research suggests that cognitive biases that show up in voting decisions and laboratory experiments largely disappear in conditions that more closely approximate real-world market decisions.[70] Economists Charles Plott and Kathryn Zeiler have shown that one of the most often-cited cognitive biases—the "endowment effect," which supposedly causes people to overvalue items they already own relative to ones they might acquire in the future—might well be an artifact of faulty experimental procedures.[71] Much has been made in recent years of possible irrationality by consumers in financial markets, such as those for credit cards and those in markets with standard form contracts.[72] However, the available evidence suggests that participants in these markets make relatively few mistakes and often correct the errors they do make quickly.[73]

This certainly does not prove that consumers never suffer from serious irrationality. To the contrary, some probably do, especially those with low cognitive ability and little relevant experience and training.[74] The key point, however, is not that consumers and other foot voters are completely rational, but that they have stronger incentives to avoid cognitive biases than voters do.[75] As Nobel Prize–winning economist F. A. Hayek put it more than thirty years ago:

> [R]ational behavior is not a premise of economic theory, though it is often presented as such. The basic contention of theory is rather that competition will make it necessary for people to act rationally in order to maintain themselves. It is based not on the assumption that most or all the participants in the market process are rational, but, on the contrary, on the assumption that it will in general be through competition that a few relatively more rational individuals will make it necessary for the rest to emulate them in order to prevail. In a society in which rational behavior confers an advantage on the individual, rational methods will progressively be developed and be spread by imitation. *It is no use being more rational than the rest if one is not allowed to derive benefits from being so.*[76]

Hayek's point is particularly relevant to the comparison between voters on the one hand and market participants on the other. Voters are almost a paradigmatic example of Hayek's category of people for whom "[i]t is no use being more rational than the rest." Market participants, despite their very real flaws, have quite different incentives.

The very different responses of voters and market participants to the Bush administration's massive 2003 prescription drug bill provides a dramatic example of the difference. At the time the plan was adopted by Congress, some 70 percent of the public did not even realize that it had passed, despite the fact it was the biggest new government program in decades.[77] As a result of the program, however, senior citizens were now able to choose from among several different prescription drug plans available through the government's Medicare system. Unlike the other members of the public, who were in the position of evaluating the prescription drug plan solely as voters, these senior citizens had to make decisions within it as consumers, albeit in an artificial market with choices limited by the government.

The options offered by the new law were extremely complex and difficult for nonexperts to evaluate; they involved choosing when and whether to enroll in the new Medicare Part D system, which enables participants to purchase discounted coverage for prescription drugs through private insurers.[78] Economist Daniel McFadden found that over 70 percent of a sample of eligible seniors surveyed in 2006 (soon after the new pre-scription drug benefits first became available) intended to enroll in the new plan at a time that would effectively minimize the expected present value (EPV) of their out-of-pocket expenses on the plan.[79] Some of the 19 percent who planned to enroll too early to minimize their EPV might still have been acting rationally, if they were highly risk averse.[80]

Senior citizen consumers certainly were not perfectly rational or perfectly informed about the new Medicare prescription drug options. McFadden concludes that a significant minority made mistakes due to ignorance or irrationality and recommends "paternalistic" intervention to address their problems.[81] Yet the contrast between market participants and ballot box voters is still striking. Even though the former faced a very "complex" choice,[82] the vast majority of them acquired enough informa-tion to make rational decisions at a time when the program was still new and unfamiliar. On the other hand, the vast majority of eligible ballot box voters did not even learn enough to know that the massive prescription drug bill had passed. As a result, they did not realize that this program was a potentially major issue on which to evaluate the performance of incumbent politicians.

FOOT VOTING AND PRIVATE PLANNED COMMUNITIES

Private sector foot voting is already a reality for many services tradition-ally performed by local government in the United States. As of 2004, over fifty-two million Americans lived in private planned communities such as condominium associations.[83] These organizations often provide security, trash removal, environmental protection, local zoning rules, and other services that are usually the responsibility of local government.[84] Similar enterprises have proven popular in Europe, Latin America, and parts of Asia.[85]

Competing private planned communities have significant advan-tages over traditional interjurisdictional competition between regional and local governments.[86] A single metropolitan area can contain many more private common interest communities than government bodies. This makes it easier for each potential resident to find the community that best fits his or her needs, and also cuts down on potential moving costs by reducing the distance most movers would have to travel.

Unlike state and local governments, which are often subsidized by higher-level governments,[87] most private planned communities are exclusively dependent on residents for their revenues. This increases their incentive to compete for residents and meet their demands. Should they fail to do so, the property values of current owners are likely to fall, and they cannot use tax revenue collected in other areas to make up the difference. By contrast, state and local government officials usually have a much weaker stake in attracting migrants and incentivizing current residents to stay. While lower-level governments do have some incentive to attract migrants in order to raise revenue from taxpayers,[88] the existence of massive subsidies from higher-level governments reduces this incentive to compete relative to that faced by private planned communities.

Finally, potentially irrational attachments to a state or locality might inhibit decisions to move out of a political jurisdiction, especially in cases when that jurisdiction is closely associated with an ethnic or religious group with which the decision-maker feels a strong sense of identity.[89] By contrast, few people have strong emotional or ideological attachments to a private planned community. This factor might make "foot voting" decisions involving private planned communities more rational, on average, than those where potential movers choose between competing governmental jurisdictions.

The relative advantages of private planned communities over government might be even more significant for the production of goods and services not tied to particular physical locations. In such cases, people can vote with their feet without actually moving at all, thereby eliminating moving costs from the equation. Here too, the informational advantages of foot voting suggest that private provision has an important advantage over government.

Swiss economist Bruno Frey has argued that regional and local governments can take on some of the characteristics of private sector firms, breaking the link between territory and jurisdiction.[90] Frey claims that various government bodies specializing in different issue areas could have overlapping jurisdictions, and that individual citizens can change government service providers without a physical move. It is too early to give a definitive verdict on these proposals. If Frey's theories turn out to be viable, they could provide a blueprint for ensuring that foot voting will often be as effective in the public sector as the private. Something resembling Frey's idea already exists in the field of commercial transactions in the United States, where businesses and others are often able to choose for themselves which state's law will govern their dealings with each other, often without making a physical move.[91]

Both Frey's proposals and the case for devolving greater power to private communities dovetail with recent scholarship that promotes "federalism all the way down," the devolution of greater authority to cities and other local governments as opposed to larger subnational units, such as American states.[92] Advocates argue that such devolution can help ensure that government policy better reflects the diverse preferences of local communities, especially those where minority groups have substantial influence. Devolution to private communities and individuals allows for even more fine-grained decision-making that reflects the views of a still wider range of individuals and groups. It may also allow for more effective exploitation of specialized local knowledge than is possible through devolution to local government bodies alone.[93]

A complete comparison of private planned communities and political bodies is outside the scope of this chapter. The key point made here is to note a potentially important and underanalyzed advantage of private communities over ones controlled by political bodies. This advantage does not necessarily outweigh all competing considerations. Yet to the extent that the informational benefits of foot voting are even greater in the case of private sector institutions than political jurisdictions, they argue for increasing the authority of the former relative to the latter.

POLITICAL IGNORANCE AND THE SIZE OF GOVERNMENT

In addition to alleviating knowledge problems by transferring decision-making power to foot voters, reductions in the size and complexity of government might also reduce information problems with respect to issues that still remain subject to the ballot box. The debate over voter ignorance has focused on how much voters know but rarely on the question of how much government there is for them to know about. Yet it is clear that the greater the size and scope of government, the more voters have to know to control its policies through the ballot. As James Madison put in *Federalist* 62, "[i]t will be of little avail to the people that the laws are made by men of their own choice if the laws be so voluminous that they cannot be read, or so incoherent that they cannot be understood."[94]

In most advanced industrial democracies, government spending now constitutes at least a third and sometimes over one half of GDP.[95] In the United States, government spending at all levels accounted for some 36.8 percent of GDP in 2007, and increased to 42.3 percent in 2010, as a result of the explosion of new spending generated by the political response to the financial crisis.[96]

But it is not the size of government alone that so greatly increases the likelihood of voter ignorance as the extraordinary scope of government activity. A government that commits enormous resources to a narrow range of readily comprehensible activities is not necessarily much more difficult for voters to keep track of than one that commits only small amounts to them.

Yet the growth of government over the past century has been characterized by an immense expansion of the domain of government power as well as by increased activity in areas of traditional state responsibility.[97] This process has reached the point at which areas of social life completely outside the control of government are arguably no longer the rule but the exception.

In the United States, the executive branch of the federal government alone has fifteen cabinet-level departments, fifty-six independent regulatory agencies and government corporations, and four "quasi-official" agencies.[98] They range in function from the United States Information Agency to the Farm Credit Administration to the National Mediation Board. It is doubtful that voters could keep adequate track of all their activities even if they paid far more attention to political information than they do today.

Current surveys of political knowledge usually do not even ask about the functions of specific government agencies, instead opting for questions about very basic aspects of government structure and opinions about whether government should do "more" in broadly defined issue areas such as "education" or "helping the poor." The omission is in part the result of researchers' reluctance to use questions that may prove intimidating to ill-informed survey respondents. The few questions requiring more detailed issue knowledge that have found their way into surveys unsurprisingly show even greater levels of ignorance than those about more basic information.[99]

A government of strictly limited powers might reduce the problem of public ignorance by reducing the number of issues to be decided by government to a level which voters would find more manageable. Even if the total stock of voter knowledge does not increase, it is spread over fewer issues and therefore more likely to be adequate in each given case. For example, if the average voter learns a hundred units of political knowledge and there are fifty issues on the government agenda, he or she only knows an average of two units of knowledge per issue. By contrast, if there are only ten issues, the voter knows an average of ten units per issue.

This scenario abstracts away from many real-world complexities. For example, some issues are more complicated than others and some items of information are useful in analyzing more than one issue. Even so, a given stock of information is, other things equal, more likely to be enough to handle a narrow range of issues than a broader one. In the short term, it is probably impossible to reduce the size and complexity of government to the point at which rationally ignorant voters could readily understand and assess its major functions. But incremental reductions at the margin could still ease their task.

Is there in fact any evidence that limited government eases the informational burden on voters and enables them to exercise greater control than they do today? Any answer is necessarily tentative. But nineteenth-century American history suggests that the answer may be yes.

Because of the very limited powers of the national government, nineteenth-century national politics revolved around a small set of relatively narrowly defined issues, including the spread of slavery; the disposition of newly acquired western lands; the tariff; federal support for infrastructure spending; banking; and, on a few occasions, warfare with foreign powers.

The theory presented here predicts that this limitation of government power should have allowed voters to focus in on those issues that did come onto the electoral agenda in greater detail than has been possible in the modern era. While there have as yet been no systematic tests of this prediction, some evidence supports it, even though there was clearly still a great deal of political apathy.[100]

In the case of slavery, the Lincoln-Douglas debates over slavery expansion—conducted before large audiences of ordinary voters, including a substantial proportion of illiterates—addressed in some detail such questions as the effect of slavery expansion on free labor, whether or not the Supreme Court's interpretation of the Constitution necessarily takes precedence over that of other branches of government, the moral status of blacks in the liberal ideology of the Declaration of Independence, and the true meaning of "popular sovereignty."[101] Campaign speeches of this complexity are at the very least fairly uncommon today.

Unfortunately, the lack of systematic survey evidence of political knowledge in the nineteenth and early twentieth centuries makes it very difficult to directly compare knowledge levels then to those that prevail today. Yet we can get some idea through analysis of the sophistication of political rhetoric directed at voters by politicians. Candidates and political office-holders have strong incentives to accurately gauge the level of sophistication of their audience so as to make more effective campaign appeals.

Linguistic researchers at the YourDictionary.com website used the Flesch-Kincaid scale to gauge the grade level of the language and phrasing used in every presidential inaugural address from 1789 to 2001.[102] They found that every inaugural address prior to 1900 reached what would today be considered a 12th-grade level, except for one that scored at 11.5.[103] By contrast, inaugural addresses over the past fifty years have been around a 7th- to 9th-grade level.[104]

Political scientist Elvin Lim documents a similar pattern in the evolution of presidential speeches over the past sixty years, concluding that they have become increasingly simplistic.[105] The same pattern emerges from linguist Paul JJ Payack's content analysis of political debates. In the Lincoln-Douglas debates in 1858, Douglas's speeches rated an 11.9 grade level, and Lincoln's an 11.2.[106] Recent presidential debates tended to fall somewhere between the 6th- and 9th grade-levels.[107] The difference is all the more striking in light of the much higher education levels of modern voters compared to those of the nineteenth century.

Obviously, linguistic sophistication is not the same thing as substantive sophistication. It is theoretically possible that modern politicians are simply making complex arguments using simple words. Nonetheless, linguistic complexity and substantive complexity do tend to be correlated. To the extent that is true, it would seem that politicians are directing much less sophisticated arguments at voters than did their predecessors of a century ago.

The available nineteenth-century evidence is by no means conclusive. What data we have are equivocal in nature and certainly do not suggest that nineteenth-century Americans had a very high level of political sophistication.[108] Even so, it provides some support for the proposition that voters had greater knowledge of the functions of government in an era when those functions were less numerous and complex. This is striking in light of the fact that nineteenth-century Americans had much lower education levels than we do today. Also, much political information was not as easily available as in the age of modern telecommunications.

The relationship between voter ignorance and large, complex government leads us to question the informational adequacy of even the best-informed voters. It also leads to the counterintuitive suggestion that the extension of government power to new areas of social life undercuts democracy more than it furthers it.

SOME POSSIBLE DRAWBACKS OF FOOT VOTING

Despite its informational advantages, foot voting in a decentralized political system also has significant potential drawbacks. Among the most important are moving costs, "races to the bottom," and the danger of oppression of minority groups.

All of these are sometimes genuine problems. But they are also often overstated. Here, I do not give anything approaching a comprehensive analysis of the three issues, or other potential shortcomings of foot voting. I suggest only that the problems are less severe than often thought, and that they should not lead us to ignore the informational advantages of foot voting.[109]

Moving Costs

The most obvious drawback of foot voting relative to ballot box voting is the problem of moving costs. People who migrate from one jurisdiction to another must pay the cost of transporting themselves and their possessions, as well as assume the burden of finding new jobs and social ties. In some cases, these costs will prevent foot voting even in situations where another jurisdiction might be more attractive to the potential migrant than her current home. People who face very high moving costs may simply be unable to vote with their feet. For this reason, among others, foot voting is not a comprehensive solution to all the shortcomings of government.

Yet moving costs are not so great as to preclude interjurisdictional mobility for millions of people. A 2008 Pew Research Center survey found that 63 percent of Americans have moved at least once in their lives, and 43 percent have made at least one interstate move.[110] Foot voting is quite common both within the United States and elsewhere where there is freedom of movement between jurisdictions with different policies.

In Western Europe, freedom of migration between the member states in the European Union has led to extensive foot voting. In recent years, hundreds of thousands of French citizens have moved to Britain in large part because that country has lower taxes and more open labor markets, enabling them to pursue economic opportunities.[111] During the 2007 French presidential election, the winning candidate, Nicolas Sarkozy, even campaigned in London in order to solicit the votes of the many French expatriates in that city.[112]

Tens of thousands of Germans have moved to Switzerland for similar reasons, so many that some Swiss complain of an "invasion" by "rude and arrogant" Germans.[113] Within the United States, interstate migration driven by variation in public policy is also a common occurrence, with migrants tending to prefer states with lower tax rates and greater economic freedom.[114] In the small state of New Hampshire, which has the lowest taxes and nearly the lowest levels of economic regulation in the country,[115] some 57 percent of the population now consists of out-of-state migrants, many of them drawn by the state's economic policies.[116]

Contrary to claims that foot voting is an option primarily for the affluent, census data find that households with an income under $5,000 per year are actually twice as likely to make interstate moves as the population as a whole.[117] As discussed earlier, historically poor and oppressed populations have often taken advantage of foot-voting opportunities.

Some scholars suggest that foot voting over public policy is rare because surveys show that most moves are motivated by job-related considerations, rather than by direct calculations of the quality of public services.[118] If so, this might suggest that moving costs are too high to make foot voting worthwhile. Although moves are indeed often motivated by considerations other than public policy, these arguments ignore the fact that employment prospects are heavily influenced by local and state public policy on taxation, regulation, and other issues.

Increases in societal wealth and improvements in transportation technology have made migration cheaper than ever before. While moving costs continue to be a shortcoming of foot voting, they fall far short of vitiating its informational advantages. Moreover, as we have already seen,[119] private planned communities and interjurisdictional competition that does not require physical mobility can reduce the impact of moving costs still further.

Races to the Bottom

The "race to the bottom" argument is one of the best-known long-standing criticisms of federalism.[120] Because of a desire to attract taxpaying business interests, state and local governments could lower environmental and safety regulations below reasonable minimums, thereby inflicting great harm on consumers, workers, and the general public. Such "destructive competition" could make the choices available to foot voters illusory. They could end up choosing between jurisdictions that have all been forced to sell out to narrow business interests in order to keep tax revenue up.

In a series of influential articles in the 1990s, Richard Revesz significantly undermined the theoretical rationale for the race-to-the-bottom argument in the field of environmental policy—an area where the argument was traditionally thought to be at its strongest.[121] Revesz pointed out that states compete with each other on more than one dimension, and that an attractive and healthy environment is one of the factors that is likely to attract relatively affluent taxpayers and some businesses. Thus there is no good reason to expect that state and local governments will systematically sacrifice environmental concerns to the needs of polluting businesses.[122] Indeed, higher-income citizens of the type most valuable to states as taxpayers generally assign a higher priority to environmental protection than do lower-income groups.[123] Local governments also have other forms of leverage against mobile business interests that reduce the extent to which the latter can expect to capture the lion's share of the gains from interjurisdictional competition.[124] The empirical record to a large extent supports Revesz's predictions. State governments pioneered many forms of environmental protection long before the federal government required them to do so.[125]

In addition to environmental protection, the other iconic example of a dangerous race to the bottom is the Supreme Court's 1918 decision in *Hammer v. Dagenhart*, which invalidated federal child labor laws as beyond the scope of congressional authority.[126] However, all but five states had already enacted child labor bans of their own by 1910 (though some were less strict than the federal law),[127] and industrial child labor disappeared almost completely by 1930, just twelve years after *Hammer*.[128] By the time *Hammer* was reversed by the Supreme Court in the late 1930s, the majority of states had laws comparable to the federal one the Supreme Court had invalidated.[129]

None of this suggests that genuine races to the bottom never happen. They can occur in various situations, particularly when state or local governments seek to attract a mobile asset by means that exploit an immobile one, such as property rights in land. By placing the burden on the immobile asset, states can potentially impose the costs of attracting the mobile factor on people who have no effective exit option.[130]

But while races to the bottom can and do happen, they are less likely than critics claim. Even in environmental policy and labor policy, two fields in which the problem has traditionally been thought to be especially severe, races to the bottom turn out to be far less prevalent than previously believed.

The Problem of Minority Rights

No issue has done more to discredit federalism in the United States than its association with the oppression of racial and ethnic minorities. The conventional wisdom holds that federalism was largely a disaster for African Americans and other minorities, while the growth of federal power greatly alleviated their plight.[131] As the leading political scientist William Riker put it in 1964, "[t]he main beneficiary [of federalism] throughout American history has been the Southern Whites, who have been given the freedom to oppress Negroes. . . . [I]f in the United States one approves of Southern white racists, then one should approve of American federalism."[132]

There is no doubt that American state and local governments have in fact oppressed minority groups on many occasions, and that federal intervention sometimes played a decisive role in diminishing that oppression—as with the abolition of slavery in 1865 and Jim Crow segregation in the 1960s. If federalism is generally inimical to the interests of racial and ethnic minorities, this undermines the utility of foot voting in a federal system, at least when it comes to unpopular minorities. The choices available to these groups would be very poor ones indeed.

But the conventional wisdom on the relationship between federalism and Jim Crow is at the very least overstated. Although state and local governments often oppressed African Americans and other minorities, the same can be said of the federal government throughout much of American history. And in many cases, oppressed minorities would have been worse off with a unitary state than they were under federalism.

During much of American history, a unified national policy on racial issues might well have led to greater oppression for minorities rather than less. At the time the Constitution was drafted in 1787, all but one state (Massachusetts) still had slavery, though a few others had enacted gradual emancipation laws.[133] A unitary policy on slavery at that time likely would have resulted in a nationwide law legalizing the institution. Moreover, it would have deprived antislavery forces of the example effect of states without slavery, which turned out to be more economically successful than southern slave states did.

During much of the pre–Civil War antebellum period, Congress and the presidency were controlled by pro-slavery forces, which succeeded in enacting such measures as the Fugitive Slave Acts of 1793 and 1850.[134] During this period, too, a unitary state might well have had a more pro-slavery policy than that which actually existed under federalism. The District of Columbia, the one part of the United States under complete federal control throughout the antebellum era, had legalized slavery until 1862, when it was abolished in large part because most slave state representatives had left Congress as a result of the secession of southern slave states that triggered the Civil War.[135] Overall, the federal government flexed its muscles in support of slavery much more often than against it.[136]

After the 1870s, a long period set in during which the white South was far more committed to maintaining segregation than most white Northerners were to eliminating it. It is difficult to say with certainty that a unitary United States would have repressed African Americans even more than state governments did during this period of actual history. But it is at least quite likely that a unitary national policy would have been more repressive than that of the northern states, even if not as much so as that of the South. The District of Columbia, during this period too, was striking in being as much segregated as most of the South. Other federally controlled institutions were also highly segregated, such as the armed forces and the federal civil service.[137]

In addition to its role in promoting slavery and segregation of African Americans for much of American history, the federal government also took the lead in a number of other notorious episodes of persecution of minority groups. For example, it interned over one hundred thousand Japanese Americans in concentration camps during World War II and extensively persecuted the Mormons during the nineteenth century.[138]

Finally, as we have already seen, foot voting between rival state jurisdictions played a key role in preventing the plight of African Americans and other minorities from being even worse than it was.[139] Without variation in policies created by federalism, things would likely have been worse for minority groups than they were. In more recent years, other unpopular minorities—notably gays and lesbians—have also benefited from foot voting and federalism. Sympathetic state and local governments enacted pro-gay policies such as gay marriage at a time when the federal government was at best indifferent and at worst actually hostile.[140]

In a democracy where public opinion was as much contaminated by racism as it was in the nineteenth- and early twentieth-century United States, racial minorities were likely to experience extensive oppression regardless of whether the government was federal or unitary. Foot voting facilitated by federalism was no panacea for this tragic situation. But it often made the situation substantially less bad than it might have been without it.

Foot voting under federalism can also be of great benefit to minorities if some local or state governments are controlled by the minority group in question, or at least substantially influenced by it. In such a scenario, pro-minority jurisdictions can serve as a valuable exit option for minority group members facing adverse policies elsewhere. Such jurisdictions are also likely to be more favorable to the minority group than is the majority-dominated central government. This is widely recognized in federal systems outside the United States, where the existence of national minorities that are regional majorities is one of the main justifications for the establishment of a federal system in the first place.[141]

In the United States, such majority-minority jurisdictions have historically been rare, with Mormon-dominated Utah an unusual and oft-ignored exception. As a result, state and local governments are usually seen as the enemies of minority groups rather than their friends. In recent years, however, a variety of minority groups have gained greater leverage at the state and local levels, which suggests that the U.S. situation may become less anomalous in the future.[142]

None of this suggests that federalism is always a net positive for minority groups. In situations where the national majority strongly support protection for a minority group, while a regional majority favors discrimination against them, concentration of power in the federal government may well be the most advantageous political structure for the minority in question. This, of course, is exactly what happened in the case of African Americans during the civil rights revolution of the 1960s. But such a configuration of opinion is far from a universal rule, and it is risky to design a political system on the assumption that this unusual alignment of political forces will be the norm.

Federalism is not always a boon for unpopular minority groups, and sometimes centralization can serve their interests better. Yet foot voting in a decentralized political system is often at least as valuable for minority groups as for the majority, and in particularly oppressive situations, even more so.

IMPLICATIONS FOR CONSTITUTIONAL DESIGN

Widespread political ignorance and irrationality strengthen the case for constitutional limits on the powers of central governments, and also for constitutional constraints on the size and scope of government power.

Foot voting has major informational advantages over ballot box voting. It reduces incentives for both ignorance and irrationality. Even if this conclusion is accepted, however, it is possible that the benefits of foot voting can be left to legislatures to balance as they see fit. Since determining the size and degree of centralization of government involves many complex tradeoffs, it is possible that legislatures will be in a better position to balance the relevant considerations than constitutional drafters or courts exercising the power of judicial review.

Despite this concern, there is reason to believe that ordinary legislative activity will undervalue the informational benefits of both decentralization and limited government. Perhaps the famous "political safeguards of federalism" would make constitutional limits on central government power unnecessary. Some scholars argue that the political power of state governments is sufficient to prevent excessive centralization, because the regions can use their clout to prevent it, and voters will punish overcentralization at the polls.[143]

Unfortunately, the very political ignorance that makes decentralization and limited government desirable also reduces the chance of achieving it through the ordinary political process. Most voters have little understanding of federalism, and fewer still are likely to be aware of the interconnection between limits on federal government power and "foot voting."[144] For these reasons, they are unlikely to punish elected officials who promote overcentralization.

This might not be a problem if central and regional governments had other incentives that would lead them to avoid excessive centralization. In fact, however, both regional and federal governments often have strong political incentives to concentrate power at center. Central governments have incentives to expand their power in order to capture more revenue and use it to buy political support; subnational governments have incentives to lobby for central government grants and to use the central government as a cartel enforcer that suppresses competition between them.[145] Strikingly, subnational governments in most federal systems get the vast majority of their funds from central government grants.[146] This occurs despite the fact that dependence on central government grants severely reduces state incentives to compete for foot voters in order to attract tax revenue, and increases the central government's ability to use grants to suppress regional policy diversity.[147]

The political reality that overexpansion of central government power often advances the interests of regional governments undermines claims that "political safeguards" are enough to ensure an optimal level of decentralization. Virtually all such arguments rely on the political power of regional governments to serve as a check on the center. But if regional governments actually help promote centralization, their influence in the national legislature becomes a liability for federalism rather than an asset.

Ordinary political processes also often cannot be relied on to prevent government from growing unduly at the expense of the private sector. Political ignorance may prevent voters from being able to effectively monitor government interventions that benefit narrow interest groups at the expense of the general public. Many of the items in government budgets are ones that the majority of voters are probably not even aware of.[148] Even when voters are aware of the existence of a given program, "rational irrationality" will often prevent them from making effective use of the information they possess.

For these reasons, widespread voter ignorance and irrationality are likely to prevent the political process from producing the appropriate level of decentralization and limits on government needed to restrict the harm caused by ignorance and irrationality themselves. This suggests that constitutional restraints on centralization and the growth of government are needed.

How strict should those constraints be? Unfortunately, analysis of the dangers of political ignorance does not in and of itself provide an answer to this question. Obviously, political ignorance is not the only factor that must be considered in determining the optimum level of constitutional constraints on government power. A wide range of other considerations—some of which vary from one society to another—must be weighed. However, my analysis does suggest that the need to combat the effects of political ignorance justifies stronger constitutional constraints on centralization and the growth of government than we might otherwise wish to impose.

THE CASE FOR FOOT VOTING

The informational advantages of foot voting over ballot box voting have important implications. Perhaps the most significant is the way in which they reinforce the argument for political decentralization. The more policy issues are under the control of regional or local governments as opposed to the national governments, the greater the range of policy choices over which citizens can exercise leverage through foot voting and make use of its informational benefits.

In addition to strengthening the case for decentralization more generally, the informational benefits of foot voting also bolster the argument for competitive as opposed to cooperative federalism.[149] The greater the incentive for regional governments to compete with each other for citizens, taxpayers, and businesses, the greater the likely effectiveness of foot voting as a tool for imposing democratic accountability on government.

This consideration strengthens the argument for policies associated with competitive federalism, such as limiting central government subsidies to regional governments, so that the latter have stronger incentives to compete.[150]

Further, the ability of even a severely oppressed minority such as Jim Crow–era blacks to acquire the knowledge necessary for effective foot voting suggests the need for a partial rethinking of the conventional view that such groups necessarily benefit from political centralization.[151] While central government intervention to protect minority groups is often desirable, this potential advantage of centralization should be weighed against the disadvantages of eliminating foot voting. This point is especially important in light of the fact that the historic impact of federalism on minorities in the United States is far less negative than conventional wisdom suggests.

To the extent that oppressed minority groups often have lower income and education levels and therefore lower political knowledge levels than others, the relative informational advantages of foot voting for them may be even greater than for other citizens. Such benefits of decentralization are even more important in periods when the central government has little or no interest in alleviating the plight of oppressed regional minorities— as was certainly true of the United States during much of the Jim Crow era.[152] The gains for oppressed groups from foot voting within a federal system imply that there may be even greater foot-voting benefits from international migration.[153] The differences in quality between regional governments within one society are generally much smaller than those between nations. Foot voting through international migration may be the best hope for many of the most oppressed people in the world.

At the same time, it is essential to recognize that the argument of this chapter is limited in scope. The informational benefits of foot voting are likely to vary from issue to issue, from nation to nation, and perhaps also from group to group. Interjurisdictional foot voting cannot be used by people who are unable to leave a particular area, or by those who seek to protect immobile assets such as land. Examples include people with very high moving costs because they cannot find employment for their special skills outside a given locality and those precluded from moving by serious health problems. Similarly, foot voting may not be effective for "network industries" that must operate in every part of a nation simultaneously in order to operate anywhere.[154] Such people and industries can, however, sometimes make effective use of foot voting in the private sector, which often does not require a physical move.

Finally, foot voting and political ignorance are far from the only issues that must be taken into account in determining the degree of decentralization that a society should have.[155] A variety of other considerations may in some situations outweigh the advantages of foot voting. For example, local governments and private sector actors often cannot effectively handle large-scale "externality" problems when activities in one area have spillover effects on others. Interstate pollution that crosses boundary lines is a good example.[156] The fact that devolution of power to local governments facilitates foot voting does not mean they are capable of handling a massive externality such as global warming. Some scholars also contend that subnational governments cannot effectively engage in redistribution to the poor, for fear of becoming "welfare magnets" that attract migrants who consume more in welfare services than they pay in taxes.[157]

The argument advanced here is not a comprehensive theory of federalism or the appropriate role of government in society. It does, however, raise an important consideration that is too often ignored.

Decentralization is not, however, the only institutional mechanism by which we can limit the impact of political ignorance. In the next chapter, we look at the possible role of judicial review as an additional tool for achieving the same purpose. Although long-standing conventional wisdom holds that judicial review is undemocratic because it imposes constraints on elected officials, it might actually help reinvigorate democratic accountability by mitigating the impact of political ignorance. In some situations, a strong system of judicial review might help accomplish that goal precisely by promoting the sort of political decentralization discussed in this chapter.

CHAPTER SIX

Political Ignorance and Judicial Review

[J]udicial review is a deviant institution in the American democracy.

—ALEXANDER BICKEL[1]

LIMITING AND DECENTRALIZING government power can mitigate the problem of political ignorance. The institution of judicial review can also help with that task. By constraining the power of the elected branches of government, judicial review can reduce the complexity of the task facing voters, and also help empower citizens to "vote with their feet." Recognition of these potential advantages of judicial review also weakens the force of one of the main traditional objections to judicial invalidation of legislation: the so-called "countermajoritarian difficulty."

The countermajoritarian difficulty has long been considered the most fundamental issue in American constitutional law.[2] It is "the central obsession of modern constitutional scholarship."[3] As legal scholar Alexander Bickel famously put it in his classic work *The Least Dangerous Branch*,[4] "the root difficulty is that judicial review is a counter-majoritarian force in our system."[5] For Bickel and innumerable later writers, judicial review was an anomaly because it enabled an unelected judiciary to override the majoritarian will of the people represented by elected legislatures.[6] Since Bickel published *The Least Dangerous Branch* in 1962, a vast academic literature has addressed the countermajoritarian difficulty.[7]

Both conservative and liberal legal scholars have advocated the abolition or severe restriction of judicial review to prevent an unelected institution from overriding the will of a democratic majority.[8] According to Robert Bork, the most prominent conservative critic of judicial review, the judicial invalidation of legislation is objectionable because it creates "new disabilities for democratic government."[9] Neal Katyal, a leading liberal constitutional law scholar, echoes Bork's concern, expressing his fear that "[f]or those worried about the vigor of popular rule in America, there is much to fear from judicial interpretation [of the Constitution]."[10]

The idea of the countermajoritarian difficulty rests on the premise that laws enacted by legislatures reflect the will of electoral majorities, which in turn relies on the assumption that the latter possess sufficient political knowledge to control what their representatives do. Yet most of the vast literature on this subject ignores the relevance of political ignorance.

An understanding of the depth and pervasiveness of voter ignorance should lead us to reconsider the countermajoritarian difficulty in several fundamental ways. If most of the electorate has little or no information on politics and government policy, it is likely that legislative output does not represent the will of the majority in the way that Bickel and later theorists assumed. Judicial invalidation of such legislation is not nearly as "countermajoritarian" as generally supposed. This important point is only the first of several important implications for voter ignorance on the central question of constitutional theory.

This chapter does not provide a comprehensive solution to the countermajoritarian difficulty or address the full range of issues raised in the prior scholarly literature on the subject. It also does not address the full range of interactions between judicial decisions, government policy, and public opinion; for example, it does not take into account the danger that overly aggressive judicial review might undermine the judiciary's legitimacy in the eyes of the public.[11] The analysis here focuses on the claim that judicial review is "countermajoritarian" because it undercuts popular democratic control of public policy. I hope to show that voter ignorance greatly weakens the validity of this claim, and in some cases turns it on its head by facilitating foot voting.

IMPLICATIONS OF WIDESPREAD IGNORANCE
FOR THE COUNTERMAJORITARIAN DIFFICULTY

As we have seen, political knowledge levels among American citizens are so low that they fail to meet the prerequisites of any of the theories of representation that might underpin the countermajoritarian difficulty.[12] This state of affairs seems deeply rooted and is likely to persist for a long time to come.[13] In this section, I explore the implications of low aggregate levels of political knowledge for the countermajoritarian difficulty. The most radical interpretation of these implications is that the countermajoritarian difficulty should not be weighed at all as a consideration against judicial invalidation of legislative enactments. Although the radical view is not without force, the moderate position is sufficient for the purposes of this book: countermajoritarian considerations probably should not be ignored completely. But in most cases, they should be outweighed by other considerations if the latter support judicial invalidation of a law. Sometimes, judicial invalidation of laws may actually *increase* the majoritarianism of the political system by reducing the knowledge burden on voters.

The Radical Approach

The radical interpretation of the impact of political ignorance on the countermajoritarian difficulty is that countermajoritarian considerations should not be given any weight in constitutional theory at all. If most citizens often lack basic political knowledge, it may be the case that a high proportion of the legislation produced by Congress and state legislatures fails to represent the will of "the people" in any meaningfully majoritarian way.

For most legislation, the vast majority of voters will not have heard of its existence, much less have an informed opinion on its merits.[14] In the rare cases when legislation is prominent enough to generate widespread citizen awareness, most citizens often have only a vague grasp of what the legislation actually does. Two of the most prominent and controversial domestic policy legislative initiatives of the 1990s—President Clinton's health care plan and the 1995 Republican Contract with America—were sufficiently poorly understood by the public that politicians in both cases adopted strategies of building public support by manipulating voter ignorance rather than either adjusting their proposals to reflect public opinion more closely or trying to persuade the public that their proposals were right on the merits.[15] In a 2003 article, I presented evidence that much of the most prominent legislation adopted during the New Deal period, which supposedly represented a period of particularly intense political attentiveness and mobilization, actually also involved manipulation of voter ignorance.[16]

If this was the case with some of the most prominent legislation in recent history and with some of the most important policy innovations of the New Deal "constitutional moment,"[17] it is difficult to avoid the conclusion that such an outcome is even more likely to occur with run-of-the mill legislation, for which political leaders do not need to make much effort to avoid unwanted majoritarian scrutiny.

Although this conclusion in some ways follows naturally from what has been said thus far, it is important to understand how much of a break the radical argument makes from the traditional framework of the countermajoritarian difficulty. Both legal scholars[18] and prominent jurists across the political spectrum have assumed that there is a deep conflict between judicial review and majoritarianism. To cite just a few examples, Franklin Roosevelt's attorney general and future prominent Supreme Court Justice Robert Jackson flatly claimed that "[e]ither democracy must surrender to the judges or the judges must yield to democracy."[19]

In more recent years, Justice Antonin Scalia, arguably the leading conservative jurist on the Supreme Court, has repeatedly raised the countermajoritarian difficulty in criticizing judicial reversals of legislation, claiming that "the sphere of self-government reserved to the people . . . is progressively narrowed" when the Court overturns legislation.[20] Liberal justices have raised similar concerns in criticizing decisions they oppose.[21] Although such rhetoric may sometimes be disingenuous, the very fact of its recurrent use testifies to the appeal of the countermajoritarian critique of judicial review.

The radical interpretation of the impact of voter ignorance suggests that all such claims should be rejected because political ignorance prevents legislation from truly reflecting the will of the majority. Although the legislation still does, of course, represent the will of the majority of legislators, these officials no more represent the will of the people than judges do.[22] As Barry Friedman puts it, the "countermajoritarian theory rests explicitly on the notion that the other branches of government 'represent' majority will in a way the judiciary does not."[23] If the fact of massive political ignorance falsifies this assumption, the countermajoritarian difficulty becomes no difficulty at all.

Even the radical approach, of course, has limits. It does *not* hold that judges can simply overturn legislation anytime they wish, merely that they should not refuse to overturn it for fear of acting in a countermajoritarian fashion. Judicial modesty may still be desirable because judges lack competence to make public policy in a given area,[24] because courts lack the power to impose their will on other powerful political actors,[25] or because they should hew narrowly to the text and original meaning of the Constitution.[26] Nonetheless, the radical argument is still radical indeed in so far as it rejects the single most widely used criticism of judicial review.

The (Relatively) Moderate Approach

Although the radical view is not without force, it is still inferior to a less sweeping alternative. There are two shortcomings in the radical view that counsel prudence. First, some legislative output does, in fact, reflect majority will. Public opinion does often influence policy. This is especially true of legislation that is both widely publicized and relatively simple in its effects. In such cases, legislation may reflect the impact of effective retrospective voting, which often works well in cases when there is a large and obvious problem that can readily be traced to mistakes made by political incumbents.[27]

Second, even in cases when this is not true, there is always a small chance that the legislation in question has penetrated the barriers of political ignorance despite the odds against such an occurrence. At the very least, the public might still have at least a partial understanding of what has happened. Although much legislation will have only a weak connection to majoritarian will, a weak connection is not the same thing as none at all.

The main informational barriers to majoritarian control of legislation on specific issues are the facts that (1) much legislation is completely unknown to most citizens and (2) even when this is not the case, the effects of much legislation are often sufficiently complex that voters cannot readily tell whether the legislation in question will advance their values and interests or not.[28] A related difficulty is that the majority of citizens often do not know where the opposing parties stand on a given issue and cannot vote effectively on their issue positions.[29]

If it is indeed the combination of obscurity and complexity that prevents majoritarian control of most legislation, it follows that legislation that is both simple and highly prominent might be an exceptional case, at least if voters clear the additional information barrier of learning the parties' relative stances on the issue in question. Examples of such legislation do in fact exist. For example, 76 percent of survey respondents were aware of the passage of Medicare legislation when it was enacted in 1965, though it is less clear that they understood how the legislation actually worked.[30]

Similarly, the majority of respondents were aware of the Supreme Court's 1989–90 decisions holding that flag burning was a protected form of expression under the First Amendment,[31] and many favored attempts to reverse the decision by constitutional amendment.[32] Even more than the Medicare case, the flag-burning example is an especially clear case of legislation that truly reflected majoritarian preferences. In addition to being highly prominent, it was also—unlike Medicare— fairly simple in its ramifications. This is not to suggest that the Supreme Court was wrong to decide the flag burning cases as it did. In my view, the Court was right to hold that the flag burning bans violate the First Amendment. But these decisions did represent a clear example of truly countermajoritarian judicial review.

Most legislation is unlike either the flag burning or Medicare examples in terms of public recognition and understanding. Rarely, therefore, will a Supreme Court decision invalidating a statute be as clearly countermajoritarian as in the flag-burning cases. However, even ordinary legislation might, on unusual occasions, be the subject of unusual public scrutiny. Therefore, it does raise the possibility that legislation sometimes reaches the public consciousness in the face of widespread general political ignorance.

The radical interpretation of political ignorance and its impact on the countermajoritarian difficulty must therefore be moderated by the recognition that a small number of statutes that are both highly prominent and relatively simple to understand usually do reflect majoritarian preferences. In addition, the mass of more ordinary legislation also includes a few items that may penetrate the public consciousness and thereby reflect majority will, albeit to a more limited degree, since mere knowledge of the existence of legislation is not enough to ensure majoritarian control of policy outcomes.[33]

For these reasons, a more moderate approach suggests that the problem of political ignorance does not completely eliminate the countermajoritarian difficulty, but does greatly reduce its significance. Although the moderate view does not prove that the difficulty will never arise, it does show that most legislation represents majority will only to a minor degree, if at all. What we might call the "countermajoritarian cost" of overruling that legislation should be low, even if not zero.

Although the moderate view does not wholly discount the countermajoritarian difficulty in the way that the radical approach did, it does conclude that there is little countermajoritarian cost to the invalidation of the vast majority of legislation. This conclusion still represents a major revision of the traditional view of the countermajoritarian difficulty, which posits a constant and high countermajoritarian cost for nearly all judicial review.

The moderate view, therefore, has important implications for how the judiciary approaches the countermajoritarian difficulty. Since most legislation has only limited majoritarian significance, if any at all, countermajoritarian concerns should be far more easily outweighed by other considerations than earlier theories suggest. A complete theory of the range of values that should influence constitutional decision-making by the judiciary is outside the scope of this chapter. But taking voter ignorance seriously leads to the conclusion that countermajoritarian concerns should usually be given comparatively little weight relative to whatever other considerations the "correct" theory of constitutional law finds relevant—whether they be fidelity to original intent, adherence to text,[34] moral commitments to individual rights,[35] or some other competing value.

The second implication of the moderate view is to cast doubt on various proposals that use avoidance doctrines such as judicial abstention from deciding "political questions"[36] and various forms of "judicial minimalism"[37] to avoid making broad constitutional decisions. To the extent that the exercise of what Bickel called "the passive virtues" is motivated by countermajoritarian considerations,[38] their usefulness is greatly overestimated. This is not to say that judicial decisions should always be "maximalist." A variety of considerations might justify judicial caution. For example, judges might choose to make a narrow ruling because they are too uncertain about the likely effects of a broad one. Political ignorance does, however, show that a justification for minimalism and avoidance must be based on something other than the countermajoritarian difficulty.

POLITICAL IGNORANCE AND

REPRESENTATION-REINFORCEMENT

In addition to not *diminishing* majority rule as much as is often claimed, judicial review sometimes actually *increases* the majoritarianism of the political system by reducing the anti-majoritarian impact of voter ignorance. It would be wrong to suppose that judicial review can come close to fully eliminating the distortions caused by ignorance. It may, however, be able to reduce them at the margin.

As discussed earlier in this book, the persistence of widespread political ignorance in the face of rising education levels and drastically lower information costs shows that most citizens are willing to devote only very limited amounts of time and effort to acquiring political knowledge.[39] Thus it is unlikely that most citizens can follow more than a small number of issues simultaneously.

For this reason, there is an inverse relationship between the size, scope, and complexity of government on the one hand and the ability of voters to have sufficient knowledge to exercise majoritarian control over its operations on the other.[40] Given a relatively constant level of public attention to political issues, the more functions government undertakes, the higher the percentage that will escape the notice of most citizens, and thus the lower the degree of majoritarian control over government.[41] The size and complexity of the modern state is therefore one of the factors that exacerbate the problems caused by political ignorance. As noted in Chapter 5, in most Western democracies, government spending constitutes over one-third of gross domestic product,[42] and most human activity is subject to one form or another of government regulation. In 2010, government spending accounted for some 42 percent of U.S. GDP.[43] Obviously, the vast expansion of government expenditures since the 1930s has been accompanied by an at least equally great expansion in the scope of its regulatory activities.[44] As noted earlier, the federal government alone has fifteen cabinet level departments with regulatory authority, as well as fifty-six independent regulatory agencies.[45] It is unlikely that most citizens can even name more than a few of these agencies, much less keep track of their activities.

The problems caused by the combination of a large and complex government and severely limited public knowledge of and attention to its activities cannot be solved by judicial review; nor should the judiciary even attempt a comprehensive solution. However, judicial review can sometimes alleviate the problem by limiting the scope of government activity. For example, if judicial review blocks government from undertaking content-based restriction of speech[46] or from intervening in the internal affairs of religious groups,[47] this means that voters need not devote time and effort to learning about government activities in these areas and can focus their limited attention on other issues. At least at the margin, the information burden on voters has been reduced, and their ability to pay adequate attention to the remaining functions of government increased.

What is true for these two well-established and widely accepted judicial restrictions on government power should also hold true for other, more controversial, ones. To take an extreme case, the information burden on voters would be vastly reduced and their ability to control remaining functions of government considerably increased in the unlikely event that the Supreme Court were to adopt Richard Epstein's position that most post–New Deal economic legislation is unconstitutional.[48] More realistically, it is possible that a more modest, but nonetheless significant, reduction in political knowledge burden would occur if the Supreme Court were able to expand and enforce its efforts to constrain federal regulation of "noneconomic . . . intrastate activity."[49] Depending on how broadly this category is defined, the resulting constraint on the scope of government regulation might potentially have an important impact on the knowledge burden placed on voters.

In this way, judicial restrictions on the scope of government power might not only avoid exacerbating the countermajoritarian difficulty but could actually strengthen majoritarian control of government. In John Hart Ely's terminology, they could be "representation-reinforcing."[50] So long as we accept that majoritarian control of government requires a substantial degree of citizen knowledge of public policy and that citizens have only a severely limited willingness and ability to acquire political information, this conclusion necessarily follows. Empirical evidence on voter participation in government before the vast post-Depression expansion of the state provides some modest support for the proposition that ordinary citizens were able to follow public policy better when there was less public policy to follow.[51]

Judicial enforcement of limits on government power can also alleviate knowledge problems in a different way. By extending the range of decisions left to the private sector rather than government, it can help ensure that more issues are decided by foot voting rather than ballot box voting. And, as discussed in Chapter 5, the latter creates much better incentives for the acquisition and unbiased evaluation of knowledge.

SOME CAVEATS TO THE REPRESENTATION- REINFORCEMENT ARGUMENT

At this point we should note a few caveats to the representation-reinforcement argument for judicial power. First and foremost, the argument does not, by itself, justify all conceivable judicial limitations on government power. Indeed, by itself, it does not justify *any* such limitations. Whether or not a particular judicial decision is justified does not depend solely on its possible representation-reinforcing effects. It also depends on a wide range of other factors, including adherence to constitutional text, history and precedent, and other considerations. My argument claims only that, to the extent that the countermajoritarian difficulty is an important issue in constitutional adjudication, we must consider the fact that judicial restraints on government power actually reinforce majoritarianism by reducing voters' knowledge burdens, rather than undermining it.

The second caveat is that my analysis applies only to judicial actions that limit the powers of other branches of government over the private sector. Judicial decisions that replace the power of other branches with judicial control would not have such a representation-reinforcing effect, though they may of course be justified for other reasons. Examples of such *power-transferring* rather than *power-limiting* decisions include well-known cases in which judges took over the management of public schools[52] and prisons.[53] Power-transferring decisions are more vulnerable to the countermajoritarian criticism than power-limiting ones because they render government decision-making less subject to control by elected officials without simultaneously reducing voters' information burdens. In some instances, they may even exacerbate voters' knowledge burdens by introducing new levels of complexity in public policy.[54]

Third, in some cases, judicial restriction of government power in one area may create political incentives for more sweeping or more complex government intervention in other areas of society. For example, Adrian Vermeule has argued that moderate judicial limits on federal regulatory power that only forbid regulation of a narrow category of activities might give Congress an incentive to adopt broader regulatory statutes.[55] If Vermeule's argument is correct, judicial intervention in this area will only have a representation-reinforcing effect if courts are able to impose more stringent limits on Congress's authority. More broadly, we would also have to consider the possible countermajoritarian and representation-reinforcing effects of judicial decisions created by the interaction of different policies. A comprehensive assessment of such interaction effects is beyond the scope of this book. For present purposes, it is enough to show that there is a substantial class of cases in which judicially imposed limits on government power would have representation-reinforcing effects due to the impact of judicial review on voter knowledge burdens.

FOOT VOTING AND JUDICIAL REVIEW
OF FEDERALISM ISSUES

With the possible exception of *Bush v. Gore*,[56] no recent Supreme Court decision has drawn as much criticism on countermajoritarian grounds as the effort to reestablish judicial review of federalism-based constraints on congressional power. The argument has been repeatedly advanced by both judicial[57] and academic[58] critics of judicial enforcement of federalism. In the 2005 case of *Gonzales v. Raich*, the Supreme Court pulled back from efforts to enforce limits on federal power by ruling that Congress's authority to regulate interstate commerce was broad enough to uphold a law criminalizing the possession of small amounts of medical marijuana that had never been sold in any market or left the confines of the state where it was grown.[59] Nonetheless, the debate over judicial review of federalism questions continues. Most recently, it was rekindled by the Supreme Court's near-invalidation of the Obama administration's massive Affordable Care Act health care legislation in the high-profile case of *NFIB v. Sebelius*.[60]

This book does not resolve the broader debate over the legitimacy and desirability of judicial enforcement of federalism.[61] Resolution of these issues depends on a variety of factors in addition to political ignorance. But taking political ignorance into account does weaken the claim that judicial review of federalism is undemocratic and countermajoritarian. Indeed, judicial enforcement of federalism-based limits on national power may actually strengthen majoritarianism. It does so by reinforcing citizens' ability to "vote with their feet," leaving states with policies they dislike for those with more favorable ones.

Once political ignorance is taken into account, the countermajoritarian cost of judicially enforced federalism is seen to be low and often almost nonexistent. There are three reasons for this conclusion.

The first is that most of the advantages of decentralized federalism over centralized control of the federal government have to do with broad structural and ideological theories of intergovernmental relations.[62] Some of the most important of these advantages, interstate competition for people and goods[63] and state responsiveness to diverse local preferences,[64] depend on interrelationships between a wide range of policy areas rather than on a small number of discrete and easy-to-grasp policy decisions.

Unfortunately, research shows that political ignorance is at its most severe in dealing with broad ideological issues and complex interrelationships between policies.[65] For decades, large majorities of survey respondents have expressed hostility to what they perceive as excessive concentration of power in the federal government, but have, however, lacked the knowledge to link this general perception to specific policy issues, on which majorities often favor expanding the federal role.[66] Since many citizens do not understand even basic aspects of liberal and conservative ideology,[67] it is unlikely that more than a small fraction of voters understand the more complex arguments surrounding issues of federalism and decentralization. Because political ignorance prevents voters from understanding the arguments for decentralized federalism—as well as those against it—it is unlikely that legislative policy on federalism reflects informed majoritarian preferences to any noteworthy degree.

This conclusion might not have held true in an era when most federalism issues arose from a single, highly prominent policy dispute, such as slavery. But it is surely the case today, when federalism questions cut across a wide range of issues, with no one predominating. And even in those earlier, atypical periods when one issue dominated state-federal relations, the prominence of the issue might have obscured broader federalism questions as much as highlighted them. During the antebellum period, for instance, southern political leaders routinely took an anti-centralization position when such a stance favored slavery and a pro-centralization view when the reverse was true, as in their uncompromising insistence on enforcement of the federal Fugitive Slave Law.[68] By contrast, northern state governments seeking to protect the rights of fugitive slaves insisted on a narrow construction of federal power.[69] Understandably, the overriding importance of the specific issue of slavery prevented consistency on the broader but less immediately significant question of federalism.

The second critical link between judicial review of federalism and political ignorance is the fact that voters seeking to use the political process to promote decentralization must coordinate across a wide range of policies in wholly disparate policy areas. Federal authority impinges on state authority in an almost infinite variety of ways. To take one especially important example, federal grants to state government account for almost 30 percent of all state revenue, and include funds earmarked for a tremendous variety of different programs.[70] Keeping track of these grants; their attached conditions;[71] and their impact on state autonomy, interstate competition, and responsiveness to diverse preferences is itself a full-time job for voters.[72] This does not even consider the many other issues involved in the Supreme Court's federalism jurisprudence, such as federal "commandeering" of state governments[73] and limits on federal power under the Commerce Clause,[74] to name only two of the most controversial.

To impose majoritarian control over federalism policy, voters would have to keep track of and understand the connections between a vast range of policies. Given the present and likely future state of political knowledge, it does not seem reasonable to suppose that they will actually do so.

There is an even more basic reason why countermajoritarian theory is not a compelling argument against judicial review of federalism questions. As Steven Calabresi puts it, judicial review of federalism involves not a rejection of majoritarianism per se but "choosing which majority should govern on which issue."[75] If federal power is blocked, then the decision will be made by state-level majorities and vice versa. Almost by definition, it is impossible to have majoritarian control over the question of who counts as part of the relevant group that gets to vote. The question of who gets to participate in democracy cannot itself be decided democratically because the institution of any majority vote procedure requires prior resolution of this problem.[76]

To the extent that judicial review of federalism is limited to deciding the question of which majority controls, it cannot be countermajoritarian, since that question is by definition one that cannot be decided in a majoritarian fashion. This argument does not apply to all judicial review of federalism. For example, it may be that some policies, if they are to function at all, can only be adopted at a national level because a single holdout state could otherwise block their implementation.[77] Judicial invalidation of federal policy in such cases would preclude most state-level variation as well. However, there is no reason to believe that this state of affairs holds true for the vast majority of public policy issues.

The choice-of-majorities point is not, of course, directly related to political ignorance. It is, however, connected because the prior decision on which majorities control which issues also determines the issues on which a given set of voters needs to be informed. If the Supreme Court's federalism jurisprudence can provide a clear dividing line between federal and national authority—something that it is far from doing at present—it could limit the knowledge burden on voters by allowing them to ignore issues left to the discretion of neighboring state governments.

CONCLUSION

For several generations, jurists and legal scholars have argued that the "countermajoritarian difficulty" is the most important shortcoming of judicial review. The debate over this issue has taken little or no account of political ignorance. Once we recognize that ignorance is a pervasive element of modern democracy, the countermajoritarian difficulty turns out to be a much less significant problem than previously assumed. Much of the legislation subject to judicial review is not actually a product of informed democratic consent. There may be good reasons for courts to leave it alone nonetheless. But the countermajoritarian difficulty isn't one of them.

In some ways, judicial review might actually alleviate the impact of political ignorance, and thereby strengthen popular control of government rather than undermine it. Judicial enforcement of federalism constraints on the central government can facilitate the sorts of foot voting discussed in Chapter 5. This enables citizens to choose the government policies they prefer to live under in a framework in which rational ignorance is much less of a danger than at the ballot box.

CHAPTER SEVEN

Can Voter Knowledge Be Increased?

I know no safe depositary of the ultimate powers of the
society but the people themselves; and if we think them
not enlightened enough to exercise their control with a
wholesome discretion, the remedy is not to take it from
them, but to inform their discretion by education.

—THOMAS JEFFERSON[1]

THE RATIONAL AND LONG-STANDING NATURE of political ignorance
suggests that the problem will be difficult to solve. Greater education
levels and introduction of new technology making information easier
to access have not significantly increased political knowledge over the
past fifty years.[2]

Yet many still hope that political ignorance might potentially be
mitigated by a substantial increase in the average knowledge level of
the electorate. There are two general ways this could be achieved. The
first is to make the mass of voters more knowledgeable. The second
is to concentrate political power in the hands of those who are well-
informed already. Unfortunately, both solutions are difficult to implement effectively.

This chapter evaluates several of the best-known proposals for either
increasing voter knowledge levels or concentrating power in the hands
of the better informed: increasing political knowledge through education, the "deliberation day" proposal developed by Bruce Ackerman and
James Fishkin, restrictions on the franchise, transferring political power
to knowledgeable experts, and reform of media coverage of politics. It also
briefly considers the lesser-known but intriguing possibility of increasing
knowledge by paying voters to learn about politics. Unfortunately, all of
these approaches are unlikely to be as effective as their advocates hope.

INCREASING POLITICAL KNOWLEDGE
THROUGH EDUCATION

The idea of increasing voter knowledge through education is perhaps the oldest and best-known method of reducing political ignorance. Thomas Jefferson, one of the leading early advocates of public education as a way to increase voter knowledge, wrote that "the remedy" for voter ignorance is "to inform their discretion by education."[3] Later political theorists such as John Stuart Mill also emphasized the importance of education as a way of increasing voter knowledge, though Mill also feared that education could be used to indoctrinate the public in the ideology favored by state authorities.[4]

Government subsidization of education for the purpose of increasing political knowledge is a natural extension of public goods theory. If ignorance is rational because political knowledge is a public good that individual voters have insufficient incentive to supply through uncoordinated voluntary action, there is a rationale for government to provide the good itself. Even some strong free market advocates such as Milton Friedman have accepted this justification for government subsidization of education.[5] In principle, government could simply require public schools to teach whatever political knowledge voters need to acquire in order to meet the requirements of the "correct" version of democratic theory.[6]

Increasing Education Levels Have Not
Increased Political Knowledge

Empirical studies almost uniformly show that education and political knowledge are highly correlated, even when controlling for other variables.[7] Not surprisingly, those people with the highest education levels also tend to have greater political knowledge. Unfortunately, however, there is a major fly in the education-increases-knowledge ointment: massive rises in education over the past fifty years have not led to significant increases in political knowledge.[8] From 1972 to 1994, average educational attainment for Americans over the age of thirty grew from eleven years of schooling to thirteen, while measured political knowledge remained roughly constant.[9] On an education-adjusted basis, political knowledge may actually have declined, with 1990s college graduates having knowledge levels comparable to those of high school graduates in the 1940s.[10] It is also noteworthy that rising education levels have failed to increase political knowledge despite the fact that measured intelligence has been rising, with IQ scores increasing substantially over the past century.[11]

The stagnation of political knowledge levels in the face of greatly augmented educational attainment suggests that further raising of education levels cannot be counted on to increase political knowledge in the future.

Why has the rise in average educational attainment failed to increase political knowledge? The answer remains uncertain. One possibility is that education correlates with knowledge primarily because it is relative education and not absolute levels that increase political knowledge. The most highly educated people tend to be near the top of social networks that give them access to political knowledge.[12] If education correlates with political knowledge primarily for this reason, raising the average level of education is unlikely to produce future gains in knowledge.

An alternative but not mutually exclusive explanation is that education correlates with political knowledge in large part because it is a proxy for intelligence. When IQ is controlled for, the correlation between education and economic knowledge is sharply reduced, and intelligence turns out to have the greater effect of the two.[13] Political knowledge may function similarly. Yet rising IQ scores over the last several decades have also seemingly failed to increase political knowledge.

The failure of rising education levels to raise political knowledge levels is also consistent with the rational ignorance theory. Education may provide *opportunities* to acquire political knowledge. But rationally ignorant citizens may choose not to make effective use of those opportunities because the individual benefit to them isn't great enough. This point applies even to relatively altruistic individuals who care about the welfare of society as well as their own; they too realize that learning more political knowledge is unlikely to help them achieve their goals.[14] They could instead devote their efforts to mastering material that is more interesting or more relevant to their future professional advancement.

In any event, if the massive improvements in educational attainment of the past fifty years were not enough to appreciably increase political knowledge, we must be at least relatively pessimistic about the prospects for increasing political knowledge by this means in the future.

Prospects for Reform

Even if current educational practices do not lead to increased political knowledge as a result of greater educational attainment, it is possible that alternative institutional arrangements might do so. In theory, nothing prevents state or federal governments from mandating that schools teach political knowledge and giving teachers and administrators strong incentives to ensure that as many students as possible leave high school with at least minimum levels of political information.

The problem, of course, is one of incentives. Political leaders chosen by an electoral process heavily influenced by ignorance and irrationality lack strong incentives to enact measures that will increase knowledge levels and potentially make their own reelection less likely. Even if increased political knowledge comes too slowly to be a threat to current incumbents, they still have little positive incentive to push for curriculum reforms that will increase it in the future. If, as seems likely, the benefits will not be attained until many years later, current political leaders are unlikely to reap any electoral rewards for achieving them.

The Danger of Indoctrination

In addition to lack of positive incentives to promote political learning, public officials may often have interests that actually cut against efforts to increase voter knowledge. John Stuart Mill, otherwise a leading advocate of using education to increase political knowledge, presciently warned that "a general state education" is likely to lead to indoctrination in whatever ideology "pleases the predominant power in the government."[15]

Governments routinely seek to use their control over public education to indoctrinate students in values that tend to support their ideologies. Indoctrination in nationalist and religious ideologies favored by ruling elites was one of the main motives for the establishment of public education in Europe and the United States in the nineteenth century, and has continued to be an important objective of public schooling in many nations ever since.[16] Today, both government and private sector interest groups of the right and the left lobby actively to use public education to indoctrinate students in their preferred values.[17] Often, this results in indoctrination that teaches factually dubious material. For example, right-wing groups have lobbied, sometimes successfully, for the removal of textbooks that accurately portray the theory of evolution or provide a critical view of American history.[18] Left-wing groups, in turn, have lobbied for inaccurate curricular reforms of their own.[19]

The danger of indoctrination is heightened when one considers the importance of political irrationality, as well as simple ignorance. Even if a given school curriculum increases factual knowledge, it might simultaneously decrease the quality of voters' evaluation of information by promoting illogical analysis of those facts. Both the government itself and various pressure groups often have strong incentives to indoctrinate students in such ways.

For example, Jim Crow–era southern state governments indoctrinated public school students in racist ideology, which would then affect the students' perceptions of any facts they might learn. For many years, the communist government of East Germany indoctrinated its citizens in hostility to market transactions. Despite the fact that most East Germans welcomed the collapse of communism, the effects of such indoctrination manifested themselves even years after German reunification made a great deal of contrary factual information available to former East Germans.[20]

When such indoctrination occurs, its effects may be exacerbated by rational irrationality. Because most voters have little incentive to rationally evaluate their beliefs, they may not reconsider false theories they have been indoctrinated in even if they are later exposed to contrary evidence.

Indoctrination isn't always effective. It is unlikely to blind people to facts that are highly visible and extremely obvious. No amount of communist propaganda was able to persuade the majority of East Germans to love the Berlin Wall. But it is likely to be much more effective in influencing people's views on more complex issues, such as the costs and benefits of markets, social welfare policy, free trade, race relations, and others.

The same concerns about incentives and indoctrination apply to proposals to use the education system to teach citizens to avoid the cognitive biases that lead many to do a poor job of evaluating the political knowledge they learn.[21] Government officials may have little incentive to combat such biases, and may even actively exploit them in cases where they facilitate indoctrination.

In principle, a knowledgeable electorate could force political leaders to ignore pressure groups and their own desire to indoctrinate students. Voters could potentially force political leaders to enact school curricula that are focused on increasing political knowledge without engaging in indoctrination. In reality, however, the very political ignorance and irrationality that good civic education is intended to cure will likely be an obstacle to its implementation.

Ignorant or irrational voters may be unable to force officials to change the curriculum in the necessary ways, partly because they may not know that current curricula are flawed and partly because they may actually share some of the irrational or factually inaccurate views in which interest groups and the government seek to indoctrinate the next generation. Thus, even if alternative public school curricula might increase political knowledge,[22] the current prevalence of political ignorance is a major obstacle to their implementation.

The failure of higher education levels to increase political knowledge levels may be closely related to the general shortcomings of modern public education. Over the past forty years, massive increases in education spending have also failed to significantly improve student achievement in mathematics, English, and other subjects not directly related to political knowledge.[23]

It is possible that new technological breakthroughs will radically improve the quality of education in the near to medium-term future.[24] Even if this happens, however, it is not clear that the new technology will be used to combat the problem of political ignorance. As we have seen, neither government officials nor voters are strongly motivated to push for increases in political knowledge. Moreover, as long as the vast majority of schools remain under government control, it is not clear that there will be much incentive to use the new technology effectively.

A possible alternative to trying to improve civic education in public schools is for government to subsidize private schooling through vouchers instead. Some data suggest that students in private schools, and especially Catholic schools, attain higher levels of political knowledge than their public school counterparts (even after controlling for standard demographic variables such as race, gender, and parental income).[25] This result supports Milton Friedman and John Stuart Mill's view that government can best promote civic education not by funding government-owned schools but by subsidizing the consumption of private education.[26]

Unfortunately, the political obstacles to widespread adoption of private school vouchers are almost as daunting as those preventing the adoption of effective political knowledge curricula in public schools.[27] Moreover, even if the adoption of a voucher system might increase political knowledge *relative* to that attained through public schools, it is still not clear whether the *absolute* levels of political knowledge achieved will be high enough to offset the dangers of rational political ignorance.

Parents choosing private schools for their children in a voucher program are unlikely to emphasize training in political knowledge in making their decisions. For the same reason that it is rational for individual voters to devote little or no effort to learning political information, it will be rational for individual parents to choose schools in a voucher system for reasons other than their impact on students' political knowledge. Private schools might still increase political knowledge relative to public schools as a by-product of providing a generally higher quality of education. But the difference may not be great enough to make a major impact on societal political knowledge levels.

Finally, even the most effective political-knowledge-oriented school curriculum can only do so much. It may not be enough to enable students to understand anything close to the full range of issues controlled by modern government. And even if a high school graduate is well versed on all the issues on the political agenda at the time she graduates at the age of eighteen, she still has only very limited reason to acquire knowledge about the many new issues that will surely arise during her lifetime as a voter. Knowledge of old issues and of the basic structure of government can help her to understand the new ones to some degree. But as new issues continually supplant older ones and the political system develops over time, the initial base of knowledge acquired in school will be less and less useful.

Despite these caveats, both school choice and efforts to improve civic education in public schools are surely worth pursuing. To the extent that they achieve marginal increases in political knowledge, that will be to the good. The same goes for technological advances in education. But it is unlikely that these strategies will lead to a major increase in political knowledge in the foreseeable future.

THE DELIBERATION DAY PROPOSAL

Unlike the traditional approach of increasing the political knowledge levels by educating children, Bruce Ackerman and James Fishkin's "Deliberation Day" strategy seeks to directly increase the political knowledge levels of adults.[28] Ackerman and Fishkin recognize the problem of rational ignorance and its tendency to keep political knowledge at very low levels.[29] They thus propose to give voters stronger incentives to become informed.

Many Americans already discuss politics on a regular basis. In a recent study, some 68 percent reported discussing political issues at least several times per month, and 25 percent reported participating in more formal meetings on political issues.[30] However, the ubiquity of political ignorance suggests that regular participation in political discussions often fails to increase knowledge much, if at all. This is not surprising in light of the fact that the motive for many such discussions may not be to learn new information or get at the truth.[31] Much political conversation may be the result of a desire for entertainment or for validation of one's preexisting views. The latter may be one reason why most people who regularly discuss politics do so overwhelmingly with those who agree with them.[32]

The Deliberation Day proposal seeks to overcome these problems by putting voters into a deliberative setting where they will be exposed to a range of new political information presented by advocates of competing viewpoints.

How Deliberation Day Would Work

Prior to each election day, Ackerman and Fishkin would have the government declare a national holiday called "Deliberation Day," during which all voters will be given an opportunity to gather in groups of five hundred and hear presentations on key issues by representatives of the major political parties. Afterward, the voters could ask questions and discuss the issues among themselves.[33]

Ackerman and Fishkin recognize that rationally ignorant voters might choose not to attend the Deliberation Day discussions, and therefore propose to pay each attendee $150 for coming.[34] At the same time, the establishment of a national holiday combined with "heavy penalties" for employers who "compel their labor force" to stay on the job that day will greatly reduce any financial disincentives to attendance resulting from potential lost income.[35]

Ackerman and Fishkin argue that the Deliberation Day proposal will lead voters to become better informed than before, leading to better decisions when they cast their ballots on election day a few days later. They cite extensive research by Fishkin on "deliberative polling," in which he and colleagues conducted what were in effect mini-deliberation days with randomly selected groups of voters addressed by experts. The research shows that many deliberative poll participants changed their minds about the issues discussed during the course of the day, after hearing opposing arguments.[36]

Ackerman and Fishkin's approach should be commended for taking the problem of rational ignorance seriously and attempting to provide a relatively low-cost solution. They estimate the cost of each Deliberation Day at roughly $520 million in addition to the $150 paid to each voter who chooses to attend.[37] The latter would amount to $15 billion if a hundred million voters choose to come. Even if this estimate is overoptimistic, a substantial reduction in political ignorance would likely be a bargain at several times that price. A second merit of the Deliberation Day idea is that it probably would indeed raise knowledge, at least to some degree. It is difficult to imagine that voters would come away from a day of presentations and discussions on policy issues without any increase in knowledge at all.

Would Deliberation Day Improve Deliberation?

Despite its genuine attractions, the Deliberation Day proposal is unlikely to increase political knowledge anywhere near enough to fully offset rational ignorance and irrationality.[38] One major problem is that there simply will not be enough time to address more than a small fraction of the many policy issues handled by the federal government. As discussed in Chapter 5, the modern state deals with an almost infinite variety of issues, spending nearly 40 percent of GDP and regulating almost every aspect of society.[39] Ackerman and Fishkin propose that the attendees will first watch a seventy-five-minute televised debate between the two major parties' presidential candidates, followed by live discussion and question-and-answer sessions with local representatives of the two parties.[40] The entire process would last about eight hours, including a break for lunch.[41]

Given that most of the participants are likely to have little previous knowledge of the issues discussed, it is difficult to believe that more than a handful can be covered in any depth. For Deliberation Day to increase political knowledge about more than a small fraction of the total government agenda, descriptions of the functions of the state would have to be radically reduced or simplified. Alternatively, one can envision several deliberation days during each election cycle, covering a much wider range of issues. In that event, however, the costs of the process would increase enormously, and its enactment in the first place would become far less likely.

A second problem with the Deliberation Day proposal is that incumbent political leaders would have to enact it and determine its structure. In particular, they would have to determine the methods for selecting the issues to be discussed and the spokespersons for the opposing parties. This process would create numerous opportunities for manipulation. For instance, if the Republicans have control of Congress at the time when the Deliberation Day bill is passed, they could try to focus the process on issues where they know the Republican Party would have an edge. Similarly, the parties and their spokespeople could use the process to appeal to voters' rational irrationality, competing with each other in reinforcing the citizens' preexisting biases rather than genuinely informing them. Such manipulations were unlikely to be as serious a problem in Fishkin and his colleagues' previous deliberative poll experiments, when the political stakes were not so high.

More generally, the incumbent legislators who would have to enact the Deliberation Day bill would be unlikely to vote for it in any form that might reduce their own chances of getting reelected. This would greatly diminish the chances of enacting anything seen as likely to significantly alter the status quo political balance of power.

As with proposals to increase political knowledge by improving civic education, a well-informed electorate could potentially force elected officials to enact a relatively unbiased Deliberation Day, one that would at least genuinely increase political knowledge on as many issues as could reasonably be covered within the allotted time. Knowledgeable voters could detect and punish incumbent politicians' efforts to manipulate the framework of Deliberation Day for their own benefit. However, an electorate that knowledgeable would likely have little need for Deliberation Day in the first place.

These reservations do not lead me to categorically reject Deliberation Day–like proposals. There might still be value to experimentation along these lines. For example, a Deliberation Day–like framework could first be tried for a local or state election, in order to better understand the possible effects. Deliberation Day could also be more useful as part of a referendum process in states with ballot initiatives. Each referendum addresses only a single issue, so there would be less danger of agenda manipulation by excluding important policies from the scope of the discussion. Overall, however, it seems unlikely that Deliberation Day could have more than a minor impact on the problem of political ignorance.

The Ackerman-Fishkin plan is not the only proposal to increase political knowledge through structured deliberation.[42] It is merely the most thoroughly developed large-scale plan in the recent academic literature. But other ideas along similar lines suffer from the same weaknesses. All run afoul of the difficulties created by the large number of issues on the political agenda, and the need for government officials to select the issues chosen for discussion and to choose the people who will have the right to make presentations to the deliberators.[43]

RESTRICTING THE FRANCHISE

If we are unlikely to solve the problem of political ignorance by greatly increasing the knowledge levels of the electorate, an obvious alternative is to try to solve it by transferring electoral power to a subset of the population that has greater than average knowledge. Possible options include limiting the franchise to voters with a relatively high level of education or requiring voters to take and pass a political knowledge exam before being allowed to vote.

Alternatively, we could stick with the universal franchise, but grant "extra" votes to citizens with higher knowledge levels—either those with more education, those who can score high on a political knowledge exam, or both. John Stuart Mill proposed giving extra votes to the highly educated in his 1861 book *Considerations on Representative Government*.[44] Mill argued that "[i]t is not useful but hurtful that the constitution of the country should declare ignorance to be entitled to as much political power as knowledge."[45]

The idea of limiting the franchise seems shocking to modern sensibilities, as it runs against reigning assumptions of democratic egalitarianism. Yet it is not quite as radical as it seems. We already exclude major portions of our population from the right to vote at least in large part because they are believed to lack adequate knowledge. Everyone under the age of eighteen is denied the right to vote primarily for that very reason, as are many of the mentally ill.[46] Similarly, legal immigrants are not allowed to become citizens unless they can pass a relatively simple civics test that covers some basic facts about American history and government.[47] Some of the questions on the test are ones that many native-born Americans do not know the answers to.[48] Presumably, immigrants are required to pass the test because doing so is thought to demonstrate at least minimal competence for taking part in the democratic process.

If children, at least some of the mentally ill, and legal immigrants who fail to pass the citizenship test can be excluded from the franchise because of their presumed lack of political knowledge, why should others be immune from the same treatment? In theory, using a test or other similar approach to exclude the ignorant from the electorate might greatly alleviate the problem of political ignorance.

An ignorant electorate poses a danger not only to the ignorant voters themselves but to the country as a whole.[49] Thus it is difficult to defend allowing the ignorant to vote on the grounds that they have a right to vote as they please, without reference to the impact on others. As economist Bryan Caplan puts it, "A test of voter competence is no more objectionable than a driving test. Both bad driving and bad voting are dangerous not merely to the individual who practices them, but to innocent bystanders."[50]

Nonetheless, there are good reasons to avoid trying to solve the problem of political ignorance by imposing radical new restrictions on the franchise. Historically, literacy tests and other similar restrictions on the right to vote were used to exclude minorities despised by the majority, especially African Americans in the Jim Crow–era South and non-Anglo-Saxon immigrants in the nineteenth- and early twentieth-century North.[51] As is now well known, these laws excluded already disadvantaged groups from the political process and helped pave the way for harshly oppressive policies that victimized what were for a long time politically powerless populations.

It might be argued that today's voters are far less likely to be racist than their predecessors of a century ago, and thus that modern-day voting tests would not seek to exclude vulnerable minority groups. Even if such minorities were excluded disproportionately for unintentional reasons (for example, because of their lower average levels of education), the remaining electorate might not take advantage of the resulting decline in their voting power because most voters today try to cast ballots "sociotropically" on the basis of their estimate of the best policies for society as a whole.[52]

I am not convinced that racism and other similar prejudices have disappeared completely enough for us to be confident that a disproportionate exclusion of minority groups from the franchise poses no risks.[53] But even if that view is too pessimistic, the broader point is that grave dangers arise from the fact that any voting test or scheme for giving "extra" votes to the best informed must be approved by incumbent legislators. These officials will have obvious incentives to try to design a test that will tend to exclude as many of their likely political opponents as possible while keeping their supporters on the voting rolls. For example, Democrats could seek to design a test that would disproportionately exclude Republicans, and vice versa. If the test were sufficiently effective, the designers could convert a temporary political majority into a long-term effective one-party state.

This scenario is hardly a danger today, at a time when the electorate is likely to respond with outrage to any scheme that seems to disenfranchise a large fraction of the population.[54] But in a world where voting tests and other similar restrictions on the franchise were a realistic possibility, it would potentially be a serious threat.

DELEGATING POWER TO EXPERTS

A more politically realistic way to transfer political power to the politically knowledgeable would be to leave the franchise alone but shift more policymaking authority to unelected experts, insulated as much as possible from the democratic process. This is the idea behind such institutions as the Federal Reserve Board and the United States Supreme Court, both of which are staffed by experts who wield great power and have at least a substantial degree of insulation from electoral politics.

In recent years, scholars such as Supreme Court Justice Stephen Breyer and Cass Sunstein have endorsed this approach as a possible way to help alleviate the dangers of political ignorance and irrationality.[55] A complete analysis of the pros and cons of delegation to insulated experts is beyond the scope of this book. Here, I limit myself to a few brief comments suggesting that it is unlikely to be a panacea for the problem of ignorance.

To some extent, this approach is similar to my own argument in Chapter 6 that widespread political ignorance weakens the case against judicial review, which is of course a mechanism for allowing insulated experts to overturn the decisions of democratic processes. In the complex modern state, a substantial degree of delegation to experts is inevitable, given the size and scope of government. Yet the rule of experts goes far beyond the idea of judicial review. The latter usually only enables judges to block the initiatives of other branches of government, not institute major new regulatory policies of their own.[56]

We must be cautious about endorsing the "rule of experts" as a comprehensive solution to the problem of voter ignorance. One danger is that political ignorance is likely to reduce the quality of any delegations to experts that are enacted into law. In a democratic government, any power delegated to experts insulated from subsequent political pressure must first be granted by legislators. Obviously, public ignorance influences the process by which this occurs, which can easily lead to delegations that don't actually accomplish the purposes for which they were intended in the first place. For example, the delegation could be the result of the sort of exaggerated public fears of actually insignificant safety or health risks that Breyer and Sunstein argue necessitates expert intervention to prevent in the first place.[57]

Alternatively, the delegation to experts could be the result of lobbying by interest groups who can use the new agency to advance their own interests at the expense of the general public—what economists call "rent-seeking."[58] Political ignorance and irrationality can facilitate such rent-seeking by creating opportunities for interest groups to manipulate public opinion to their advantage. Sunstein and coauthor Timur Kuran have themselves shown how public ignorance and cognitive biases sometimes enable interest groups and activists to influence public opinion into building up irresistible political pressure for vast expenditures on minor or nonexistent health risks, while other more serious risks go unaddressed.[59]

A closely related problem is the question of "who guards the guardians" after the insulated experts have been granted their power. If the guarding is to be done by elected officials, the problem of political ignorance reenters by the back door. Voters are likely to be poor monitors of elected officials' supervision of the experts for the very same reasons that necessitated the experts' insulation in the first place. Moreover, subjecting the experts to political control ensures that they may not really be insulated after all. If, on the other hand, the experts are given "slack" that allows them to do as they wish without fear of political retribution, it is not clear what incentive they will have to use their power to protect the public interest as opposed to pursuing unrelated objectives of their own.

Finally, expert regulators face serious knowledge problems themselves. As F. A. Hayek famously argued, it may be impossible for them to determine the true preferences of the people they wish to serve.[60] A public health expert probably knows more than I do about the risks of drinking or smoking. But only I know how much enjoyment I derive from drinking a beer or smoking a cigarette. For that reason, the expert cannot easily tell whether trying to limit my smoking or drinking will improve my welfare or not.[61]

These points are not universally decisive criticisms of the rule of experts. In particular situations, it may be possible to design and enact incentives that suitably constrain experts on the one hand, while giving them necessary autonomy on the other. Political ignorance does not fully preclude this particular solution to the problems it causes. But it does certainly limit its potential effectiveness. Moreover, resorting to the rule of experts is less an attempt to raise the knowledge levels of voters than an effort to dispense with democratic control of government itself, at least with respect to whatever issues the expert regulators are tasked with deciding.

MEDIA REFORM

For some, the most obvious way to increase political knowledge is to improve media coverage of politics. If only the media would provide voters more and better information, perhaps they would learn it and make better choices at the ballot box.[62]

Criticism of media coverage of politics is very common, and some of it is surely warranted. But it is difficult to blame the media for low levels of political knowledge. Over the past thirty years, the rise of twenty-four-hour cable news and the Internet has made it easier and cheaper than ever to acquire political knowledge through media sources. Some media, most notably the C-SPAN cable network, provide lengthy and detailed coverage of public policy issues in addition to "horse race" coverage of elections—precisely the sort of programming that many reformers advocate.[63] Yet there has been little or no actual increase in public knowledge of politics.[64] Those who have used the new media to increase their knowledge seem to be primarily members of the minority who already had a strong preexisting interest in politics and were already likely to know the basics from other sources.[65] Moreover, if there were a strong audience demand for more detailed and substantive coverage of policy issues, one would expect profit-oriented media sources to provide more of it.

All of this suggests that low political knowledge levels are primarily caused by lack of demand for information, not lack of supply. In a world in which the functions of government are numerous and complicated, and most voters are rationally ignorant, few will take the time and effort to assimilate more than a small amount of political information. That will be true even if that information is readily available from media sources. This reluctance is also probably reinforced by the availability of numerous entertainment-oriented media, many of which are more appealing to citizens with limited interest in politics than political coverage is.[66]

Despite these reservations, we should not categorically rule out the possibility that changes in the media might increase political knowledge. Some evidence suggests that political knowledge levels are higher in countries where public or private TV stations are required to devote more time to public service programming, including coverage of political issues.[67] However, most of the knowledge differences between the United States, which has few such requirements, and European nations that have more falls in the area of international news.[68] This could easily be the result of a lower level of interest in international events in a large nation such as the United States, which historically has had a more insular culture than those of smaller European countries.

Moreover, laws requiring more extensive media coverage of political news face some of the same constraints as structured deliberation.[69] It is difficult for news coverage to reach more than a small fraction of the many issues controlled by modern government—at least if the amount of coverage citizens are expected to watch is to be kept to a realistic level.

Furthermore, the government would have to decide what qualifies as appropriate news coverage, and perhaps which of the many available political issues should receive more coverage compared to others. Such decisions create obvious opportunities for indoctrination and manipulation of public opinion, as is also the case with political education in public schools.[70] These considerations apply even more strongly to proposals to assign a greater political role to publicly funded media,[71] which are likely to be even more susceptible to government pressure than privately funded media outlets.

It is also worth noting that mandated public service programming may be of only limited usefulness in increasing political knowledge if few voters choose to watch it. In a modern media environment with numerous other entertainment options, that is a real possibility. Those least interested in politics—who tend to be the ones with the lowest levels of political knowledge[72]—are also especially likely to prefer entertainment programming to "hard" news.[73]

Although it is possible that either public service programming mandates or other changes in media coverage can increase political knowledge levels substantially, at this point such a result seems unlikely. The fundamental cause of political ignorance is not an inadequate supply of information, but low demand.

Nonetheless, future technological breakthroughs might still significantly increase political learning through the media. This is particularly likely if future technologies make it possible for people to assimilate new information with less time and effort than is possible at present. Rationally ignorant voters may continue to limit the resources they are willing to devote to learning about politics. But more advanced information technology might make it possible for them to learn more without devoting any more effort to the task than at present.[74]

In order to break through the barriers of rational ignorance, new technology must do more than make larger quantities information available at lower financial cost, as have the major innovations of the last several decades. It must make it easier and less time-consuming for citizens to learn, understand, and evaluate the huge amounts of information *already* available to them. Otherwise, future breakthroughs may not raise political knowledge levels any more than those of the last century.[75] Unless and until the right kinds of technological advances do occur, it is unlikely that changes in media coverage of politics will greatly increase political knowledge levels.

This point is well-illustrated by the example of "prediction markets"— markets which enable people to place bets on future events in government and public policy. Because bettors have strong incentives to make correct predictions in order to get a larger payoff, such markets can potentially provide voters and policymakers with a great deal of useful information about the likely effects of different policy options.[76] In the same way, conventional stock markets can give us valuable information about the likely future success of different industries and firms.

But even if prediction markets make high-quality data readily available for free, rationally ignorant voters may pay little or no attention to it, just as they currently ignore vast amounts of information available from other sources. There is no evidence that more than a tiny fraction of voters have been paying attention to prediction markets over the last few years that the data has been available; and prediction market data have had little if any electoral impact. Even those voters who do pay some attention to prediction markets may not evaluate their results with anything approaching objectivity, thanks to the effects of rational irrationality.

Political ignorance even makes it more difficult for prediction markets to function at all. In part because most of the public is either unaware of prediction markets or does not understand their value, there was little outcry over the U.S. government's December 2012 crackdown on Intrade, one of the largest prediction market sites. The Commodity Futures Trading Commission forced Intrade to stop taking bets from Americans.[77] Ironically, political ignorance may itself be an obstacle to the development of technologies that might over time help to dispel it.

This is not to suggest that prediction markets are useless. People can still use the data to make private sector decisions and for "voting with their feet" between states and local governments. In these situations, rational ignorance is far less of a problem.[78] Prediction market data can also sometimes be used to good effect by government officials and policy experts. But it is unlikely to be a solution to the problem of voter ignorance.

PAYING VOTERS TO LEARN

The strategies described in the preceding sections are all long-standing mainstays of the literature on efforts to alleviate political ignorance. There is, however, another, simpler option that is usually overlooked:

paying voters to increase their own knowledge. Instead of denying the franchise to citizens who fail to pass a political knowledge test, the government could instead reward those who do pass with monetary prizes. This approach would give citizens the sorts of individual incentives to acquire political information that they otherwise lack. In effect, it strikes at the very root of rational ignorance by making the acquisition of political knowledge "pay."

A 2008 study by Arthur Lupia and Markus Prior showed that offering experimental test subjects a modest payment of $1 for every correct answer on a test of basic political knowledge significantly improved performance.[79] Even when respondents had to give answers immediately, offering this incentive increased the proportion of correct answers by 11 percent.[80] The combination of monetary incentives and giving respondents twenty-four hours to come up with the answers caused a 24 percent increase.[81]

The authors argue that this experiment shows that conventional measures of political knowledge underestimate the true level of information known to voters. But their evidence actually supports the opposite conclusion. Real-world voters are *not* given financial incentives to increase their political knowledge and also don't generally spend significant amounts of time searching for political information. Lupia and Prior's experiment actually supports the theory of rational ignorance by proving that voter knowledge increases when individuals are given a financial incentive to become better-informed.

Be that as it may, the more interesting implication of their study is that even small financial incentives can have a significant impact on political knowledge. Obviously, we cannot know how large payments might need to be to achieve really great increases in knowledge for the citizenry as a whole. Further research is surely required.

Paying citizens to increase their own political knowledge is at least a potentially effective way to alleviate political ignorance. At the same time, several caveats are in order. First, it may be difficult or even prohibitively expensive to incentivize citizens effectively enough to learn about the full range of issues addressed by modern government. Second, as with voting tests that would exclude the less-knowledgeable from the franchise, tests with financial incentives would also have to be approved by incumbent legislators. This would create many opportunities for manipulation, similar to those that arise with the exclusionary voter knowledge tests discussed earlier.[82]

Any proposal to pay citizens for increasing their political knowledge might well get a hostile reception from public opinion. The idea of paying people to do their "civic duty" better is unlikely to prove immensely popular. Here too, political ignorance could turn out to be a major obstacle to its own alleviation. At the same time, the public has come to accept the need to pay people to perform other civic obligations, such as jury service. Perhaps public opinion could gradually come to accept the idea of payment for becoming a better-informed voter as well.

Despite these caveats and doubts, payment for performance is a proposal that at least deserves further consideration and research. Future studies could try to determine how much of an incentive would be needed to increase political knowledge on a variety of issues and within particular subgroups of the population.

THE LIMITED PROSPECTS FOR
INCREASING POLITICAL KNOWLEDGE

Overall, the prospects for a major increase in political knowledge in the foreseeable future seem relatively bleak. Major proposals for radically increasing political knowledge are likely to be either ineffective, politically infeasible, or both. It is possible that a breakthrough in education policy, media technology, or some other field will reverse this generally pessimistic prognosis. For the moment, however, it seems likely that the problem of political ignorance will be with us for a long time to come.

That does not mean that we should abandon all efforts to increase political knowledge. Even if major improvements cannot be achieved, modest advances are still worth pursuing. For example, small-scale deliberative polling might increase political knowledge at the margin. Similarly, it may be possible to achieve marginal improvements in school curricula or media coverage of politics that will increase knowledge to some degree. In the longer term, it may also be possible to give voters selective incentives to increase their political knowledge levels. While this today seems a radical idea, it is not fundamentally different from paying citizens to perform other civic duties.

At the same time, the painful reality is that we cannot count on any major increase in political knowledge in the foreseeable future. Instead of creating a vastly more knowledgeable electorate, we will—at least for a long time to come—have to make the best of the one we have.

Conclusion

The liberal believes that the limits which he wants democracy to impose upon itself are also the limits within which . . . the majority can truly direct and control the actions of government. . . .

Though democracy is probably the best form of limited government, it becomes an absurdity if it turns into unlimited government. Those who profess that democracy is all-competent and support all that the majority wants at any given moment are working for its fall.

—F. A. HAYEK[1]

THE CENTRAL ARGUMENT of this book is that widespread political ignorance is a serious problem for democracy, one that should lower our confidence in the effectiveness of the modern democratic state as a tool for making important policy decisions. It also questions whether the modern electorate even comes close to meeting the requirements of democratic theory.

Not all the implications of my analysis for democracy are negative. Voter ignorance is unlikely to be a serious problem in situations when the electorate is confronted with a clear, easy-to-recognize policy failure that can readily (and correctly) be ascribed to incumbent officials. In such a situation, even generally ignorant voters can effectively impose electoral punishment on the offending leaders.[2] This is a major advantage of democracy over authoritarianism, under which political leaders often get away with massive failures and atrocities without losing power. But few public policy issues in modern democracies are so clear-cut as famine or mass murder inflicted by a government on its own people.

Overall, recognition of the dangers of political ignorance should lead to greater pessimism about democratic government and a willingness to leave more decisions under the control of the market, civil society, and decentralized political institutions in which citizens can "vote with their feet." In any given situation, political ignorance should make us more skeptical of government intervention than we would be otherwise. Political ignorance also strengthens the case for constitutional limitations on the power of government, and their enforcement through judicial review.

At the same time, political ignorance does not by itself justify absolute libertarianism or any other theory of the appropriate size and scope of government. In any given case, opposing considerations could outweigh the risks of political ignorance. Some market failures are even worse than the political failures that ignorance helps facilitate.

The continuing relevance of these countervailing factors must, however, be viewed in light of the impact of ignorance. Before concluding that a given power should be assigned to democratic government, it is important to consider whether that authority can be used effectively despite the influence of political ignorance and irrationality. There are likely some tasks that a democratic government could carry out well if monitored by a well-informed electorate but that it will do badly with a relatively ignorant one.

A government with well-informed voters might be able to surgically implement only those few protectionist measures that genuinely improve the economy as a whole, even as it maintains an overall policy of free trade—as recommended by most economists.[3] But in light of the public's ignorance of basic economics and strong "antiforeign bias,"[4] it may be more prudent to eliminate or severely restrict elected officials' power to erect trade barriers.

A final downside of political ignorance is that it is an obstacle to its own alleviation. In Chapter 7, we saw how political ignorance makes it difficult to enact policies that would increase political knowledge directly. Rationally ignorant or irrational voters might also oppose policies such as decentralization and limits on government power that would reduce the range of decisions influenced by political ignorance. Considering the ways in which this vicious circle can be alleviated is an important objective for future research.

If political ignorance is rational and most voters choose not to learn much about politics for that reason, democracies will have to live with widespread ignorance for the foreseeable future. The challenge is to find ways to minimize the harm that ignorance causes.

IMPLICATIONS FOR PUBLIC POLICY

Widespread political ignorance has several important policy implications, only some of which have been considered in detail in this book. One is that it counts against efforts to increase voter turnout. The desirability of increasing voter turnout is an almost unquestioned bipartisan truism in American politics. But increasing turnout may reduce the average knowledge level of the electorate, thereby exacerbating the dangers of political ignorance. That does not prove that all efforts to increase turnout are always wrong. For example, it may be reasonable to promote turnout among a group that has been systematically excluded from politics by a hostile majority, as in the case of southern blacks until the 1960s. In other circumstances, however, large increases in turnout might simply reduce the average knowledge levels of the electorate.

A second policy implication of widespread political ignorance is that simple, transparent policies and institutions may be easier for voters to monitor than highly complex ones. As discussed in Chapter 4, retrospective voting can be an effective information shortcut in situations in which a highly visible problem is easy to connect to the policies of incumbent office-holders. The more complex the policy in question and the more indirect the connections between policy and outcome, the harder retrospective voting becomes.

Complex policy proposals are also likely to be unusually difficult for voters to assess. For example, a September 2009 survey found that only 37 percent of Americans said that they "understand" President Barack Obama's health care reform proposal,[5] despite the fact that the plan had been extensively covered in the media for months. The highly complex nature of the plan made it difficult or impossible for rationally ignorant voters to understand it well enough to make an informed assessment of its merits.

This is not to suggest that simple policies are always best. Some degree of policy complexity is unavoidable. But the tradeoff between policy complexity and voter understanding is one that must be carefully weighed.

Perhaps the most important implication of widespread political ignorance is that it strengthens the case for settling issues through foot voting rather than ballot box voting. Foot voting can be facilitated either
by decentralizing government functions to state or local governments or
by leaving more issues to be decided outside of government altogether.
Relative to ballot box voting, foot voting creates much stronger incentives for both acquiring relevant information and evaluating it in a more
rational way.

Especially in the short term, it is neither possible nor desirable to
fully decentralize all functions of government. Still, many small democracies seem to function well despite being only a tiny fraction of the size
of the United States. These include nations such as Switzerland, Luxembourg, Liechtenstein, and Denmark, several of the most successful
democratic states in the world. In the case of Switzerland, many crucial
government powers are devolved to cantons, most of which are no bigger than modest-size American cities.[6]

If economies of scale or other factors make it essential to conduct
important government activities on a large scale, these nations would
not rank among the world's most prosperous and successful democratic states—even though none of them have unusually great natural
resource endowments.[7] More systematic research also fails to find that
large democracies function better than small ones.[8] The success of small
democracies suggests that larger democracies such as the United States
may be able to take advantage of foot voting by decentralizing many
government powers without sacrificing much in the way of economies
of scale and other advantages.

Sadly, political ignorance may be an important obstacle to the kind
of decentralization and limitation of government power that might help
alleviate its impact. For example, economist Bryan Caplan finds that
voters have a strong "anti-market bias" that leads them to oppose many
reductions in government regulation.[9]

Given the self-perpetuating nature of the problem of political ignorance,
readers might wonder whether there is much purpose to a book such as
this one. Even if the case for limiting and decentralizing government is

correct, rationally ignorant voters could easily ignore it, just as they do a great deal of other relevant information.

The challenge is indeed a daunting one. Nonetheless, there is at least some reason for cautious optimism. Past experience in several countries suggests that substantial liberalization and decentralization can be achieved in modern democracies. In the 1980s and 1990s, for example, New Zealand greatly reduced the role of government in its economy, achieving unprecedented prosperity as a result.[10] Between 1985 and 1995, Ireland went from a 6.1 rating in the Cato Institute and Fraser Institute's "economic freedom" rankings to an 8.6.[11] This is a massive increase on the measure's 10-point scale. During the 1990s and early 2000s, a left-liberal Canadian government also managed to push through massive reductions in government spending.[12] Switzerland has remained a highly decentralized—and highly successful—federal state for decades.

Ireland, New Zealand, and Switzerland all ranked ahead of the United States on the Cato Institute-Fraser Institute economic liberties index as of 2007, even before the massive increases in federal spending and regulation resulting from the financial crisis and recession that began in 2008.[13] Canada's ranking was statistically indistinguishable from that of the United States and has since pulled ahead.[14]

These examples suggest that substantial reductions in the size, scope, and centralization of government are at least possible in a modern democracy, even if often politically difficult. It may not be possible to reduce government to the point where rationally ignorant voters can readily understand all of its major functions. But it is at least possible to make their task easier at the margin, and to increase the range of decisions that are made through foot voting rather than ballot box voting. By contrast, there is little if any evidence to suggest that we can achieve massive increases in political knowledge.

In the United States, surveys show that Bryan Caplan's "anti-market bias" coexists with a considerable suspicion of government. A 2010 *Washington Post*/ABC News survey found that 58 percent of Americans prefer a "smaller government with fewer services" to a "larger government with more services" (preferred by 38 percent).[15] A majority have consistently preferred "smaller government with fewer services" on this question for the past twenty years.[16] Similarly, an August 2009 Gallup poll showed that 57 percent of Americans believe that "the government is trying to do too many things that should be left to individuals and businesses."[17] Even on the day of the November 2012 presidential election, an important victory for the Democratic Party, CNN exit polls found that 51 percent of voters believe that government is doing "too much" that should be left to the private sector, compared to 43 percent who state that it should do "more" to solve problems.[18]

Such general anti-government sentiments are balanced by strong public support for many specific types of government intervention. For example, an extensive July 2011 survey conducted by the Pew Research Foundation found that large majorities of the public oppose cuts in the benefits provided by Medicare and Social Security, two of the largest federal spending programs.[19] The point is not that major reductions in the size and scope of government are easy to achieve or likely to occur soon. Neither is true. I suggest only that they are probably more feasible than major increases in political knowledge.

Some decentralization and reductions in the size of government might be brought about by persuading either political elites or the small subset of voters who are unusually well informed. The existence of widespread political ignorance helps give these groups a measure of "slack" and autonomy from public opinion.[20]

But even the less-knowledgeable general public might gradually come to support greater privatization and decentralization. At the very least, it is easier to convince rationally ignorant voters to support generalized reductions in government than to invest the vast amounts of time and energy needed to increase their knowledge of numerous individual government programs, so as to facilitate effective monitoring of government's performance at its current size. If consistently applied, suspicion and distrust of government can be a useful information shortcut—especially for voters who are aware of the limitations of their knowledge and judgment at the ballot box. Over time, arguments like those presented in this book might help make more people aware of those limitations.

IMPLICATIONS FOR THEORIES OF
DEMOCRATIC PARTICIPATION

The problem of political ignorance also has important implications for normative theories of democratic participation. A particularly important one is that there may be a tradeoff between the quantity and quality of participation. There are two dimensions to this problem: the number of issues on the government agenda and the number of people who take part in the democratic process. The more issues voters must consider, the less likely they are to acquire and rationally evaluate the information they need to vote on them in an informed way. Likewise, the greater the percentage of the population that has the right to vote, the higher the proportion of those with relatively low interest in politics and low levels of political knowledge.

This does not mean that universal adult suffrage is undesirable. For reasons discussed in Chapter 7, it may be dangerous to try to mitigate political ignorance by restricting the franchise. At the same time, however, universal suffrage increases the difficulty of achieving high levels of political knowledge.

The empirical evidence suggests that it is extremely difficult to achieve even the levels of political knowledge in the electorate demanded by relatively modest theories of participation, such as retrospective voting.[21] In light of this reality, it is likely impossible to achieve the much higher knowledge levels demanded by more stringent theories, such as deliberative democracy. Not only do these theories demand a high level of factual knowledge, they also require voters to demonstrate considerable sophistication in analyzing the information they have.[22] Unfortunately, advocates of deliberative democracy have failed to provide a convincing account of how their theory can be realized with an electorate characterized by widespread rational ignorance and irrationality. At least for the foreseeable future, it seems unlikely that deliberative democracy is a realistic possibility. The combination of rational ignorance and irrationality is a powerful obstacle to the achievement of the deliberative ideal.

However, it may still be possible to achieve higher-quality deliberation in making important social decisions. As discussed in Chapter 5, foot voters have much stronger incentives than ballot box voters to acquire information and analyze it rationally. The deliberative decisions made by foot voters may not meet the most stringent requirements of political philosophers. But they come closer to doing so than the choices of ballot box voters.[23] Paradoxically, the best way to improve democratic deliberation may be to rely on it less.

THE FUTURE OF DEMOCRACY

It is conceivable that future technological or economic developments will lead to a major increase in political knowledge. So far, however, political ignorance and irrationality have proven extremely resistant to technological change. The rise of radio, television, and most recently the Internet has made political information more easily available than ever before. Rising education levels and IQ scores have also made knowledge acquisition easier for voters.[24] Yet political knowledge levels have grown only slightly, if at all, over the past several decades.[25] Nor is there any reason to believe that voters have become more rational in making use of the knowledge they do possess. Limits on demand rather than supply seem to be the most important causes of political ignorance.

Over the past four years, the political reaction to the recent financial crisis and recession has led to a major increase in the size and scope of government. It is too early to say whether political knowledge levels will increase to compensate for the added information burden this creates for voters. Past experience, however, does not counsel optimism.

Despite political ignorance, democracy retains many advantages over rival systems of government, such as dictatorship.[26] Nonetheless, political ignorance will probably continue to be a serious weakness of democratic government. We are unlikely to eliminate that weakness completely. But we can reduce its dangers by limiting and decentralizing the role of government in society.

The government that governs least is not always best in every way. Yet it is the form of democracy least vulnerable to political ignorance. Democratic control of government works better when there is less government to control.

Reference Matter

Appendix

Correlates of political knowledge in the 2000
American National Election Studies survey

Variable Name	Unstandardized Coefficients	Standard Error	Standardized Coefficients	T-Statistic	Significance
Constant	−2.555	.770		−3.318	.001
Region (South = 1)	−.351	.285	−.024	−1.229	.219
Watching TV News (Number of days per week)	.127	.053	.050	2.391	.017
Newspaper (Number of days per week)	.114	.049	.047	2.312	.021
Age (6-pt. scale)	−2.987E-02	.107	−.006	−.280	.780
Education (7-pt. scale)	1.289	.101	.292	12.818	.000
Working Full Time (30+ hrs./week)	−.658	.314	−.045	−2.099	.036
Union Member in Household	−2.490E-02	.380	−.001	−.066	.948
Household Income (5-pt. scale)	.849	.164	.119	5.193	.000
Race (Black = 1)	−1.522	.454	−.065	−3.353	.001
Hispanic (Hispanic = 1)	−1.440	.647	−.042	−2.227	.026
Gender (Female = 1)	−2.284	.282	−.160	−8.112	.000
Political Acts Beyond Voting (9-pt. scale)	.348	.122	.059	2.847	.004
Listening to Political Talk Radio (4-pt. scale)	.461	.116	.077	3.969	.000
Seeing Election News on the Internet	.701	.321	.046	2.184	.029
External Efficacy (10-pt. scale)	7.414E-02	.062	.024	1.193	.233
Interest in Politics (9-pt. scale)	1.390	.091	.359	15.362	.000

NOTES: OLS regression, N = 1,349; adjusted R^2 = 0.538.

Dependent variable: Political knowledge (30-point scale)

Notes

INTRODUCTION

1. James Madison, "Letter to William T. Barry, Aug. 4, 1822," in *Writings*, ed. Jack N. Rakove (New York: Library of America, 1999), 790.

2. See Table 1.1.

3. Ibid.

4. Siegel-Gale survey, September 18, 2009, http://www.siegelgale.com/media_release/new-poll-americans-still-confused-by-president-obama%E2%80%99s-health-care-plan/. The figure probably overstates the true level of knowledge because many survey respondents are reluctant to admit ignorance. See discussion in Chapter 1.

5. Rassmussen Reports, "Toplines—Cap & Trade I—May 7–8, 2009," http://www.rasmussenreports.com/public_content/politics/toplines/pt_survey_toplines/may_2009/toplines_cap_trade_i_may_7_8_2009.

6. Ibid.

7. See Chapter 1.

8. Abraham Lincoln, "Gettysburg Address," in *Abraham Lincoln: His Speeches and Writings*, ed. Roy P. Basler (New York: Da Capo Press, 2001), 734.

9. See, e.g., Charles Beitz, *Political Equality: An Essay in Democratic Theory* (Princeton, NJ: Princeton University Press, 1989); Thomas Christiano, *The Rule of the Many* (Boulder, CO: Westview Press, 1996).

10. See, e.g., Richard J. Arneson, "Democracy Is Not Intrinsically Just," in *Justice and Democracy: Essays for Brian Barry*, ed. Keith Dowding, Robert E. Goodin, and Carole Pateman (New York: Cambridge University Press, 2004), 40–58.

11. See Jason Brennan, *The Ethics of Voting* (Princeton, NJ: Princeton University Press, 2011); Jason Brennan, "The Right to a Competent Electorate," *Philosophical Quarterly* 61 (2011): 700–24.

12. Robert H. Bork, *The Tempting of America* (New York: Free Press, 1990), 139.

13. H. L. Mencken, *A Little Book in C Major*, (New York: John Lane, 1916), 19.

14. John Stuart Mill, *Considerations on Representative Government* (Indianapolis: Bobbs-Merrill, 1958 [1861]), 154–55 (emphasis added). For a modern elaboration of an argument similar to Mill's, see Brennan, *The Ethics of Voting*.

15. See, e.g., Mancur Olson, *The Logic of Collective Action* (Cambridge: Harvard University Press, 1965); James M. Buchanan, *The Demand and Supply of Public Goods* (Indianapolis: Liberty Press, 1999 [1968]); Paul A. Samuelson, "The Pure Theory of Public Expenditure," *Review of Economics and Statistics* 36 (1954): 387–401.

16. See George Akerlof, "The Market for Lemons: Quality Uncertainty and the Market Mechanism," *Quarterly Journal of Economics* 84 (1970): 488–500.

17. For evidence that voters systematically overestimate the economic benefits of protectionism, see Bryan Caplan, *The Myth of the Rational Voter: Why Democracies Choose Bad Policies* (Princeton, NJ: Princeton University Press, 2007), 50–52.

18. See, e.g., James L. Stimson, *Tides of Consent: How Public Opinion Shapes American Politics* (New York: Cambridge University Press, 2006); Stuart N. Soroka and Christopher Wlezien, *Degrees of Democracy: Politics, Public Opinion, and Policy* (New York: Cambridge University Press, 2009); Robert Erikson, et al., *Statehouse Democracy: Public Opinion and Policy in the American States* (New York: Cambridge University Press, 1993); Lawrence R. Jacobs, *The Health of Nations: Public Opinion and the Making of American and British Health Policy* (Ithaca: Cornell University Press, 1993); Benjamin Page and Robert Shapiro, *The Rational Public* (Chicago: University of Chicago Press, 1992).

19. See Chapters 2 and 6.

20. See discussion of retrospective voting in Chapter 4. See also R. Douglas Arnold, *The Logic of Congressional Action* (New Haven: Yale University Press, 1990), 48–51, 72–74.

21. See the discussion in Chapter 3.

22. See, e.g., F. A. Hayek, "The Use of Knowledge in Society," *American Economic Review* 4 (1945): 519–30; Jeffrey Friedman and Wladimir Kraus, *Engineering the Financial Crisis: Systemic Risk and the Failure of Regulation* (Philadelphia: University of Pennsylvania Press, 2011).

23. See, e.g., David Schultz, *American Politics in the Age of Ignorance: Why Lawmakers Choose Belief Over Research* (New York: Palgrave Macmillan, 2012).

24. See Jennifer Tolbert Roberts, *Athens on Trial: The Antidemocratic Tradition in Western Thought* (Princeton, NJ: Princeton University Press, 1994), 48–92. For an excellent recent argument suggesting that ancient Athenian democracy was able to overcome the problem of ignorance, see Josiah Ober, *Democracy and Knowledge: Innovation and Learning in Classical Athens* (Princeton, NJ: Princeton University Press, 2008). I have argued that Athens' relative success in this regard depended on advantages not enjoyed by modern democracies. See Ilya Somin, "Democracy and Political Knowledge in Ancient Athens," *Ethics* 119 (2009), 585–90, available at Social Science Research Network, http://papers.ssrn.com/sol3/papers.cfm?abstract_id=1428612.

25. Plato, *The Gorgias*, trans. Walter Hamilton (New York: Penguin, 1971). The great historian Thucydides blamed popular ignorance for the failures of democracy. He believed it was responsible for the decision to undertake the invasion of Sicily during the Peloponnesian War in 415 B.C.—a choice that led to the worst defeat in Athenian history and caused the loss of most of its armed forces and eventually its empire. According to Thucydides, the citizen-voters undertook the Sicilian expedition because they were "ignorant of the size of the island" and the power of Syracuse and its allies. Thucydides, *History of the Peloponnesian War*, trans. Rex Warner (New York: Penguin, 1954), section 6.1.1.

26. Aristotle, *The Politics*, trans. T. A. Saunders, rev. ed. (New York: Penguin, 1981), book III.xi, 202–03.

27. Ibid., book III.iv–v, 181–86.

28. James Madison, "Federalist 63," *The Federalist*, ed. Clinton Rossiter (New York: Mentor, 1961), 384.

29. Mill, *Considerations on Representative Government*, 140–42.

30. Vladimir I. Lenin, *Chto Delat? [What Is to Be Done?]* (Moscow: Lenin Institute, 1925 [1902]), chs. 2–4.

31. Adolf Hitler, *Mein Kampf*, trans. Ralph Mannheim (New York: Houghton-Mifflin, 1971), 180.

32. See works discussed in Chapter 4.

33. Benjamin Barber, *Strong Democracy* (Berkeley: University of California Press, 1984), 234.

34. For a summary, see Morton H. Halperin, Joseph T. Siegle, and Michael M. Weinstein, *The Democracy Advantage: How Democracy Promotes Prosperity and Peace*, rev. ed. (New York: Routledge, 2010), chs. 1–2.

35. Ibid.

36. See the discussion in Chapter 4.

37. Ibid.

38. A May 2007 Gallup poll found that 35 percent of Americans believed that homosexuality is caused by "upbringing and environment" while 42 percent answered (correctly) that it is a condition "a person is born with." People giving the former answer were far more likely to believe that homosexuality is morally unacceptable and that homosexual sex should be against the law. Of those giving the second answer, 78 percent believed that homosexuality is "an acceptable alternative lifestyle," compared with only 30 percent of the former group. Gallup Poll, May 10–13, 2007.

39. See Laurence H. Tribe, *Abortion: The Clash of Absolutes* (New York: Norton, 1991).

40. For a recent survey of the relevant evidence showing that most major political disagreements turn on disputes over factual issues, see Michael Murakami, "Paradoxes of Democratic Accountability: Polarized Parties, Hard Decisions, and No Despot to Veto," *Critical Review* 20 (2008): 91–114.

41. See ibid., and Morris Fiorina, *Culture War? The Myth of a Polarized America*, 3rd ed. (New York: Longman, 2010).

42. According to some estimates, up to one million women per year sought to obtain black market abortions before the Supreme Court forced the nationwide legalization of abortions in 1973. Tribe, *Abortion*, 140. Many pro-lifers might still support banning abortion even if aware of this problem, though others perhaps might not. But the existence of a massive black market is surely relevant to determinations of what sorts of pro-life policies should be adopted, even from the standpoint of those whose values condemn abortion as immoral.

43. Ian Shapiro, *Democracy's Place* (Ithaca: Cornell University Press, 1996), 9. Shapiro partially qualifies this by adding that democracy must be defended on "consequentialist grounds," which implies that there might be external standards for evaluating its output after all. But he then undermines the qualification by suggesting that only democratic procedures can determine which policies to adopt in situations when "the desirability of the consequences in question is *debatable*," which presumably includes virtually all political issues on which people are likely to disagree (ibid). For similar rejection of the possibility of judging democracy by external standards, see Barber, *Strong Democracy*, 117–18. For a different criticism of such arguments, see Caplan, *Myth of the Rational Voter*, 187–89.

44. Most of those scholars who argue that we cannot evaluate democratic processes by external standards also argue that democracy is superior to alternative regimes. See, e.g., Ian Shapiro, *The State of Democratic Theory* (Princeton, NJ: Princeton University Press, 2003), 1–2; Barber, *Strong Democracy*, ch. 1.

45. Anthony Downs, *An Economic Theory of Democracy* (New York: Harper & Row, 1957), ch. 13.

46. Caplan, *Myth of the Rational Voter*, ch. 5.

CHAPTER ONE

1. John Ferejohn, "Information and the Electoral Process," in *Information and Democratic Processes*, ed. John Ferejohn and James Kuklinski (Urbana: University of Illinois Press, 1990), 3.

2. For the classic studies of this era, see, e.g., Angus Campbell, et al., *The American Voter* (New York: John Wiley & Sons, 1960); Bernard Berelson, et al., *Voting* (Chicago: University of Chicago Press, 1954), and especially Philip Converse, "The Nature of Belief Systems in Mass Publics," in *Ideology and Discontent*, ed. David Apter (New York: Free Press 1964). For more recent surveys of the evidence, see especially Michael X. Delli Carpini and Scott Keeter, *What Americans Know About Politics and Why It Matters* (New Haven: Yale University Press, 1996); Scott L. Althaus, *Collective Preferences in Democratic Politics* (New York: Cambridge University Press, 2003); and Richard Shenkman, *Just How Stupid Are We? Facing the Truth About the American Voter* (New York: Basic Books, 2008).

3. John Sides and Lynn Vavreck, "Independents and Undecided Voters on Paul Ryan: More Unfavorable than Favorable, but Most Unsure," *Monkey Cage*, August 11, 2012, http://themonkeycage.org/2012/08/11/independents-and-undecided-voters-on-paul-ryan-more-unfavorable-than-favorable/

4. Pew Research Foundation, "As Fiscal Cliff Nears, Democrats Have Public Opinion on their Side," December 13, 2012, http://www.people-press.org/files/legacy-pdf/12-13-12%20Political%20Release.pdf. CNN exit polls indicate that 60 percent of voters supported this proposal on election day. CNN Exit Poll, November 6, 2012, http://www.cnn.com/election/2012/results/race/president#exit-polls.

5. Peter Schroeder, "Hill Poll: Likely Voters Prefer Lower Individual, Business Tax Rates," *The Hill*, February 27, 2012, http://thehill.com/polls/212643-hill-poll-likely-voters-prefer-lower-tax-rates-for-individuals-business.

6. Pew Research Center, *What Americans Know, 1989–2007: Public Knowledge of Current Affairs Changed Little by News and Information Revolutions* (Washington, DC: Pew Research Center, 2007), 25.

7. See Table 1.3, further on.

8. See Suzanne Mettler, *The Submerged State: How Invisible Government Policies Undermine American Democracy* (Chicago: University of Chicago Press, 2011); Christopher Howard, *The Hidden Welfare State: Tax Expenditures and Social Policy in the United States* (Princeton, NJ: Princeton University Press, 1999).

9. Mettler, *Submerged State*, 4–6, 8–29.

10. Data calculated from the American National Election Studies(ANES) 2002, variable 025083. Data from the 2002 study is available from the author or from the ANES website at http://www.electionstudies.org. 11. See, e.g., W. Russell Neumann, *The Paradox of Mass Politics* (Cambridge: Harvard University Press, 1986), 15–16; Stephen E. Bennett and Linda Bennett, "Out of Sight Out of Mind: Americans' Knowledge of Party Control of the House of Representatives, 1960–1984," *Political Research Quarterly* (1992), 67–81.

12. Ilya Somin, "Voter Ignorance and the Democratic Ideal," *Critical Review* 12 (1998): 413–58, at 417.

13. Benjamin Page and Robert Shapiro, *The Rational Public* (Chicago: University of Chicago Press, 1992), 10.

14. Delli Carpini and Keeter, *What Americans Know About Politics*, 62.

15. Ibid., 94; Neumann, *Paradox of Mass Politics*, 15.

16. See, e.g., Althaus, *Collective Preferences*; Delli Carpini & Keeter, *What Americans Know About Politics*, ch. 2.

17. Delli Carpini & Keeter, *What Americans Know About Politics*, 70–71.

18. Zogby Poll, July 21–27, 2006.

19. McCormack Tribune Freedom Museum, "Americans' Awareness of First Amendment Freedoms," January 20–22, 2006, http://www.freedomproject.us/files/pdf/survey_results_report_final.pdf.

20. Michael Dorf, "Whose Constitution Is It Anyway? What Americans Don't Know About Our Constitution—and Why It Matters," *Findlaw*, May 29, 2002, http://writ.corporate.findlaw.com/dorf/20020529.html.

21. See, e.g., works cited in Somin, "Voter Ignorance and the Democratic Ideal," 417–18; see also David RePass, "Searching for Voters Along the Liberal-Conservative Continuum: The Infrequent Ideologue and the Missing Middle," *The Forum* 6 (2008): 1–49.

22. Anthony Downs, *An Economic Theory of Democracy* (New York: Harper & Row, 1957), ch. 7.

23. See, e.g., Samuel Popkin, *The Reasoning Voter* (Chicago: University of Chicago Press, 1991), 52.

24. Neumann, *Paradox*; Donald Kinder and Lynn Sanders, "Mimicking Political Debate with Survey Questions: The Case of White Opinion on Affirmative Action for Blacks," *Social Cognition* 8 (1990): 73–103.

25. For studies showing little or no change over time, see Delli Carpini and Keeter, *What Americans Know About Politics*, 62–134; Eric R.A.N. Smith, *The Unchanging American Voter* (Berkeley: University of California Press, 1989); Stephen E. Bennett, "'Know-Nothings' Revisited: The Meaning of Political Ignorance Today," *Social Science Quarterly* 69 (1988): 476–92; Stephen E. Bennett, "'Know-Nothings' Revisited Again," *Political Behavior* 18 (1996): 219–31; Stephen E. Bennett, "Trends in Americans' Political Information, 1967–87," *American Politics Quarterly* 17 (1989): 422–35; Michael X. Delli Carpini and Scott Keeter, "Stability and Change in the U.S. Public's Knowledge of Politics," *Public Opinion Quarterly* 55 (1991): 583–96. For an exception, see Althaus, *Collective Preferences*, 215, which shows a very small increase in knowledge when comparing the 1980–88 period to 1990–98. The increase shown in Althaus's study is very small (from an average of 52 percent correct answers in the earlier period to 54 percent in the later one), and may be an artifact of the particular questions studied (ibid).

26. For evidence that increasing education levels over the past several decades have not led to higher levels of political knowledge, see Norman H. Nie, et al., *Education and Democratic Citizenship in America* (Chicago: University of Chicago Press, 1996), 111–66.

27. See, e.g., Pew Research Center, *What Americans Know*.

28. Markus Prior, *Post-Broadcast Democracy: How Media Choice Increases Inequality in Political Involvement and Polarizes Elections* (New York: Cambridge University Press, 2007), 74–84.

29. Ibid., ch. 4.

30. Bruce Bimber, *Information and American Democracy: Technology in the Evolution of Political Power* (New York: Cambridge University Press, 2003), 229–30; Markus Prior, "News vs. Entertainment: How Increasing Media Choice Widens Gaps in Political Knowledge and Turnout," *American Journal of Political Science* 49 (2005): 577–92; see also John Hindman, *The Myth of Digital Democracy* (Princeton, NJ: Princeton University Press, 2008), 60–61; Prior, *Post-Broadcast Democracy*, chs. 4 and 8.

31. See John Stuart Mill, *Considerations on Representative Government* (Indianapolis: Bobbs-Merrill, 1958 [1861]).

32. The 2000 ANES study was an extensive nationwide survey of over 1,800 respondents that included thirty political knowledge items covering a wide range of subjects, an unusually large number of knowledge items for a single survey. A total of 1,545 respondents had complete data on answers to all thirty knowledge items. Data from the 2000 study is available for downloading from the University of Michigan Interuniversity Consortium on Political and Social Research, at http://www.icpsr.umich.edu/icpsrweb/landing.jsp. The 2000 study is data set number 3131. A modified version of the data set with recoded variables for purposes of the present study is available from the author.

33. See the discussion of public knowledge of Republican vice-presidential nominee Paul Ryan, and of tax rates, earlier in this chapter.

34. CNN/Opinion Research poll, Oct. 27–30, 2010.35. David M. Herszenhorn, "Components of Stimulus Vary in Speed and Efficiency," *New York Times*, January 29, 2009.

36. 130 S.Ct. 876 (2010).

37. Reid also was up for reelection in 2010, eventually narrowly defeating Republican candidate Sharron Angle.

38. Many survey respondents will even express opinions about nonexistent legislation rather than admit they have never heard of it. For a notorious example, see Stanley Payne's famous finding that 70 percent of respondents expressed opinions regarding the nonexistent "Metallic Metals Act." Stanley Payne, *The Art of Asking Questions* (Princeton, NJ: Princeton University Press, 1951), 18. In a more recent study, 43 percent of respondents expressed opinions about the proposed repeal of the fictitious "Public Affairs Act" rather than admit that they didn't know what it was. George Bishop, *The Illusion of Public Opinion* (New York: Rowman & Littlefield, 2004), 28. For some additional recent evidence, see Patrick Sturgis and Patten Smith, "Fictitious Issues Revisited: Political Interest, Knowledge and the Generation of Nonattitudes." *Political Studies* 58 (2010): 66–84.

39. Stephanie Condon, "Five Health Care Promises Obama Won't Keep," *CBS News Special Report*, September 21, 2009, http://www.cbsnews.com/stories/2009/09/21/politics/main5326987.shtml.

40. *Newsweek*, September 29, 2008. The issue had hit the newsstands several days earlier.

41. Public Interest Project/Greenberg Quinlan Rosner Research Poll, June 17–26, 2008.

42. See the discussion of guessing earlier in this chapter.

43. Indeed, the *Wall Street Journal* reported in July 2004 that "discussions of a jobless recovery evaporated" after the Labor Department reported a gain of 308,000 jobs during the month of March alone, on April 2. Aaron Luchetti, "Bond Rally Ends as Economy, Job Market Spur Fed to Move," *Wall Street Journal*, July 1, 2004, C12.

44. Pew Research Center Survey, February 11–16, 2004.

45. Ibid.

46. I have chosen not to include a relevant but methodologically flawed question about the identity of the chief justice of the Supreme Court that has been discredited by recent research. See James L. Gibson and Gregory Caldeira, "Knowing the Supreme Court: A Reconsideration of Public Ignorance About the High Court." *Journal of Politics* 71 (2009): 429–41.

47. There were significantly fewer knowledge questions in the 2004 ANES study and the 2008 ANES study.

48. The potential exceptions are the home states of vice-presidential candidates Dick Cheney and Joe Lieberman (Wyoming and Connecticut, respectively), and possibly being able to name a second House candidate in one's congressional district, especially in cases when the House race was not close. Eliminating these three items would not significantly change any of the results analyzed in this chapter. Moreover, the first two were repeatedly mentioned in the press during the campaign and likely would have been picked up by anyone who followed the campaign at all closely.

49. These items were the reduction in the federal deficit in the Clinton years, the reduction in crime, and increased government spending to help the poor.

50. Delli Carpini and Keeter, *What Americans Know About Politics*, 138–52.

51. Data calculated from questions listed in Table 1.4.

52. Bennett, "'Know-Nothings' Revisited," 483.

53. Data calculated from answers to items listed in Table 1.4.

54. These seventeen were the twelve items comparing Bush's and Gore's or Democratic and Republican issue positions, the three questions asking about changes in the crime rate, the deficit, and spending on the poor in the 1992–2000 period, and the two questions regarding identification of Bush's and Pat Buchanan's ideology (moderate, liberal, or conservative). Although some of these questions had more than three options on the original survey, I collapsed them into three for recoding purposes, with the result that respondents who guessed randomly would have had a one-in-three chance of getting the correct answer. For the questions regarding Bush's and Gore's ideologies, I gave half credit to respondents who picked "moderate," even though, arguably, most knowledgeable observers would not agree with such answers. Al Gore ran an explicitly liberal campaign emphasizing the theme of "the people versus the powerful." See, e.g., John F. Harris and Ceci Connolly, "Shaking Off the Clinton Strategy, Too; With Populist Push, Gore Looks Toward a Different Group of Swing Voters," *Washington Post*, August 24, 2000, A1. Bush famously described himself as a "compassionate conservative" and prominently proposed a number of strongly conservative policies, including a large income tax cut and the privatization of social security.

55. These were the two questions regarding party control of the House of Representatives and Senate prior to the election.

56. I decided to code as correct answers both "moderate" and "liberal" on the question asking the respondent to identify Bill Clinton's ideology.

57. Guessing, albeit with low probabilities of success, was possible on the questions asking for identification of the four candidates' home states, Joe Lieberman's religion, and the positions held by Lott, Blair, and Reno.

58. Half points were possible because I allowed half credit for certain answers on two questions.

59. I assume that a respondent guessing randomly would have gotten right, on average, 5.67 of the 17 questions with three possible answers, one of the two binary questions, and 0.66 points on the question regarding Clinton's ideology (where two of three possible answers were counted as correct—both "liberal" and "moderate"),and on average one more question from the remaining nine, for a total score of 8.33.

60. Bennett, "'Know-Nothings' Revisited," 483.

61. See Scott L. Althaus, "Information Effects in Collective Preferences," *American Political Science Review* 92 (1998), 545–46.

62. See the calculation in Note 59 above.

63. See the discussion in Note 38.

64. This finding replicates similar results from earlier research (presenting evidence that the most widely known facts about politicians are personal tidbits with little real information value). Delli Carpini and Keeter, *What Americans Know About Politics*, 10. For example, among the most widely known facts about the first President Bush were his distaste for broccoli and the fact that he had a dog named "Millie" (ibid).

65. These were the home states of Lieberman (30 percent correct) and Republican vice presidential nominee Dick Cheney (19 percent). Ironically, these two items probably had greater informational value than at least two of the three similar questions that many more respondents answered correctly. Lieberman's issue positions were reasonably representative of moderately liberal Connecticut, while Cheney's conservatism was certainly representative of majority political opinion in Wyoming.

66. If we also eliminate the Clinton ideology question, we are left with a slightly lower average score of 10.5 out of 24 (44 percent correct).

67. This figure was calculated using the methodology outlined in the notes above. I continue to assume that respondents employing random guessing would get about 5.67 correct answers out of the seventeen questions with three options, 1 point from the two binary questions, and 0.66 points from the Clinton ideology question. However, because the number of other items has been reduced from ten to five, I have assumed that they would get only 0.5 correct answers from these items by guessing rather than 1.0 as in the model for the thirty-item scale. Thus a total of just under eight predicted correct answers. A total of 35 percent of respondents scored eight correct answers or fewer on the twenty-five-point scale.

68. See, e.g., Gibson and Caldeira, "Knowing the Supreme Court"; Jon A. Krosnick, Arthur Lupia, Matthew DeBell, and Darrell Donakowski, "Problems with ANES Questions Measuring Political Knowledge," *ANES Report*, March 2008; Jeffery J. Mondak and Mary R. Anderson, "The Knowledge Gap: A Reexamination of Gender-Based Differences in Political Knowledge," *Journal of Politics* 66 (2004): 492–512; Jeffery J. Mondak and Belinda Creel Davis, "Asked and Answered: Knowledge Levels When We Will Not Take 'Don't Know' for an Answer," *Political Behavior* 23 (2001): 199–224.

69. See Robert Luskin and John Bullock, "'Don't Know' Means 'Don't Know': DK Responses and the Public's Level of Political Knowledge," *American Political Science Review* 73 (2011): 547–57, esp. 555–56.

70. See the discussion in Note 38 above.

71. See Gibson and Caldeira, "Knowing the Supreme Court." For a partial defense of this question, showing that correcting its flaws may only lead to modest increases in estimated knowledge levels, see Luskin and Bullock, "'Don't Know' Means 'Don't Know,'" p. 555.

72. As Luskin and Bullock point out, "the knowledge questions we ask, a distinctly nonrandom sample of the universe of potential knowledge questions, are on the grand scale of things extremely easy. The universe includes many items only policy specialists, if anyone, would know. Thus all survey questionnaires, including ours and the ANES's, involve a severe item sampling bias, toward easy knowledge items." Luskin and Bullock, "'Don't Know' Means 'Don't Know,'" 556.

73. See, e.g., William Galston, "Political Knowledge, Civic Engagement, and Civic Education," *Annual Review of Political Science* 4 (2001): 217–34 for a discussion of the relevant evidence.

74. See, e.g., Stephen Ansolabehere and Eitan Hersh, "Validation: What Big Data Reveal About Survey Misreporting and the Real Electorate," *Political Analysis* 20 (2012):

437–59; Brian D. Silver, Barbara Anderson, and Paul Abramson, "Who Overreports Voting?" *American Political Science Review* 80 (1986): 613–24.

75. Ansolabehere and Hersh," Validation"; Silver, Anderson, and Abramson, "Who Overreports Voting?"

76. For the correlates of political knowledge, see the Appendix, and also the discussion of interest in politics in Chapter 3.

CHAPTER TWO

1. Joseph A. Schumpeter, *Capitalism, Socialism, and Democracy*, 3d ed. (New York: Harper Perennial, 1950), 262.

2. For the most prominent theories of retrospective voting, see V. O. Key, *The Responsible Electorate* (Cambridge: Belknap Press, 1966); and Morris Fiorina, *Retrospective Voting in National Presidential Elections* (New Haven: Yale University Press, 1981).

3. For a well-known analysis of the Burkean trusteeship theory, see Hanna F. Pitkin, *The Concept of Representation* (Berkeley: University of California Press, 1967), 168–89.

4. Much of the political science literature on government responsiveness to majoritarian control adopts this perspective. See, e.g., Robert Erikson, et al., *Statehouse Democracy: Public Opinion and Policy in the American States* (New York: Cambridge University Press, 1993); Lawrence R. Jacobs and Robert Y. Shapiro, *Politicians Don't Pander: Political Manipulation and the Loss of Democratic Responsiveness* (Chicago: University of Chicago Press, 2000); Lawrence R. Jacobs, *The Health of Nations: Public Opinion and the Making of American and British Health Policy* (Ithaca: Cornell University Press, 1993). For my assessment of some of this literature, see Ilya Somin, "Do Politicians Pander?" *Critical Review* 14 (2001) 147–59.

5. This book was written before I could take full account of Jamie Terence Kelly's recent classification of various normative theories of democracy based on their epistemic demands. See Jamie Terence Kelly, *Framing Democracy: A Behavioral Approach to Democratic Theory* (Princeton: Princeton University Press, 2012), ch. 4. Kelly focuses primarily on the extent to which various theories require citizens to be able to avoid "framing effects" in their analysis of information rather than on the factual knowledge the theories require them to know.

6. For more detailed discussion of this point, see Ilya Somin, "Voter Ignorance and the Democratic Ideal," *Critical Review* 12 (1998): 413–58, 415–16; Ilya Somin, "Resolving the Democratic Dilemma?" *Yale Journal on Regulation* 16 (1999): 401–16, 410–11.

7. For a rare exception, see Bryan Caplan, *The Myth of the Rational Voter: Why Democracies Choose Bad Policies* (Princeton, NJ: Princeton University Press, 2007), 172–76.

8. See Chapter 4.

9. See the description of Plato and Aristotle's views in the Introduction.

10. Schumpeter, *Capitalism, Socialism, and Democracy*, 272. Schumpeter himself did not use the term *retrospective voting*, which comes from later political science literature. I have used the modern term for convenience. For an important recent defense of the Schumpeterian theory, see Richard A. Posner, *Law, Pragmatism, and Democracy* (Cambridge: Harvard University Press, 2003); for my critique of Posner's analysis, see Ilya Somin, "Richard Posner's Democratic Pragmatism and the Problem of Ignorance," *Critical Review* 16 (2004): 1–14.

11. William H. Riker, *Liberalism Against Populism: A Confrontation Between the Theory of Democracy and the Theory of Social Choice* (Long Grove, IL: Waveland Press, 1982), 9, 11.

12. Riker, *Liberalism Against Populism*, 11.

13. Fiorina, *Retrospective Voting in National Presidential Elections*, 5. Fiorina himself has since qualified this view; see Somin, "Voter Ignorance and the Democratic Ideal," 447 n. 6.

14. Riker, *Liberalism Against Populism*, 11.

15. Fiorina, *Retrospective Voting in National Presidential Elections*, 10; see also Key, *The Responsible Electorate*, 60–61.

16. For a more detailed analysis of the limitations of retrospective voting as a device for reducing the amount of knowledge required of voters, see Somin, "Voter Ignorance and the Democratic Ideal," 426–27, and the discussion of retrospective voting in Chapter 4.

17. See Table 1.1.

18. See Table 1.4.

19. For all three questions, the original survey instrument allowed the respondent to say that the relevant variable had gotten only "somewhat" larger or smaller since 1992, as opposed to "much larger" or "much smaller." Such responses were coded as correct so long as they trended in the right direction. It could, however, be argued that they should have been coded as incorrect or only partially correct because the declines in crime and the deficit and the increase in spending on the poor were all very large relative to previous levels.

20. See Thomas Holbrook and James Garand, "Homo Economicus? Economic Information and Economic Voting," *Political Research Quarterly* 49 (1996): 351–72, at 361; Larry Bartels, "Uninformed Votes: Information Effects in Presidential Elections," *American Journal of Political Science* 40 (1996): 194–217.

21. See the discussion of this issue in the section on retrospective voting in Chapter 4.

22. Edmund Burke, "An Appeal from the New to the Old Whigs [1791]," in *Burke's Politics*, ed. Ross J. S. Hoffman and Paul Levack (New York: Knopf, 1949), 397–98.

23. Ibid., 398. This brief summary deliberately ignores many internal contradictions and qualifications in Burke's own views because my interest is not in Burke per se, but in the knowledge requirements of the trusteeship theory of representation more generally. For a more nuanced analysis of Burke's theory of trusteeship representation, see Pitkin, *The Concept of Representation*, 127–31, 168–89.

24. Ibid., 183–89.

25. For a good discussion of this disagreement and its impact on the impeachment fight, see Richard A. Posner, *An Affair of State: The Impeachment of Bill Clinton* (Cambridge: Harvard University Press, 1999), 132–59, 199–216.

26. It is also worth pointing out that few modern theorists fully subscribe to the Burkean trusteeship model. As Hannah Pitkin notes, Burke's elitist theory of trusteeship implicitly assumes that the trustees can effectively represent the "true" interests of the people because those interests can be determined in an "objective" and unbiased manner. Pitkin, *The Concept of Representation*, 186–89. Once this assumption is dropped or questioned, Burke's elitist conclusions become more problematic. Nonetheless, I have discussed Burke's model because elements of it—particularly the emphasis on the need for personal virtue in political leaders—persist in modern thought. Some modern scholars endorse Burke's notion that personal character traits are a vital element to be taken account of in the selection of political leaders. See, e.g., James David Barber, *The Presidential Character: Predicting Performance in the White House*, 4th ed. (New York: Prentice-Hall, 1992).

27. See Table 1.1.

28. Ibid.

29. See Table 1.4.

30. Delli Carpini and Keeter, *What Americans Know About Politics*, 94.

31. See Table 1.4. The low profile of Lott is telling in light of the trusteeship theory's emphasis on personal virtue. Even before his eventual resignation as majority leader in December 2002 on charges of racism, Lott had often been criticized, even by some fellow conservatives, for his long-standing ties to the racist Council of Conservative Citizens. See, e.g., Jeff Jacoby, "Renounce the Racists," *Boston Globe*, April 19, 1999, A19.

32. Amy King and Andrew Leigh, "Beautiful Politicians," *Kyklos* 62 (2009): 579–93; Gabriel Lenz and Chapell Lawson, "Looking the Part: Television Leads Less-Informed Citizens to Vote Based on Candidates' Appearance," *American Journal of Political Science* 55 (2011): 574–89; Alexander Todorov, Anesu N. Mandisodza, Amir Goren, and Crystal C. Hall, "Inferences of Competence from Faces Predict Election Outcomes," *Science* 308 (2005): 1623–26.

33. See the discussion of retrospective voting in Chapter 4.

34. For an elaboration of this idea, see Phillip Pettit, "Three Conceptions of Democratic Control," *Constellations* 15 (2008): 46–55, at 52–53.

35. Angus Campbell, et al., *The American Voter* (New York: John Wiley & Sons, 1960), 168–87.

36. See Somin, "Voter Ignorance and the Democratic Ideal," 415–16; Somin, "Resolving the Democratic Dilemma?" 410–11.

37. This example is adapted from Somin, "Resolving the Democratic Dilemma?" 410–11.

38. See discussion of this issue in Chapter 5.

39. For the most thorough summary, see Delli Carpini and Keeter, *What Americans Know About Politics*, 62–104.

40. See Table 1.1.

41. Ibid.

42. See Table 1.2 and related discussion in Chapter 1.

43. See Table 1.3.

44. 545 U.S. 469 (2005).

45. Ilya Somin, "The Limits of Backlash: Assessing the Political Response to *Kelo*," *Minnesota Law Review* 93 (2009): 2100–78.

46. Ibid., 2108–10.

47. See ibid., 2101–2, which summarizes the reform laws enacted by forty-three states. One more state, Mississippi, enacted reform legislation after this article was written. See Ilya Somin, "Referendum Initiatives Prevent Eminent Domain Abuse," *Daily Caller*, November 9, 2011. The state of Virginia, which had earlier adopted reforms through its state legislature, adopted additional reforms by referendum in November 2012.

48. Somin, "Limits of Backlash," 2155–59.

49. Ibid.

50. Ibid., 2120–30.

51. Fifty-seven percent knew that the Democrats favor a higher level of government spending on services than the Republicans, and 51 percent knew that Gore was more supportive of gun control than Bush.

52. See data cited in Chapter 4 in the discussion of the party identification information shortcut.

53. Ibid.

54. See Delli Carpini and Keeter, *What Americans Know About Politics*, 138–52.

55. For various works advocating deliberative democracy or the closely related theory of "republicanism," see, for example, Cass R. Sunstein, *The Partial Constitution* (Cambridge: Harvard University Press, 1993), 25–29; Robert Goodin, *Reflective Democracy* (New York: Oxford University Press, 2005); Frank Michelman, "Law's Republic," *Yale Law Journal* 97 (1988): 1493; Cass R. Sunstein, "Beyond the Republican Revival," *Yale Law Journal* 97 (1988): 1539; Cass R. Sunstein, "Naked Preferences and the Constitution," *Columbia Law Review* 84 (1984): 1689; Ethan R. Lieb, *Deliberative Democracy in America: A Proposal for a Deliberative Branch of Government* (University Park: Pennsylvania State University Press, 2004). For works by political theorists along similar lines, see James Bohman, *Public Deliberation: Pluralism, Complexity, and Democracy* (Boston: MIT Press, 1996); John S. Dryzek, *Deliberative Democracy and Beyond: Liberals, Critics, Contestations* (New York: Oxford University Press, 2002); Amy Gutmann and Dennis Thompson, *Why Deliberative Democracy?* (Princeton, NJ: Princeton University Press, 2004); Amy Gutmann and Dennis Thompson, *Democracy and Disagreement* (Cambridge: Belknap Press, 1996); Seyla Benhabib, "Toward a Deliberative Model of Democratic Legitimacy," in *Democracy and Difference*, ed. Seyla Benhabib (Princeton, NJ: Princeton University Press, 1996); James S. Fishkin, "Deliberative Democracy and Constitutions," *Social Philosophy and Policy* 28 (2011): 242–60. I have previously criticized deliberative democracy advocates for their insufficient response to the challenge of voter ignorance. See Ilya Somin, "Deliberative Democracy and Political Ignorance," *Critical Review* 22 (2010): 253–79; and Somin, "Voter Ignorance and the Democratic Ideal," 438–42. For a criticism of republican theory along different lines, see Richard A. Epstein, "Modern Republicanism—Or the Flight from Substance," *Yale Law Journal* 97 (1988): 1633–48.

56. The phrase is borrowed from Sunstein, "Naked Preferences."

57. Bohman, *Public Deliberation*, 25.

58. See also Somin, "Deliberative Democracy and Political Ignorance," 268–69.

59. For examples of several different criteria advanced in the literature, see Somin, "Voter Ignorance and the Democratic Ideal," 439–40.

60. Gutmann and Thompson, *Democracy and Disagreement*, 57–58. Gutmann and Thompson further elaborate their theories in Gutmann and Thompson, *Why Deliberative Democracy?*, chs. 2–3.

61. Samuel Freeman, "Deliberative Democracy: A Sympathetic Comment," *Philosophy and Public Affairs* 29 (2000): 371–418, 375. Freeman's article summarizes areas of commong ground between many deliberative democrats. Ibid., 375–76. Other deliberative democrats believe that self-interested voting can still play a role in deliberative democracy, if properly constrained. See, e.g., Jane Mansbridge, "The Place of Self-Interest and the Role of Power in Deliberative Democracy," *Journal of Political Philosophy* 18 (2010): 64–100.

62. Freeman, *Deliberative Democracy*, 377.

63. John Rawls, "The Idea of Public Reason Revisited," *University of Chicago Law Review* 64 (1997): 765–84, at 777; see also John Rawls, *Political Liberalism* (New York: Columbia University Press, 1993), 212–47. For similar arguments by Dworkin, see generally Ronald Dworkin, *Life's Dominion* (New York: Vintage Press, 1993), in which he argues that the political debate over abortion and the right to die should exclude arguments derived from religious viewpoints, a category he describes very broadly.

64. Rawls, *Political Liberalism*, 243. The condition is stringent enough that, in Rawls's view, it would rule out comprehensive moral doctrines that, for example, would require banning first trimester abortions.

65. Jürgen Habermas, *Moral Consciousness and Communicative Action*, trans. Christian Lenhardt and Shierry Weber Nicholson (Cambridge: MIT Press, 1990), 75–76, 100.

66. David Estlund, *Democratic Authority: A Philosophical Framework* (Princeton, NJ: Princeton University Press, 2007), 176. Estlund recognizes that "ideal" deliberation that incorporates these conditions is unrealistic and "is not a goal to strive for" (ibid., 182–83). But he also argues that "[r]eal democratic deliberation" must be judged by whether or not "it could, under nonutopian assumptions . . . tend to produce roughly the same conclusions as the ideal epistemic deliberation."

67. See, e.g., Gutmann and Thompson, *Why Deliberative Democracy?* 13–17.

68. Joshua Cohen, "Deliberation and Democratic Legitimacy," in *Deliberative Democracy*, ed. James Bohman and William Rehg (Cambridge: MIT Press, 1997), 274.

69. Fishkin, "Deliberative Democracy and Constitutions," 251–52.

70. This example is taken from Guido Pincione and Fernando Teson, *Rational Choice and Democratic Deliberation: A Theory of Discourse Failure* (New York: Cambridge University Press, 2006), 10–13.

71. Gutmann and Thompson, *Democracy and Disagreement*, 56–65.

72. Habermas, *Moral Consciousness and Communicative Action*, 75–76.

73. For a more detailed discussion of the extent to which political knowledge levels fall short of the requirements of deliberative democracy, see Somin, "Deliberative Democracy and Political Ignorance," 257–62; see also Mark Pennington, "Democracy and the Deliberative Conceit," *Critical Review* 22 (2010): 159–85.

74. This issue is discussed in greater detail in Chapter 3.

75. Gutmann and Thompson, *Why Deliberative Democracy?* 20.

76. Somin, "Deliberative Democracy and Political Ignorance," 262–66.

77. For a critical discussion of some of them, see ibid., 266–72. See also Chapter 7.

78. See, e.g, Dryzek, *Deliberative Democracy and Beyond*, 40–42.

79. I evaluate and criticize proposals of both types in Chapter 7. For a discussion of possible knowledge-increasing policies proposed by deliberative democrats, see Somin, "Deliberative Democracy and Political Ignorance," 266–72.

80. David M. Ryfe. "Does Deliberative Democracy Work?" *Annual Review of Political Science* 8 (2005), 49–71, 63–64.

81. For a description of pure proceduralist defenses of democracy, see Thomas Christiano, "The Authority of Democracy," *Journal of Political Philosophy* 12 (2004): 266–90.

82. For example, some assume that the procedures are just only if they are "properly deliberative." Ibid., at 266–67. See also Fabienne Peter, *Democratic Legitimacy* (New York: Routledge, 2008). As discussed earlier, however, deliberation requires a considerable degree of knowledge.

83. This point is noted in Thomas Christiano, "Knowledge and Power in the Justification of Democracy," *Australasian Journal of Philosophy* 79 (2001): 197–215, at 197.

84. As political philosopher Jamie Terence Kelly points out, "many (if not all) theories of democracy that claim to be *purely* procedural cannot, in the end maintain this claim." Kelly, *Framing Democracy*, 74.

85. See the discussion of such policies in Chapter 5. See also C. Vann Woodward, *The Strange Career of Jim Crow* (New York: Oxford University Press, 1955), 70–76, which notes several examples of prominent early twentieth century white southern political leaders who switched their positions on racial issues in response to public opinion, which favored harsh segregation policies.

86. Dan T. Carter, *The Politics of Rage: George Wallace, the Origins of the New Conservatism, and the Transformation of American Politics* (Baton Rouge: Louisiana State University Press, 1995), 95–96.

87. Ibid., 96.

88. See the discussion of such beliefs in Chapter 5.

89. See Avraham Barkai, *Nazi Economics: Ideology, Theory, and Policy* (London: Berg Publishers, 1990); Adam Tooze, *The Wages of Destruction: The Making and Breaking of the Nazi Economy* (New York: Viking, 2006).

90. Gallup Poll, May 10–13, 2007. For a summary of the scientific evidence showing that homosexuality is caused by genetic factors, see Matt Ridley, *Nature Via Nurture: Genes, Experience, and What Makes Us Human* (New York: HarperCollins, 2003), 159–62.

91. Some 78 percent of those who believe that homosexuality is genetic endorse the view that it is an "acceptable alternative lifestyle" compared to only 30 percent of those who believe that it is caused by upbringing or environment. Gallup Poll, May 10–13, 2007.

92. For one prominent model of this kind, see Sam Peltzman, "The Growth of Government," *Journal of Law and Economics* 23 (1980): 209–88. For a survey of the economic literature on rent-seeking, see Dennis Mueller, *Public Choice III* (Cambridge: Cambridge University Press, 2003), 333–58.

93. For reviews of the relevant literature, see Caplan, *Myth of the Rational Voter*, 148–53, 198, 229, and David Sears and Carolyn Funk, "Self-Interest in Americans' Political Opinions," in *Beyond Self-Interest*, ed. Jane Mansbridge (Chicago: University of Chicago Press, 1990). For some examples, see Leif Lewin, *Self-Interest and Public Interest in Western Democracies* (Oxford: Oxford University Press, 1991); Carolyn Funk, "The Dual Influence of Self-Interest and Societal Interest in Public Opinion," *Political Research Quarterly* 53 (2000): 37–62; and Thomaas Holbrook and James Garand, "Homo Economicus? Economic Information and Economic Voting," *Political Research Quarterly* 49 (1996): 351–75.

94. See Holbrook and Garand, "Homo Economicus." For a list of studies reaching this conclusion, see Caplan, *Myth of the Rational Voter*, 229. Caplan notes that voters who cast their ballots on the basis of societal economic welfare might have their own narrow self-interest in mind, hoping to benefit from general prosperity (ibid.).

95. See Dennis Mueller, *Constitutional Democracy* (New York: Oxford University Press, 1996), 237–47.

96. See James W. Ely Jr., *The Guardian of Every Other Right: A Constitutional History of Property Rights*, 3d. ed. (New York: Oxford University Press, 2008), 42–57.

97. Mueller, *Public Choice III*, 104–6.

98. Caplan, *Myth of the Rational Voter*, 50–51, 69–71.

99. John Palmer, "Obama and McCain Offer Voters a Choice on Trade," Reuters, June 2, 2008.

100. Susan Ferrechio, "Obama Backs Away from Reforming Free Trade Deal," *Washington Examiner*, May 17, 2009.

101. Jonathan Weisman, "Obama, in Canada, Warns Against Protectionism," *Wall Street Journal*, February 20, 2009.

102. A September 2010 NBC/*Wall Street Journal* poll found that 53 percent of Americans believe that "free trade agreements" have, in general, "hurt the United States," compared to only 17 percent who say they have "helped the United States." "NBC/*Wall Street Journal* Survey," Study #101061, September 22–26, 2010, http://online.wsj.com/public/resources/documents/WSJNBCPoll09282010.pdf.

CHAPTER THREE

1. Tony Blair, *A Journey: My Political Life* (New York: Knopf, 2010), 70–71.

2. See, e.g., Richard Shenkman, *Just How Stupid Are We? Facing the Truth About the American Voter* (New York: Basic Books, 2008).

3. Average American IQ rose fifteen points during the last half of the twentieth century. Michael R. Flynn, *Are We Getting Smarter? Rising IQ in the Twenty-First Century* (New York: Cambridge University Press, 2012), pg. 6.

4. Blair, *A Journey*, 70.

5. Barack Obama, *The Audacity of Hope* (New York: Crown, 2006), pg. 4.

6. William H. Riker and Peter Ordeshook, "A Theory of the Calculus of Voting," *American Political Science Review* 62 (1968): 25–42; Andrew Gelman, Nate Silver, and Aaron Edlin, "What Is the Probability That Your Vote Will Make a Difference? *Economic Inquiry* 50 (2012): 321–26. The economist Anthony Downs formulated the theory of rational ignorance back in the 1950s. See Anthony Downs, *An Economic Theory of Democracy* (New York: Harper & Row, 1957), ch. 13.

7. Andrew Gelman, et al., "What Is the Probability that Your Vote Will Make a Difference?", 322–24.

8. Mancur Olson, *The Logic of Collective Action* (Cambridge, MA: Harvard University Press, 1965); Russell Hardin, *Collective Action* (Chicago: University of Chicago Press, 1982).

9. For an argument that an unselfish person committed to the "public good" would acquire greater knowledge about politics than people who are rationally ignorant about information relevant to the pursuit of "individual goods," see Gerry Mackie, "Rational Ignorance and Beyond," in *Collective Wisdom: Principles and Mechanisms*, ed. Hélène Landemore and Jon Elster (Cambridge: Cambridge University Press, 2012). Mackie ignores the reasons why even an altruistic person would rationally devote little time to acquiring political information, discussed further on.

10. See, e.g., Brian Barry, *Economists, Sociologists, and Democracy*, 2nd ed. (Chicago: University of Chicago Press, 1978).

11. For studies showing little or no increase in political knowledge over time, see works cited in Chapter 1.

12. Riker and Ordeshook, "Calculus of Voting."

13. See, e.g., Jeffrey Friedman, "Popper, Weber, and Hayek: The Epistemology and Politics of Ignorance." *Critical Review* 17 (2005): i–lviii.

14. Russell Hardin, *How Do You Know? The Economics of Ordinary Knowledge* (Princeton, NJ: Princeton University Press, 2009), 74 (emphasis in the original); see also Hardin, "Ignorant Democracy," *Critical Review* 18 (2006): 179–95, 186–87.

15. Derek Parfit, *Reasons and Persons* (Oxford: Clarendon Press, 1984), 73–75; Aaron Edlin, Andrew Gelman, and Noah Kaplan, "Voting as a Rational Choice: Why and How People Vote to Improve the Well-Being of Others," *Rationality and Society*, 19 (2007): 293–314. This assumption of modest altruism is plausible. Empirical evidence suggests that most Americans are at least mildly altruistic. Americans spend some 3 percent of their household income on charity. See Arthur Brooks, *Who Really Cares? America's Charity Divide* (New York: Basic Books, 2006), 3; Richard B. McKenzie, "Was It a Decade of Greed?" *Public Interest* 27 (1992): 91–96. This is very likely a far greater sum than—judging by survey evidence of the results—individual voters spend on acquiring political information.

16. This equation is modified from Parfit, *Reasons and Persons*, 74.

17. This equation may overstate the degree of altruism most people have in so far as it implies that they may be willing to make truly enormous sacrifices when it is possible to generate very large benefits for others. Changing the equation to assume that people's willingness to sacrifice for others is nonlinear when the magnitude of the sacrifice becomes a large fraction of their total wealth would not alter the conclusions we focus on here.

18. Assuming the slightly better odds of 1 in 60 million that was estimated as the average in the recent study by Gelman and colleagues would make the likelihood of voting even greater, but without significantly increasing the incentive to acquire information.

19. See Blake Aued, "Two Elections Decided by One Vote," *Athens Banner-Herald*, November 6, 2009, http://www.onlineathens.com/stories/110609/new_513141849.shtml.

20. John Aldrich, "Rational Choice and Turnout," *American Journal of Political Science* 37 (1993): 246–78.

21. See Terry M. Moe, *The Organization of Interests* (Chicago: University of Chicago Press, 1980), 70–72.

22. For these two findings, see Edlin, et al., "Voting as a Rational Choice." See also Aldrich, "Rational Choice and Turnout."

23. Poll taxes of just $1–2 per year reduced turnout in late-nineteenth-century Georgia by approximately 16 to 28 percent. J. Morgan Kousser, *The Shaping of Southern Politics: Suffrage Restriction and the Establishment of the One-Party South, 1880–1910* (New Haven: Yale University Press, 1974), 67–68. See also studies cited in Bryan Caplan, *The Myth of the Rational Voter: Why Democracies Choose Bad Policies* (Princeton, NJ: Princeton University Press, 2007), 132.

24. Donald R. Kinder and Cindy Kam, *Us Against Them: Ethnocentric Foundations of American Opinion* (Chicago: University of Chicago Press, 2009).

25. See, e.g., Jason Brennan, *The Ethics of Voting* (Princeton, NJ: Princeton University Press, 2011), 23–24; Geoffrey Brennan and Loren Lomasky, *Democracy and Decision* (New York: Cambridge University Press, 1993), ch. 4.

26. See Gelman et al., "What Is the Probability that Your Vote Will Make a Difference?"

27. The potential benefits might be saving the time and effort of voting (if the relatively low-probability model turns out to be correct) or the expected utility of voting under Equation 3.1 or 3.2 (if Gelman is right).

28. See the second part of this chapter.

29. Caplan, *Myth of the Rational Voter*, 103–4.

30. For a similar argument, see Guido Pincione and Fernando Teson, *Rational Choice and Democratic Deliberation* (New York: Cambridge University Press, 2006), ch. 3.

31. For this theory, see Mackie, "Rational Ignorance and Beyond." Mackie contends that this argument undercuts the standard rational choice account of voting and the theory of rational ignorance that follows from it. His argument does not, however, consider the points I develop here.

32. See in general Lawrence J. Grossback, David A. M. Peterson, and James Stimson, *Mandate Politics* (Cambridge: Cambridge University Press, 2006).

33. While a single vote can make the difference between winning and losing when all the other votes are equally divided, it is not entirely clear whether a single vote can *ever* make the difference between a "big" mandate and a "normal" one. A one-vote difference in the winner's margin of victory will virtually always be imperceptible to public opinion, which will not even notice the difference. By contrast, an election decided by one vote is a genuine, even if highly unlikely, possibility.

34. For a more thorough discussion of the paradox of voting and its relationship to rational choice, see Aldrich, "Rational Choice and Turnout." Aldrich's argument that voter turnout is a poor test of collective action theory because the expected costs and benefits on each side are so small is a useful complement to the arguments I develop in the text.

35. Terry Moe, *The Organization of Interests*, 31–32; Hardin, *How Do You Know?* 74. For the explanation to be useful, it is not necessary that *all* voting be explained by it, merely a substantial part.

36. Ruy Teixeira, *The Disappearing American Voter* (Washington, DC: Brookings Institution, 1992), 56.

37. Irrational, I remind the reader, only in the sense that the individual voter's fulfillment of his duty does not in fact succeed in helping his countrymen. For a defense of the view that voting is motivated by "expressive utility," see Geoffrey Brennan and Loren Lomasky, *Democracy and Decision* (New York: Cambridge University Press, 1993). See also Alan Hamlin and Colin Jennings, "Expressive Political Behavior: Foundations, Scope, and Implications," *British Journal of Political Science* 41 (2011): 1–26.

38. Stefano DellaVigna, John List, and Ulrike Malmendier, "Voting to Tell Others," unpublished paper, February 27, 2013, http://elsa.berkeley.edu/~sdellavi/wp/turnout13-03-04.pdf.

39. Brennan and Lomasky, *Democracy and Decision*, 32–51.

40. For data supporting it, see David E. Campbell, *Why We Vote?* (Princeton, NJ: Princeton University Press, 2006).

41. DellaVigna, et al., "Voting to Tell Others."

42. Jeffrey Friedman, "Ignorance as a Starting Point: From Modest Epistemology to Realistic Political Theory," *Critical Review* 19 (2007): 1–22, esp. 11–13; Jeffrey Friedman and Stephen E. Bennett, "The Irrelevance of Economic Theory to Understanding Economic Ignorance," *Critical Review* 20 (2008): 195–258, esp. 206.

43. See discussion in Chapter 1.

44. Jon D. Miller "Public Understanding of, and Attitudes Toward, Scientific Research: What We Know and What We Need to Know." *Public Understanding of Science* 13 (2004): 273–94; Rafael Pardo and Felix Calvo, "The Cognitive Dimension of Public Perceptions of Science: Methodological Issues," *Public Understanding of Science* 13 (2004): 203–27.

45. Gallup poll, February 6–7, 2009. A 2006 survey found that 46 percent of Americans believe that humans did not evolve but were created by God "pretty much in their present form at one time within the last 10,000 years or so." Gallup poll, May 8–11, 2006. Some 36 percent of respondents endorsed the view that "Human beings have developed over millions of years from less advanced forms of life, but God guided this process" (ibid.).

46. National Geographic Foundation, *Final Report: National Geographic-Roper Public Affairs 2006 Geographic Literacy Study*, 2006, http://www.nationalgeographic.com/roper2006/pdf/FINALReport2006GeogLitsurvey.pdf.

47. See, e.g., Robert Lichter and Stanley Rothman, *Environmental Cancer—A Political Disease?* (New Haven: Yale University Press, 1999); Nancy Kraus, Torbjorn Malmfors, and Paul Slovic, "Intuitive Toxicology: Expert and Lay Judgments of Chemical Risks," *Risk Analysis* 12 (1992): 215–32.

48. CNN/*Time* survey, June 1997.

49. See, e.g., Friedman, "Popper, Weber, and Hayek."

50. See Delli Carpini and Keeter, *What Americans Know About Politics*, 184; Robert C. Luskin, "Explaining Political Sophistication," *Political Behavior* 12 (1990): 331–53, at 344.

51. See Tyler Cowen, "Self-Deception as the Root of Political Failure," *Public Choice* 124 (2005): 437–51. For a related comparison of political and religious commitments and sports fans, see Jonathan Haidt, *The Righteous Mind: Why Good People Are Divided by Politics and Religion* (New York: Pantheon, 2012), 246–49.

52. The authors of one recent history of the Red Sox and Yankees note that they chose not to write "a fair and balanced look at the Red Sox-Yankees 'rivalry,'" because "neither author of this book wanted to represent the Yankees [sic] point of view. . . . Neither of us could bring ourselves to say enough complimentary things about [the Yankees] to fill the back of a matchbox, let alone half a book." Bill Nowlin and Jim Prime, *Blood Feud: The Red Sox, the Yankees and the Struggle of Good vs. Evil* (Cambridge, MA: Rounder Books, 2004), 4.

53. See, e.g, Charles Lord, Lee Ross, and Mark R. Lepper, "Biased Assimilation and Attitude Polarization: The Effects of Prior Theories on Subsequently Considered Evidence," *Journal of Personality and Social Psychology* 37 (1979): 2098–2109; Charles S. Taber and Milton R. Lodge, "Motivated Skepticism in the Evaluation of Political Beliefs," *American Journal of Political Science* 50 (2006): 755–69.

54. See, e.g., Brendan Nyhan and Jason Reifler, "When Corrections Fail: The Persistence of Political Misperceptions," unpublished paper, April 22, 2009; John Bullock, "The Enduring Importance of False Political Beliefs," paper presented at the annual meeting of the Western Political Science Association, March 17, 2006.

55. Nyhan and Reifler, "When Corrections Fail," 311–15.

56. Ibid., 323–24.

57. See, e.g, Taber and Lodge, "Motivated Skepticism,"; Shenkman, *Just How Stupid Are We?* ch. 3.

58. Caplan, *Myth of the Rational Voter*, ch. 5; Bryan Caplan, "Rational Ignorance vs. Rational Irrationality," *Kyklos* 53 (2001): 3–21. For a less-developed similar argument, see George A. Akerlof, "The Economics of Illusion," *Economics and Politics* 1 (1989): 1–15.

59. Caplan, "Rational Ignorance vs. Rational Irrationality," 5.

60. Akerlof, "Economics of Illusion," 1.

61. Taber and Lodge, "Motivated Skepticism."

62. Diana Mutz, *Hearing the Other Side: Deliberative Versus Participatory Democracy* (New York: Cambridge University Press, 2006), 29–41; Alan S. Gerber, et al., "Disagreement and the Avoidance of Political Discussion: Aggregate Relationships and Differences across Personality Traits," *American Journal of Political Science* 56 (2012): 849–74.

63. Mutz, *Hearing the Other Side*, 32.

64. See Shanto Iyengar and Kyu S. Hahn, "Red Media, Blue Media: Evidence of Ideological Selectivity in Media Use," *Journal of Communication* 59 (2009): 19–39.

65. See Markus Prior, "Media and Political Polarization," *Annual Review of Political Science*, forthcoming.

66. Haidt, *The Righteous Mind*, 75–76.

67. Ibid.

68. John Stuart Mill, *On Liberty*, ed. David Spitz (New York: Norton, 1975), 36.

69. Jeffrey Friedman and Stephen E. Bennett, "The Irrelevance of Economic Theory to Understanding Economic Ignorance," *Critical Review* 20 (2008): 195–258, 206.

70. Ibid., 206–7.

71. For a similar reply to this criticism, see Bryan Caplan, "Reply to My Critics," *Critical Review* 20 (2008): 377–413, 380–82. Caplan also points out that rational irrationality can exist even in the absence of a fully conscious decision to be irrational, noting that people can choose to ignore or not seek out information that might disconfirm their beliefs without a carefully calculated plan to do so (ibid.).

72. The table in the Appendix illustrates this point by presenting the results of a regression analysis of the determinants of political knowledge in the American National Election Studies (ANES) 2000 study, the same survey data already utilized extensively in Chapter 1.

73. Consistent with other studies, the ANES 2000 study evidence also shows that women have lower levels of political knowledge than men and blacks lower levels than whites. See, e.g., Nancy Burns, et al., *The Private Roots of Public Action: Gender, Equality, and Political Participation* (Cambridge: Harvard University Press, 2001); Delli Carpini and Keeter, *What Americans Know About Politics*, 184–85, 203–9; Sidney Verba, et al., "Knowing and Caring About Politics: Gender and Political Engagement," *Journal of Politics* 59 (1997): 1051, 1054–57; also Michael X. Delli Carpini and Scott Keeter, "Gender and Political Knowledge," in *Gender and American Politics: Women, Men, and the Political Process*, ed. Jyl J. Josephson and Sue Tolleson-Rinehart (Armonk, NY: M.E. Sharp, 2000), 21, 24–30; Ilya Somin, "Political Ignorance and the Countermajoritarian Difficulty," *Iowa Law Review* 89 (2004): 1287, 1354–63.

74. The interest-in-politics variable is a nine-point scale that combines the respondents' self-reported interest in the 2000 campaign, their self-reported interest in campaigns more generally, and the ANES interviewers' assessment of the respondents' level of interest in the

interview. In this way, I am able to include both self-assessment and external assessment of the respondents' interest.

75. The data are derived from the regression analysis presented in the Appendix.

76. Previous studies have also emphasized the importance of political interest. See, e.g., Delli Carpini and Keeter, *What Americans Know About Politics*, 184; Robert C. Luskin, "Explaining Political Sophistication," *Political Behavior* 12 (1990): 331, 344, which emphasized that interest has "a huge effect" on political knowledge.

77. See Norman H. Nie, et al., *Education and Democratic Citizenship in America* (Chicago: University of Chicago Press), 11–66. For a more optimistic view of the potential of education to increase political knowledge, see William Galston, "Political Knowledge, Political Engagement, and Civic Education," *Annual Review of Political Science* 4 (2001): 217. See also the discussion in Chapter 7.

78. Figure calculated from the 2000 ANES data displayed in the Appendix.

79. Neil Malhotra and Yotam Margalit, "State of the Nation: Anti-Semitism and the Economic Crisis," *Boston Review*, May-June 2009, http://bostonreview.net/BR34.3/malhotra_margalit.php.

80. Ibid.

81. The Harris Poll, "'Wingnuts' and President Obama," March 24, 2010, http://www.harrisinteractive.com/vault/Harris-Interactive-Poll-Research-Politics-Wingnuts-2010-03.pdf.

82. Rassmussen poll, April 30–May 1, 2007.83. Ibid.

84. Each of these examples is noted in Cass R. Sunstein and Adrian Vermeule, "Conspiracy Theories," University of Chicago Law School Law & Economics Research Paper No. 387 (2008).

85. Malhotra and Margalit, "Anti-Semitism and the Financial Crisis"; Rassmussen poll, April 30–May 1, 2007; The Harris Poll, "'Wingnuts' and President Obama."

86. A possible alternative scenario is that Jews deserve "blame" for the crisis because Jewish financiers or government officials caused it inadvertently, rather than deliberately. However, there is no evidence to suggest that Jewish officials and financiers behaved differently from gentile ones in this respect.

87. For a well-known statement of the view that public opinion in modern democracies is controlled by political elites, see Benjamin Ginsberg, *The Captive Public* (New York: Basic Books, 1986).

88. Stuart Taylor, "Campaign Lies, Media Double Standards," *National Journal*, September 20, 2008.

89. Ibid.

90. Sandler Training poll, May 2010.

91. For a similar argument, see Caplan, *Myth of the Rational Voter*, 176–77.

92. See the discussion earlier in this chapter.

CHAPTER FOUR

1. Walter Lippman, *Public Opinion* (New York: Free Press, 1997 [1922]), 174.

2. The tide has at least partially turned over the past fifteen years, however. As a 2001 literature review pointed out, there are "signs of an emerging consensus" that "there is a level of basic knowledge below which the ability to make a full range of reasoned civic judgments is impaired." William A. Galston, "Political Knowledge, Political Engagement, and Civic Education," *Annual Review of Political Science* 4 (2001): 217–34, at 221.

3. Technically, the miracle of aggregation may not be an information shortcut because it is not a tool by which voters can increase their understanding of political issues but rather an argument suggesting that they do not need to, so long as their errors are randomly distributed. I include it in this chapter anyway because it is an argument holding that voters can make informed decisions with little or no knowledge.

4. See, e.g., Richard Lau and David Redlawsk, "Advantages and Disadvantages of Cognitive Heuristics in Political Decision Making," *American Journal of Political Science* 45 (2001): 951–75, which finds that cognitive shortcuts improve decision-making by already well-informed experts but lead to worse decisions by poorly informed "novices."

5. Arthur Lupia, "How Elitism Undermines the Study of Voter Competence," *Critical Review* 18 (2006): 217–33.

6. See, e.g., Samuel Popkin, *The Reasoning Voter* (Chicago: University of Chicago Press, 1991); Donald Wittman, *The Myth of Democratic Failure* (Chicago: University of Chicago Press, 1995), ch. 1.

7. This idea dates back to Anthony Downs, *An Economic Theory of Democracy* (New York: Harper & Row, 1957), 243–44.

8. Popkin, *Reasoning Voter*, 23–24; see also Gerry Mackie, "Rational Ignorance and Beyond," in *Collective Wisdom: Principles and Mechanisms*, ed. Hélène Landemore and Jon Elster (Cambridge: Cambridge University Press, 2012), 290–91.

9. Popkin, *Reasoning Voter*, 23.

10. Thomas Holbrook and James Garand, "Homo Economicus? Economic Information and Economic Voting," *Political Research Quarterly* 49 (1996), 361.

11. Ibid., 360.

12. Ibid.

13. Diana Mutz, "Direct and Indirect Routes to Politicizing Personal Experience: Does Knowledge Make a Difference?" *Public Opinion Quarterly* 57 (1993), 483–502.

14. See Martin Gilovich, *How We Know What Isn't So: The Fallibility of Human Reason in Everyday Life* (New York: Simon & Schuster, 1991), 78–79.

15. Bryan Caplan, *The Myth of the Rational Voter: Why Democracies Choose Bad Policies* (Princeton, NJ: Princeton University Press, 2007), 36–39.

16. Ilya Somin, "Voter Ignorance and the Democratic Ideal," *Critical Review* 12 (1998): 413–58, at 421.

17. Downs, *Economic Theory of Democracy*, chs. 7–8; John H. Aldrich, *Why Parties?* (Chicago: University of Chicago Press, 1995), 47–49.

18. See., e.g., Aldrich, *Why Parties?*, 170–74.

19. D. Sunshine Hillygus and Todd Shields, *The Persuadable Voter: Wedge Issues in Presidential Campaigns* (Princeton, NJ: Princeton University Press, 2008), 31; see also Richard R. Lau and David P. Redlawsk, *How Voters Decide* (New York: Cambridge University Press, 2006), 76–82.

20. See Table 1.4.

21. On this point, see also the discussion of retrospective voting later in this chapter.

22. For example, an American voter who has been a mature adult for twenty years as of 2012 will have experienced two Democratic and two Republican presidential administrations since achieving political awareness. This counts the first two years of the Obama administration as a full case.

23. See David Schleicher, "Why Is There No Partisan Competition in City Council Elections? The Role of Election Law," *Journal of Law and Politics* 23 (2007): 419–73.

Schleicher effectively rebuts claims that partisan competition in local government is irrelevant because local governments are completely constrained by capital mobility and other factors (ibid., 420–25).

24. Schleicher, "Why Is There No Partisan Competition in City Council Elections?"

25. Lau and Redlawsk, *How Voters Decide*, 86–87.

26. See Somin, "Voter Ignorance and the Democratic Ideal."

27. Lau and Redlawsk, *How Voters Decide*, 202–3.

28. See Kathleen Bawn, et al., "A Theory of Political Parties: Groups, Policy Demands and Nominations in American Politics," unpublished paper, UCLA, September 5, 2011, http://masket.net/Theory_of_Parties.pdf, 1–2, 12–14.

29. See, e.g., Larry M. Bartels, "Beyond the Running Tally: Partisan Bias in Political Perceptions," *Political Behavior* 24 (2002): 117–150.

30. See, e.g., John Bullock, Alan Gerber, and Gregory Huber, "Partisan Bias in Responses to Factual Questions," paper presented at the Western Political Science Association, March 2010.

31. Ibid.

32. See the discussion of the miracle of aggregation later in this chapter.

33. Such elections are common at the local level. See David Schleicher, "Why Is There No Partisan Competition in City Council Elections?"

34. See Susan Herbst, *Numbered Voices: How Opinion Polling Has Shaped American Politics* (Chicago: University of Chicago Press, 1995).

35. See, e.g., James L. Stimson, *Tides of Consent: How Public Opinion Shapes American Politics* (New York: Cambridge University Press, 2006); Robert Erikson, et al., *Statehouse Democracy: Public Opinion and Policy in the American States* (New York: Cambridge University Press, 1993); Lawrence R. Jacobs, *The Health of Nations: Public Opinion and the Making of American and British Health Policy* (Ithaca: Cornell University Press, 1993); Benjamin Page and Robert Shapiro, *The Rational Public* (Chicago: University of Chicago Press, 1992).

36. For the most thorough study, see Scott L. Althaus, *Collective Preferences in Democratic Politics* (New York: Cambridge University Press, 2003).

37. Ibid.

38. See the discussion of retrospective voting in this chapter. See also Samuel DeCanio, "State Autonomy and American Political Development: How Mass Democracy Promoted State Power," *Studies in American Political Development* 19 (2005): 117–136; Samuel DeCanio, "Beyond Marxist State Theory: State Autonomy in Democratic Societies," *Critical Review* 14 (2000): 215–36.

39. For representative citations to the extensive literature defending this theory, see Somin, "Voter Ignorance and the Democratic Ideal," 424.

40. W. Russell Neuman, quoted in Popkin, *Reasoning Voter*, 47. For the most extensive defense of the opinion leader shortcut, see Arthur Lupia and Matthew McCubbins, *The Democratic Dilemma: Can Citizens Learn What they Need to Know?* (New York: Cambridge University Press, 1998); I criticized their analysis in my review of their book. See Ilya Somin, "Resolving the Democratic Dilemma?" *Yale Journal on Regulation* 16 (1999): 401–16.

41. Danny Oppenheimer and Mike Edwards, *Democracy Despite Itself: Why a System That Shouldn't Work at All Works So Well* (Cambridge: MIT Press, 2012), 183–84.

42. See the extensive analysis in Sidney Verba, et al., *Voice and Equality* (Cambridge: Harvard University Press, 1995).

43. See works cited in Somin, "Voter Ignorance and the Democratic Idea," 425; the classic analysis is Philip Converse, "The Nature of Belief Systems in Mass Publics," in *Ideology and Discontent*, ed. David Apter (New York: Free Press, 1964).

44. I have analyzed the shortcomings of opinion leaders in greater detail in Somin, "Resolving the Democratic Dilemma?" 404–11.

45. See, e.g., Arthur Lupia and Matthew McCubbins, *The Democratic Dilemma: Can Citizens Learn What They Need to Know?* (New York: Cambridge University Press, 1998), ch. 9.

46. Ibid.

47. See Somin, "Resolving the Democratic Dilemma?" 411.

48. See, e.g., Jonathan Woon, "Democratic Accountability and Retrospective Voting: A Laboratory Experiment," *American Journal of Political Science* 56 (2012): 913–30.49. See, e.g., R. Douglas Arnold, *The Logic of Congressional Action* (New Haven: Yale University Press, 1990), 28–34, 272–73. The critique of retrospective voting developed in this chapter applies just as readily to cases in which politicians try to anticipate retrospective voting as to ones in which they do not. In both scenarios, the effectiveness of retrospective voting might be affected by various kinds of ignorance. If political leaders know about the existence of ignorance, they can even build it into their calculations.

50. Morris Fiorina, *Retrospective Voting in American Presidential Elections* (New Haven: Yale University Press, 1981), 10; see also V. O. Key, *The Responsible Electorate* (Cambridge Harvard University Press, 1966), 60–61.

51. I considered the normative theory in Chapter 2.

52. See discussion of this and other such cases in the Introduction and in Chapter 1.

53. See Suzanne Mettler, *The Submerged State: How Invisible Government Policies Undermine American Democracy* (Chicago: University of Chicago Press, 2011), ch. 1.

54. See, e.g., D. Roderick Kiewet, *Macroeconomics and Micropolitics* (Chicago: University of Chicago Press, 1983).

55. Andrew Leigh, "Does the World Economy Swing National Elections?" *Oxford Bulletin of Economics and Statistics* 71 (2009): 163–81.

56. Justin Wolfers, "Are Voters Rational? Evidence from Gubernatorial Elections," working paper, University of Pennsylvania (2011).

57. Ibid.

58. Christopher H. Achen and Larry Bartels, "Blind Retrospection Electoral Responses to Drought, Flu, and Shark Attacks," UCLA International Institute, revised January 24, 2004, http://www.international.ucla.edu/media/files/PERG.Achen.pdf; Andrew Healy, Neil Malhotra, and Cecilia Hyunjung Mo, "Irrelevant Events Affect Voters' Evaluations of Government Performance," *Proceedings of the National Academy of Sciences* 107 (2010): 12804–9; Andrew Healy and Neil Malhotra, "Random Events, Economic Losses, and Retrospective Voting: Implications for Democratic Competence," *Quarterly Journal of Political Science* 5 (2010): 193–208.

59. Healy, Malhotra, and Hyunjung Mo, "Irrelevant Events Affect Voters' Evaluations of Government Performance."

60. Michael K. Miller, "For the Win! The Effect of Professional Sports Records on Mayoral Elections," *Social Science Quarterly* 94 (2013): 59–78.

61. Christopher H. Achen and Larry Bartels, "Musical Chairs: Pocketbook Voting and the Limits of Democratic Accountability," Princeton University, September 2004, http://www.princeton.edu/~bartels/chairs.pdf; Larry M. Bartels, *Unequal Democracy: The Political Economy of a New Gilded Age* (Princeton, NJ: Princeton University Press, 2010), 99–104; Christopher Achen and Larry Bartels, "Myopic Retrospection and Party Realignment in the Great Depression," working paper, Princeton University (2008).

62. Gregory Huber, Seth Hill, and Gabriel Lenz, "Sources of Bias in Retrospective Decision Making: Experimental Evidence on Voters' Limitation in Controlling Incumbents," *American Political Science Review* 106 (2012): 720–41.

63. Frederic Bastiat, *That Which Is Seen, That Which Is Not Seen: The Unintended Consequences of Government Spending* (West Valley, UT: Editorium, 2006 [1849]), 1–2.

64. See Table 1.1.

65. See Chapter 1 for citations to the evidence that voters are ignorant of government structure.

66. Fiorina, *Retrospective Voting*, 11.

67. Bryan Caplan, Eric Crampton, Wayne Grove, and Ilya Somin, "Systematically Biased Beliefs About Political Influence," *PS: Political Science and Politics*, forthcoming, available at http://ssrn.com/abstract=2241024. These differences between the public and political scientists remain after controlling for such variables as ideology, education, income, gender, race, and others. It is therefore likely to be the product of the superior knowledge of the experts.

68. Ibid.

69. For a somewhat different knowledge-based critique of economic retrospective voting, see Jose Antonio Cheibub and Adam Przeworski, "Democracy, Elections, and Accountability for Economic Outcomes," in *Democracy, Accountability, and Representation* ed. Adam Przeworski, Susan Stokes, and Bernard Manin (Cambridge: Cambridge University Press, 1999), 222–50.

70. Achen and Bartels, "Blind Retrospection," 36.

71. Ibid., 4.

72. Amartya Sen, *Development as Freedom* (Norwell, MA: Anchor Press, 1999), 178.

73. Joseph Stalin's communist government deliberately engineered a famine that killed millions in the early 1930s U.S.S.R. See Robert Conquest, *The Harvest of Sorrow* (New York: Oxford University Press, 1986). An even larger government-created famine occurred in Maoist China, taking an estimated thirty million lives. See Jasper Becker, *Hungry Ghosts: Mao's Secret Famine* (New York: Holt, 1996).

74. Rudolph Rummel, *Power Kills: Democracy as a Method of Nonviolence* (New Brunswick: Transaction, 1997); Rudolph Rummel, *Death by Government* (New Brunswick: Transaction, 1994).

75. Alastair Smith and Alejandro Quiroz Flores, "Disaster Politics: Why Earthquakes Rock Democracies Less," *Foreign Affairs*, July 15, 2010, http://www.foreignaffairs.com/articles/66494/alastair-smith-and-alejandro-quiroz-flores/disaster-politics.

76. Andrew Healy and Neil Malhotra, "Myopic Voters and Natural Disaster Policy," *American Political Science Review* 103 (2009): 387–406.

77. For a recent comparison of the American and New Zealand political traditions, see David Hackett Fisher, *Fairness and Freedom: A History of Two Open Societies: New Zealand and the United States* (New York: Oxford University Press, 2012).

78. As discussed in Chapter 5, federalism may in some ways also mitigate the problem of political ignorance.

79. See Larry Bartels, "Beyond the Running Tally"; Thomas Rudolph, "Triangulating Political Responsibility: The Motivated Formation of Responsibility Judgments," *Political Psychology* 27 (2006): 99–122; Michael Marsh and James Tilley, "The Attribution of Credit and Blame to Governments and Its Impact on Vote Choice," *British Journal of Political Science* 40 (2009) 115–34; Chistopher H. Achen and Larry M. Bartels, "It Feels Like We're Thinking: The Rationalizing Voter and Electoral Democracy," working paper (2006), http://www.princeton.edu/~bartels/papers; and Donald Green, Bradley Palmquist, and Eric Shickler, *Partisan Hearts and Minds: Political Parties and the Social Identities of Voters* (New Haven: Yale University Press, 2002), vii–viii, 85–139.

80. See the works cited above.

81. Bartels, "Beyond the Running Tally, 133–38.

82. See the discussion of "the miracle of aggregation" later in this chapter.

83. Converse, "The Nature of Belief Systems in Mass Publics."

84. Shanto Iyengar, ""Shortcuts to Political Knowledge: The Role of Selective Attention and Accessibility," in *Information and Democratic Processes*, ed. John Ferejohn and James Kuklinski (Urbana: University of Illinois Press, 1990).

85. Michael X. Delli Carpini and Scott Keeter, *What Americans Know About Politics and Why It Matters* (New Haven: Yale University Press, 1996), 138–52.

86. See, e.g., Vincent L. Hutchings, *Public Opinion and Democratic Accountability: How Citizens Learn About Politics* (Princeton, NJ: Princeton University Press, 2003).

87. Ibid., ch. 4.

88. Iyengar, "Shortcuts to Political Knowledge."

89. Somin, "Voter Ignorance and the Democratic Ideal," 429.

90. Mancur Olson, *The Logic of Collective Action* (Cambridge, MA: Harvard University Press, 1965), 165.

91. See, e.g., Matthew A. Baum, "Soft News and Political Knowledge: Evidence of Absence or Absence of Evidence," *Political Communication* 20 (2003): 173–90; Kathleen McGraw, Milton Lodge, and Patrick Stroh, "On-line Processing in Candidate Evaluation: The Effects of Issue Order, Issue Importance, and Sophistication," *Political Behavior* 12 (1990): 41–58; Milton Lodge, Kathleen McGraw, and Patrick Stroh, "An Impression-Driven Model of Candidate Evaluation," *American Political Science Review* 83 (1989): 399–419.

92. See works cited in the previous note.

93. See the discussion earlier in this chapter.

94. See the discussion in the section on retrospective voting earlier in this chapter.

95. See Daniel Kahneman, *Thinking Fast and Slow* (New York: Farrar, Straus & Giroux, 2011), 31–38.

96. Ibid., 41–48. See also the discussion of irrationality in Chapter 3.

97. See the discussion in Chapter 3.

98. See, e.g., Gabriel Lenz and Chapell Lawson, "Looking the Part: Television Leads Less-Informed Citizens to Vote Based on Candidates' Appearance," *American Journal of Political Science* 55 (2011): 574–89.

99. The phrase is taken from Philip Converse, "Popular Representation and the Distribution of Information," in *Information and Democratic Processes*, ed. John Ferejohn and James Kuklinski (Urbana: University of Illinois Press, 1990), 383.

100. For arguments in favor of the aggregation theory, see, e.g., Oppenheimer and Edwards, *Democracy Despite Itself,* 185–87; Wittman, *Myth of Democratic Failure;* Converse, "Popular Representation"; Page and Shapiro, *Rational Public;* James Stimson, "A Macro Theory of Information Flow," in *Information and Democratic Processes,* ed. John Ferejohn and James Kuklinski (Urbana: University of Illinois Press, 1990); Bernard Grofman and Julie Withers, "Information-Pooling Models of Electoral Politics," *Information, Participation and Choice,* ed. in Bernard Grofman (Ann Arbor: University of Michigan Press, 1993); James Surowiecki, *The Wisdom of Crowds: Why the Many Are Smarter Than the Few* (New York: Doubleday, 2004), ch. 12; and Robert S. Erikson, Michael B. Mackuen, and James A. Stimson, *The Macro Polity* (New York: Cambridge University Press, 2002).

101. Page and Shapiro, *Rational Public,* ch. 10.

102. Converse, "Popular Representation."

103. See Althaus, *Collective Preferences,* 129–33.

104. Ibid., 130.

105. See, e.g., Delli Carpini and Keeter, *What Americans Know About Politics,* ch. 6; Martin Gilens, "Political Ignorance and Collective Policy Preferences," *American Political Science Review* 95 (2001): 379–96.

106. Gilens, "Political Ignorance and Collective Policy Preferences," 387.

107. See the discussion in Chapter 3.

108. Ibid.

109. See Arthur Lupia, "Shortcuts vs. Encyclopedias: Information and Voting Behavior in California's Insurance Reform Elections," *American Political Science Review* 88 (1994): 63–76.

110. Caplan, *Myth of the Rational Voter;* Holbrook and Garand, "Homo Economicus"; Mutz, "Politicizing Personal Experience"; Lau and Redlawsk, "Advantages and Disadvantages of Cognitive Heuristics in Political Decision Making." See also the discussion later in this chapter.

111. See Krishna K. Lada, "The Condorcet Jury Theorem, Free Speech, and Correlated Votes," *American Journal of Political Science* 36 (1992): 617–34.

112. Krishna K. Ladha, "Information Pooling Through Majority-Rule Voting: Condorcet's Jury Theorem with Correlated Votes," *Journal of Law, Economics, and Organization* 26 (1995): 353–72.

113. For an early result of this kind, see Converse, "The Nature of Belief Systems in Mass Publics."

114. On gender and racial differences in political knowledge, see, e.g., Ilya Somin, "Political Ignorance and the Countermajoritarian Difficulty: A New Perspective on the 'Central Obsession' of Constitutional Theory," *Iowa Law Review* 87 (2004): 1354–63 and literature cited therein. For other differences, see, e.g., Delli Carpini and Keeter, *What Americans Know About Politics,* 135–77; Althaus, *Collective Preferences,* 16–17.

115. See David O. Sears and Carolyn Funk, "Self-Interest in Americans' Political Opinions," in *Beyond Self-Interest,* ed. Jane J. Mansbridge (Chicago: University of Chicago Press, 1990): 147–71; see also D. Roderick Kiewet, *Macroeconomics and Micropolitics,* (Chicago: University of Chicago Press, 1983). For a recent summary of the relevant studies, see Caplan, *Myth of the Rational Voter,* 148–51.

116. Caplan, *Myth of the Rational Voter,* 147–51.

117. Ibid., 150.

118. Robert Wolpert and James Gimpel, "Self-Interest, Symbolic Politics, and Public Attitudes Towards Gun Control," *Political Behavior* 20 (1998): 241–62.

119. See, e.g., Tali Mendelberg, *The Race Card* (Chicago: University of Chicago Press, 2001).

120. See Donald R. Kinder and Cindy Kam, *Us Against Them: Ethnocentric Foundations of American Public Opinion* (Chicago: University of Chicago Press, 2009).

121. See, e.g., Scott E. Page, *The Difference: How the Power of Diversity Creates Better Groups, Schools, Firms, and Societies* (Princeton, NJ: Princeton University Press, 2007), 182–88; Hélène Landemore, "Democracy and Reason: Why the Many Are Smarter Than the Few and Why It Matters," *Journal of Public Deliberation* 8 (2012): 1–14; Jack Knight and James Johnson, *The Priority of Democracy: Political Consequences of Pragmatism* (Princeton, NJ: Princeton University Press, 2011), 158–61. Landemore expands her argument in Hélène Landemore, *Democratic Reason: Politics, Collective Intelligence, and the Rule of the Many* (Princeton: Princeton University Press, 2013), which unfortunately came out too late to be fully considered here.

122. See, e.g., Page, *The Difference*, 152–74; Lu Hong and Scott E. Page, "Groups of Diverse Problem Solvers Can Outperform Groups of High-Ability Problem Solvers," *Proceedings of the National Academy of Sciences* 101 (2004): 16385–89, esp. 16386.

123. Hong and Page, 16386.

124. Landemore, "Democracy and Reason," 3; see also Hélène Landemore, "Democratic Reason: The Mechanisms of Collective Intelligence in Politics," in *Collective Wisdom: Principles and Mechanisms*, ed. Helene Landemore and Jon Elster (Cambridge: Cambridge University Press, 2012); see also Landemore, *Democratic Reason*, 97–99.

125. Landemore, "Democracy and Reason," 3.

126. See the discussion in Chapter 3.

127. See Chapter 3.

128. Landemore, "Democracy and Reason," 4; Hong and Page, "Groups of Diverse Problem Solvers."

129. See the discussion earlier.

130. Landemore, *Democratic Reason*, 102.

131. To her credit, Landemore recognizes that "[i]f citizens share a number of wrong views—racist prejudices or the systematic biases diagnosed by Bryan Caplan in economic matter—majority rule is simply going to amplify these mistakes and make democratic decisions dumber, if anything, than the decisions that could have been reached by a single randomly chosen citizen." Landemore, "Democracy and Reason," 5. But she does not consider the possibility that even a slightly greater prevalence of one kind of error over another can lead to this result in a large group, thereby negating most of the benefits of diversity.

132. For a more formal description of the Jury Theorem and a discussion of the recent relevant literature on it, see Kerstin Gerling, Hans Peter Grüner, Alexandra Kiel, and Elisabeth Schulte, "Information Acquisition and Decisionmaking in Committees: A Survey," European Central Bank, working paper no. 236 (2003).

133. For a helpful restatement and explanation of the theorem, see Dennis C. Mueller, *Public Choice III* (New York: Cambridge University Press, 2003), 128–29.

134. For recent defenses of this view, see Cesare Martinelli, "Would Rational Voters Acquire Costly Information?" *Journal of Economic Theory* 129 (2006): 225–51; Yukio Koriyama and Balazs Szentes, "A Resurrection of the Condorcet Jury Theory," *Theoretical Economics* 4 (2009): 227–52; and Christian List and Robert E. Goodin, "Epistemic

Democracy: Generalizing the Condorcet Jury Theorem," *Journal of Political Philosophy* 9 (2001): 277–306.

135. Under certain conditions, the theorem might hold even if voters' errors are highly correlated with each other. See Krishna K. Lada, "The Condorcet Jury Theorem, Free Speech, and Correlated Votes," *American Journal of Political Science* 36 (1992): 617–34. However, the quality of each individual voter's judgment must improve significantly the higher the correlation there is between errors (ibid.).

136. Landemore argues that Jury Theorem can work so long as voters' decisions only have a "low" correlation. Landemore, *Democratic Reason*, 153. But, in reality, the correlation is often extremely high, as shown by the existence of widespread loyalty to political parties, ideologies, ethnic groups, and other political aggregations.

137. See Gerling, et al., "Information Acquisition and Decision Making in Committees," for a survey of the literature. See also Kaushik Mukhopadhaya, "Jury Size and the Free Rider Problem," *Journal of Law, Economics, and Organization* 19 (2003): 24–44. This result may not hold if the cost of additional information acquisition gradually approaches zero as the electorate gets larger. See Martinelli, "Would Rational Voters Acquire Costly Information?" and Koriyama and Szentes, "A Resurrection of the Condorcet Jury Theory." But such an assumption is implausible in light of the fact that the main cost of acquiring information is the time and effort it takes to learn and process it. That cost is unlikely to decline merely because the size of the electorate increases.

138. Mukhopadhaya, "Jury Size and the Free Rider Problem."

CHAPTER FIVE

1. Quoted in Garabed Sarkissian, "Thoughts on the Business of Life," *Forbes*, July 2, 2007.

2. For a survey of the relevant history, see Scott Gordon, *Controlling the State: Constitutionalism From Ancient Athens to Today* (Cambridge: Harvard University Press, 2002).

3. I have myself briefly discussed these advantages in several prior publications. See, e.g., Ilya Somin, "Foot Voting, Political Ignorance, and Constitutional Design," *Social Philosophy and Policy* 28 (2011): 202–26; Ilya Somin, "Political Ignorance and the Countermajoritarian Difficulty: A New Perspective on the 'Central Obsession' of Constitutional Theory," *Iowa Law Review* 87 (2004): 1287–1371; Ilya Somin, "Knowledge About Ignorance: New Directions in the Study of Political Information," *Critical Review* 18 (2006): 255–78; and Ilya Somin, "When Ignorance Isn't Bliss: How Political Ignorance Threatens Democracy," *Cato Institute Policy Analysis* No. 525 (2004). However, this chapter is a much more extensive analysis. Viktor Vanberg and James Buchanan have analyzed the significance of rational political ignorance for the constitution-making process. See Viktor Vanberg and James Buchanan, "Constitutional Choice, Rational Ignorance and the Limits of Reason," in *Rules and Choice in Economics*, ed. Viktor Vanberg (New York: Routledge, 1994), 178–92. But this work only briefly mentions possible implications for federalism in constitutional design (ibid., 188–89). For an otherwise thorough recent survey of the implications of exit rights for democratic theory that largely ignores the issue of voter ignorance, see Mark Warren, "Voting with Your Feet: Exit-Based Empowerment in Democratic Theory," *American Political Science Review* 105 (2011): 683–701. Warren does briefly mention the problem, however (ibid., 688, 692).

4. The terms *"foot voting"* and *"ballot box voting"* used here are similar to Albert Hirschman's well-known distinction between *"exit"* and *"voice."* See Albert Hirschman, *Exit, Voice, and Loyalty: Responses to Decline in Firms, Organizations, and States* (Cambridge: Harvard University Press, 1970). However, Hirschman's concept of *voice* includes methods of influencing an organization from within other than voting. He seeks to compare exit and voice generally, whereas I only wish to compare foot voting with ballot box voting. Thus I use "foot voting" and "ballot box voting" instead of "exit" and "voice" in order to make clear that this chapter has a somewhat different focus than Hirschman's classic work.

5. Charles Tiebout, "A Pure Theory of Local Expenditures," *Journal of Political Economy* 64 (1956): 516–24.

6. For a helpful recent survey that covers much of the relevant literature in political theory, see Warren, "Voting with Your Feet."

7. Adam Przeworksi, *Democracy and the Limits of Self-Government* (Cambridge: Cambridge University Press, 2010), 101.

8. See, e.g., Michael X. Delli Carpini and Scott Keeter, *What Americans Know About Politics and Why It Matters* (New Haven: Yale University Press, 1996), 147–48, 207–8.

9. Lee Shaker, "Local Political Knowledge and Assessments of Citizen Competence," *Public Opinion Quarterly* 76 (2012): 525–37. A "know-nothing" is a survey respondent who gets as many or fewer multiple-choice knowledge questions correct than would be expected by random guessing.

10. Ibid.; Delli Carpini and Keeter, *What Americans Know About Politics*, 148–50, 207–9.

11. See, e.g., Frank Bryan, *Real Democracy: The New England Town Meeting and How It Works* (Chicago: University of Chicago Press, 2004); J. Eric Oliver, *Democracy in Suburbia* (Princeton, NJ: Princeton University Press, 2001), 42–52. However, absolute knowledge levels are low even in very small communities. See Ilya Somin, "Deliberative Democracy and Political Ignorance," *Critical Review* 22 (2010): 253–79, at 270.

12. On the latter point, see David Schleicher, "Why Is There No Partisan Competition in City Council Elections? The Role of Election Law," *Journal of Law and Politics* 23 (2007): 419–73.

13. See Bill Bishop, *The Big Sort: Why the Clustering of the Like-Minded Is Tearing Apart America* (Boston: Houghton Mifflin Harcourt, 2008).

14. See the discussion of retrospective voting in Chapter 4.

15. Ibid.

16. Lee Shaker, "Local Political Knowledge and Assessments of Citizen Competence," *Public Opinion Quarterly* 76 (2012): 525–37, esp. 531–34.

17. See Bishop, *The Big Sort*.

18. David Lowery, "Consumer Sovereignty and Quasi-Market Failure," *Journal of Public Administration Research and Theory* 8 (1998): 137–172, 152–53. For a summary of other information problems that may arise from interjurisdictional competition, see Peter J. Boettke, Christopher Coyne, and Peter Leeson, "Quasimarket Failure," *Public Choice* 149 (2011): 209–24, 213–14.

19. Lowery, "Consumer Sovereignty and Quasi-Market Failure," 148–49; Boettke, et al., "Quasimarket Failure," 213.

20. See the discussion of retrospective voting in Chapter 4.

21. See the discussion of this point in the section on retrospective voting in Chapter 4.

22. Obviously, a voter who cares only about his narrow self-interest or that of his region has no reason to consider the impact of national policies on other parts of the country. However, the evidence suggests that most voters do not adopt their political views on the basis of narrow self-interest, and many try to vote in such a way as to benefit the entire nation. See the discussion of self-interested voting in Chapter 2.

23. Quoted in Sarkissian, "Thoughts on the Business of Life.

24. See the discussion in Chapter 3.

25. Edward Rubin and Malcolm Feeley, "Federalism: Some Notes on a National Neurosis," *UCLA Law Review* 41 (1994): 903–52, esp. 936–42.

26. See, e.g., ibid., 936–51; Malcolm Feeley and Edward Rubin, *Federalism: Political Identity and Tragic Compromise* (Ann Arbor: University of Michigan Press, 2008).

27. Thomas Dye, *American Federalism: Competition Among Governments* (New York: John Wiley & Sons, 1990), 1–33; Ilya Somin, "Closing the Pandora's Box of Federalism: The Case for Judicial Restriction of Federal Subsidies to State Governments," *Georgetown Law Journal* 90 (2002): 468–71; Barry Weingast, "The Economic Role of Political Institutions: Market-Preserving Federalism and Economic Development," *Journal of Law, Economics, and Organization* 11 (1995):1–31. For an early discussion, see F. A. Hayek, *Law Legislation and Liberty*, vol. 3, *The Political Order of a Free People* (Chicago: University of Chicago Press, 1979), 146–47.

28. Somin, "Political Ignorance and the Countermajoritarian Difficulty."

29. There is a large literature on the this subject. See, e.g., Lawrence R. Jacobs and Robert Shapiro, *Politicians Don't Pander: Political Manipulation and the Loss of Democratic Responsiveness* (Chicago: University of Chicago Press, 2000); Tali Mendelberg, *The Race Card* (Chicago: University of Chicago Press, 2001); Ilya Somin, "Voter Knowledge and Constitutional Change: Assessing the New Deal Experience," *William & Mary Law Review* 45 (2003): 595–674, at 652–54.

30. See Paul Teske, Mark Schneider, Michael Mintrom, and Samuel Best, "Establishing the Micro Foundations of a Macro Model: Information, Movers, and the Market for Local Public Goods," *American Political Science Review* 87 (1993): 702–13.

31. See the discussion of the miracle of aggregation in Chapter 4.

32. For a good discussion of the federalism issues raised by the Mormons' establishment of a new state in Utah, see Sarah Barringer Gordon, *The Mormon Question: Polygamy and Constitutional Conflict in Nineteenth-Century America* (Chapel Hill: University of North Carolina Press, 2002). For a recent account of the Pilgrims' decision to leave Europe and found a new society in Massachusetts, see Nathan Philbrick, *Mayflower: A Story of Courage, Community, and War* (New York: Viking, 2006).

33. See, e.g., Adolf Ens, *Subjects or Citizens? The Mennonite Experience in Canada, 1870–1925* (Ottawa: University of Ottawa Press, 1994); Steven Nolt, *A History of the Amish*, rev. ed. (Intercourse, PA: Good Books, 2004).

34. See William Cohen, *At Freedom's Edge: Black Mobility and the Southern White Quest for Racial Control, 1861–1915* (Baton Rouge: Louisiana State University Press, 1991); Florette Henri, *Black Migration: Movement North 1900–20* (New York: Doubleday, 1975); Daniel M. Johnson and Rex R. Campbell, *Black Migration in America: A Social Demographic History* (Durham, NC: Duke University Press, 1981); David E. Bernstein, "The Law and Economics of Post–Civil War Restrictions on Interstate Migration by African-Americans," *Texas Law Review* 76 (1998): 782–85.

35. Johnson and Campbell, *Black Migration in America*, 74–75.

36. Ibid., 77.

37. Ibid., 114–23.

38. Ibid., 60–61; Cohen, *At Freedom's Edge*; Robert Higgs, *Competition and Coercion: Blacks in the American Economy 1865–1914* (New York: Cambridge University Press, 1977).

39. Price V. Fishback, "Can Competition Among Employers Reduce Governmental Discrimination? Coal Companies and Segregated Schools in West Virginia in the Early 1900s," *Journal of Law and Economics* 32 (1989): 324–41; Cohen, *At Freedom's Edge*; Robert Higgs, *Competition and Coercion*.

40. United States Bureau of the Census, *A Half-Century of Learning: Historical Statistics on Educational Attainment in the United States, 1940 to 2000* (Washington, DC: Bureau of the Census, 2000), Tables 7a and 11a.

41. James D. Anderson, *The Education of Blacks in the South, 1860–1935* (Chapel Hill: University of North Carolina Press, 1988).

42. Henri, *Black Migration*, 59–60.

43. Johnson and Campbell, *Black Migration in America*, 83.

44. Some shortcut advocates argue that rationally ignorant voters can rely on cues from "opinion leaders" more knowledgeable than themselves. I have criticized this theory in Ilya Somin, "Voter Ignorance and the Democratic Ideal," *Critical Review* 12 (1998): 413–58; and Ilya Somin, "Resolving the Democratic Dilemma?" *Yale Journal on Regulation* 16 (1999): 401–16.

45. Henri, *Black Migration*, 63–64.

46. For a detailed account of these emigrant agents and their role in providing information to southern blacks, see Bernstein, "The Law and Economics of Post–Civil War Restrictions," 782–83, 792–802. See also Henri, *Black Migration*, 60–62; Cohen, *At Freedom's Edge*, 119–27, 259–70; Ira Berlin, *The Making of African America: The Four Great Migrations* (New York: Viking, 2010), 158–59.

47. Henri, *Black Migration*, 62–63.

48. Ibid.; Bernstein, "The Law and Economics of Post–Civil War Restrictions."

49. Henri, *Black Migration*, 57–60; Johnson and Campbell, *Black Migration in America*, 84–85.

50. Frederick Douglass, *Selected Speeches and Writings*, ed. Philip S. Foner and Yuval Taylor (Chicago: Lawrence Hill Books, 1999 [1886]), 702.

51. Quoted in Michael J. Klarman, *From Jim Crow to Civil Rights: The Supreme Court and the Struggle for Racial Equality* (New York: Oxford University Press, 2004), 164.

52. Henri, *Black Migration*, 168–73.

53. See, e.g., Thomas R. Dye, *American Federalism: Competition Among Governments* (New York: John Wiley & Sons, 1990); Weingast, "The Economic Role of Political Institutions."

54. Bernstein, "The Law and Economics of Post–Civil War Restrictions," 784. See also Henri, *Black Migration*, 75–76, 170–71; Higgs, *Competition and Coercion*, 29–32, 59, 119–20, 152–53.

55. Michael J. Pfeifer, *Rough Justice: Lynching and American Society, 1874–1947* (Urbana: University of Illinois Press, 2004).

56. Henri, *Black Migration*, 57–58; Johnson and Campbell, *Black Migration in America*, 84–85.

57. Fishback, "Can Competition Among Employers Reduce Governmental Discrimination?" For a general discussion of the ability of migration to reduce discrimination in education,

see Robert A. Margo, "Segregated Schools and the Mobility Hypothesis: A Model of Local Government Discrimination," *Quarterly Journal of Economics* 106 (1991): 61–75.

58. Douglass, *Selected Speeches and Writings*, 702.

59. It should, however, be noted that its failure to do so was partly attributable to southern state governments' efforts to reduce black mobility. See Cohen, *At Freedom's Edge*, 201–72; Bernstein, "The Law and Economics of Post–Civil War Restrictions," 810–27.

60. See the discussion of retrospective voting in Chapter 4 and Ilya Somin, "When Ignorance Isn't Bliss: How Political Ignorance Threatens Democracy," Cato Institute Policy Analysis No. 525, 2004.

61. U.S. Bureau of the Census, *A Half-Century of Learning: Historical Statistics on Educational Attainment in the United States, 1940 to 2000*. Washington, DC: Bureau of the Census, 2000, Tables 7a and 11a.

62. Sandra Gunning, *Race, Rape, and Lynching: The Red Record of American Literature, 1890–1912* (New York: Oxford University Press, 1996); Pfeifer, *Rough Justice*.

63. Pfeifer, *Rough Justice*.

64. For a discussion of one of the best-known efforts to disprove this rationale for lynching, see Patricia Schechter, *Ida B. Wells-Barnett and American Reform, 1880–1930* (Chapel Hill: University of North Carolina Press, 2000).

65. We don't have any survey data documenting the precise number of southern white voters who accepted the rape myth. However, contemporary observers believed that it was widely accepted, and politicians routinely exploited it in their campaigns, and as a justification for lynching. See generally Pfeifer, *Rough Justice*.

66. Numan V. Bartley, *The New South, 1945–1980* (Baton Rouge: Louisiana State University Press, 1995), 245–60.

67. See the discussion earlier in this chapter.

68. For the classic analysis, see V. O. Key, *Southern Politics in State and Nation* (New York: Knopf, 1949), chs. 24–31; see also Earl Black and Merle Black, *Politics and Society in the South* (Cambridge: Harvard University Press, 1987), 75–77.

69. For a summary and discussion of the relevant literature on cognitive failure in private sector settings, see Cass Sunstein and Richard H. Thaler, *Nudge* (Princeton, NJ: Princeton University Press, 2008), chs. 1–4; see also Dan Ariely, *Predictably Irrational: The Hidden Forces That Shape Our Decisions* (New York: HarperCollins, 2008); Christine Jolls, Cass R. Sunstein, and Richard Thaler, "A Behavioral Approach to Law and Economics," in *Behavioral Law and Economics*, ed. Cass Sunstein (New York: Cambridge University Press, 2000).

70. See, e.g., Joshua D. Wright and Douglas H. Ginsburg, "Behavioral Law and Economics: Its Origins, Fatal Flaws, and Implications for Liberty," *Northwestern University Law Review* 106 (2012): 1–58, esp. 12–20; Lee Jussim, *Social Perceptions and Social Reality: Why Accuracy Dominates Bias and Self-Fulfilling Prophecy* (New York: Oxford University Press, 2012); Richard B. McKenzie, *Predictably Rational? In Search of Defenses for Rational Behavior in Economics* (Heidelberg, Germany: Springer, 2010); Richard A. Epstein, *Skepticism and Freedom: A Modern Case for Classical Liberalism* (Chicago: University of Chicago Press, 2003), chs. 8–9.

71. Charles R. Plott and Kathryn Zeiler, "Are Asymmetries in Exchange Behavior Incorrectly Interpreted as Evidence of Endowment Effect Theory and Prospect Theory?" *American Economic Review* 97 (2007): 1449–71; Charles R. Plott and Kathryn Zeiler,

"The Willingness to Pay-Willingness to Accept Gap, the 'Endowment Effect,' Subject Misconceptions, and Experimental Procedures for Eliciting Valuations," *American Economic Review* 95 (2005): 530–45. See also Epstein, *Skepticism and Freedom*, 210–18.

72. See, e.g., Oren Bar-Gill, "Seduction by Plastic," *Northwestern University Law Review* 98 (2004): 1373–1430.

73. For a detailed review, see Joshua D. Wright, "Behavioral Law and Economics, Paternalism, and Consumer Contracts: An Empirical Perspective," *NYU Journal of Law and Liberty 2007* (2007): 470–511.

74. On the relevance of individual differences along these lines, see Jeffrey J. Rachlinski, "Cognitive Errors, Individual Differences, and Paternalism," *University of Chicago Law Review* 73 (2006): 207–29.

75. For a related argument, see Edward Glaeser, "Paternalism and Psychology," *University of Chicago Law Review* 73 (2006): 133–57.

76. Hayek, *Law Legislation and Liberty*, 75 (emphasis added).

77. See the Introduction and Chapter 1.

78. Daniel McFadden, "Free Markets and Fettered Consumers," *American Economic Review* 96 (2006): 5–29, 17–21.

79. Ibid., 22.

80. Ibid. A highly risk-averse person might choose to purchase more insurance than a risk-neutral calculation would dictate.

81. Ibid., 23.

82. Ibid., 18.

83. Robert Nelson, *Private Neighborhoods and the Transformation of Local Government* (Washington, DC: Urban Institute, 2005), xiii.

84. Ibid.

85. See generally, Georg Glasze, Chris Webster, and Klaus Frantz, eds., *Private Cities: Global and Local Perspectives* (New York: Routledge, 2006).

86. For a related argument suggesting that private planned communities might improve the quality of decision making and deliberation relative to government bodies, see Guido Pincione and Fernando Teson, *Rational Choice and Democratic Deliberation: A Theory of Discourse Failure* (New York: Cambridge University Press, 2006), 228–47; see also Vanberg and Buchanan, "Constitutional Choice, Rational Ignorance, and the Limits of Reason," 186–90, which argues that individuals might make better-informed choices between alternative constitutional arrangements in the market than through voting.

87. Ilya Somin, "Closing the Pandora's Box of Federalism: The Case for Judicial Restriction of Federal Subsidies to State Governments," *Georgetown Law Journal* 90 (2002): 461–502.

88. See, e.g., John O. McGinnis and Ilya Somin, "Federalism vs. States' Rights: A Defense of Judicial Review in a Federal System," *Northwestern University Law Review* 99 (2004): 89–130, at 107–10.

89. See the discussion of this issue earlier in this chapter.

90. See Bruno Frey, "A Utopia? Government Without Territorial Monopoly," *Independent Review* 6 (2001), 99–112; Bruno Frey, *Happiness: A Revolution in Economics* (Cambridge: MIT Press, 2008), 189–97; Bruno S. Frey and Reiner Eichenberger, *The New Democratic Federalism for Europe: Functional, Overlapping, and Competing Jurisdictions*, new ed. (London: Edward Elgar, 2004).

91. See Erin O'Hara and Larry Ribstein, *The Law Market* (New York: Oxford University Press, 2009).

92. See, e.g., Heather Gerken, "Foreword: Federalism All the Way Down," *Harvard Law Review* 124 (2010): 6–74; Richard C. Schragger, "Cities as Constitutional Actors: The Case of Same-Sex Marriage," *Journal of Law and Politics* 21 (2005): 147–76; Heather K. Gerken, "A New Progressive Federalism," *Democracy* 24 (Spring 2012), http://www.democracyjournal.org/24/a-new-progressive-federalism.php?page=1.

93. For a more detailed discussion of these points in the special context of property rights, see Ilya Somin, "Federalism and Property Rights," *University of Chicago Legal Forum* (2011): 53–88, at 71.

94. James Madison, "Federalist 62," *The Federalist*, ed. Clinton Rossiter (New York: Mentor, 1961).

95. See International Monetary Fund, *Government Finance Statistics Yearbook 2008* (Washington, DC: IMF, 2008).

96. Organization for Economic Cooperation and Development, *Country Statistical Profile: United States, 2011–12*, http://www.oecd-ilibrary.org/economics/country-statistical-profile-united-states_20752288-table-usa. The *Economic Report of the President* gives slightly lower measures, with government spending at all levels accounting for 31.5 percent of GDP in 2007 and about 36 percent in 2010. Calculated from Council of Economic Advisers, *Economic Report of the President 2011* (Washington, DC: Government Printing Office, 2011), Tables B-1, B-82.

97. See, e.g., Robert Higgs, *Crisis and Leviathan: Critical Episodes in the Growth of American Government* (New York: Oxford University Press, 1987).

98. Figures derived from Department of Commerce, *U.S. Government Manual 2008–2009* (Washington, DC: Government Printing Office, 2008), vii–ix.

99. See, e.g., Delli Carpini and Keeter, *What Americans Know About Politics*, 91–93.

100. See Glenn Altschuler and Stuart M. Blumin, *Rude Republic: Americans and Their Politics in the Nineteenth Century* (Princeton, NJ: Princeton University Press, 2000).

101. Paul Angle, ed., *The Complete Lincoln-Douglas Debates*, 2nd ed. (Chicago: University of Chicago Press, 1991); Harry V. Jaffa, *Crisis of the House Divided: An Interpretation of the Issues in the Lincoln-Douglas Debates* (New York: Doubleday, 1959).

102. "Inaugural Address Analysis Shows Bush's Ranking Against Predecessors: YourDictionary.com Provides Linguistic Analysis in Historical Context," YourDictionary.com (January 20, 2001), http://www.yourdictionary.com/about/news038.html.

103. Ibid.

104. Ibid.

105. Elvin T. Lim, *The Anti-Intellectual Presidency: The Decline of Presidential Rhetoric from George Washington to George W. Bush* (New York: Oxford University Press, 2008).

106. Paul JJ Payack, "Presidential Debates Mirror Long-Term School Decline," YourDictionary.com (2000), http://www.yourdictionary.com/library/presart1.html.

107. Ibid.

108. For a discussion of the available evidence and its equivocal nature, see Ilya Somin, "Originalism and Political Ignorance," *Minnesota Law Review* 97 (2012): 625–68, 645–48.

109. For a more detailed discussion of some of these issues, see Ilya Somin, "Foot Voting, Federalism, and Political Freedom," *Nomos*, forthcoming, available at http://ssrn.com/abstract=2160388.

110. Pew Research Center, *Who Moves? Who Stays Put? Where's Home?* (Washington, DC: Pew Research Center, December 2008), 8, 13.

111. Mark Deen and Alan Katz, "London's French Foreign Legion Shuns Sarkozy Plea to Come Home," *Bloomberg News*, January 17, 2008, http://www.bloomberg.com/apps/news?pid=newsarchive&sid=acDlozxrk7iE.

112. Ibid.

113. Tony Paterson, "German 'Brain Drain' at Highest Level Since 1940s," *The Independent*, June 1, 2007.

114. See Nathan J. Ashby, "Economic Freedom and Migration Flows Between U.S. States," *Southern Economic Journal* 73 (2007): 677–97.

115. See William P. Ruger and Jason Sorens, *Freedom in the Fifty States: An Index of Personal and Economic Freedom* (Arlington, VA: Mercatus Center, George Mason University, 2009), 34.

116. Kenneth Johnson, *The Changing Faces of New Hamphsire: Recent Demographic Trends in the Granite State* (Durham, NH: Carsey Institute, University of New Hampshire, 2007).

117. Somin, "Political Ignorance and the Countermajoritarian Difficulty," 1351.

118. See, e.g., Robert C. Ellickson, "Legal Sources of Residential Lock-Ins: Why French Households Move Half as Often as US Households," *University of Illinois Law Review* (2012): 373–404, esp. 395–97; Paul W. Rhode and Koleman S. Strumpf, "Assessing the Importance of Tiebout Sorting: Local Heterogeneity from 1885 to 1990," *American Economic Review* 93 (2003): 1648–77, at 1649. Ellickson cites survey data showing that 16 percent of American movers and 26 percent of French movers switch locations because of jobs. Rhode and Strumpf cite an earlier and differently worded survey in which only 5 percent move because of public services (education) and 50 percent due to family or job considerations.

119. See the discussion of private planned communities and Bruno Frey's proposal for non-territorially based governments earlier in this chapter.

120. For a helpful summary and defense of the race-to-the-bottom theory, see Kirsten H. Engel, "State Environmental Standard-Setting: Is there a 'Race' and Is It 'to the Bottom'?" *Hastings Law Journal* 48 (1997): 274–369. For other modern defenses, see, e.g., Kirsten Engel and Scott R. Saleska, "Facts Are Stubborn Things: An Empirical Reality Check in the Theoretical Debate Over State Environmental Rate-Setting, *Cornell Journal of Law and Public Policy* 8 (1998): 55–88; and Joshua D. Sarnoff, "The Continuing Imperative (But Only from a National Perspective) for Federal Environmental Protection," *Duke Environmental Law and Policy Forum* 7 (1997): 225–54.

121. Richard Revesz, "Rehabilitating Interstate Competition: Rethinking the 'Race to the Bottom' Rationale for Federal Environmental Regulation," *NYU Law Review* 67 (1992): 1210–54; Richard Revesz, "The Race to the Bottom and Federal Environmental Regulation: A Response to Critics," *Minnesota Law Review* 82 (1997): 535–64.

122. Revesz, "Rehabilitating Interstate Competition."

123. For a summary of the evidence on this point, see Ilya Somin and Jonathan H. Adler, "The Green Costs of *Kelo*: Economic Development Takings and Environmental Protection," *Washington Law Review* 84 (2006): 623–66, at 663–64.

124. See generally Richard C. Schragger, "Mobile Capital, Local Economic Regulation, and the Disciplining City," *Harvard Law Review* 123 (2009): 483–540.

125. See, e.g., Jonathan H. Adler, "Judicial Federalism and the Future of Federal Environmental Regulation," *Iowa Law Review* 90 (2005): 377–474; Jonathan H. Adler,

"Interstate Competition and the Race to the Top," *Harvard Journal of Law and Public Policy* 35 (2012): 89–99.

126. 247 U.S. 251 (1918).

127. See Carolyn Moehling, "State Child Labor Laws and the Decline of Child Labor," *Explorations in Economic History* 36 (1999): 72–106, at Table 1, 76–77.

128. Michael S. Greve, *The Upside-Down Constitution* (Cambridge: Harvard University Press, 2012), 187–88. See also Moehling, "State Child Labor Laws and the Decline of Child Labor," 94–95. The 1918 federal law did not ban agricultural child labor, which remains legal to this day. Moehling argues that child labor laws had little effect on the decline in industrial child labor, which mostly followed preexisting trends. But if this is true, it is far from clear that federal laws would have had any greater effect. National child-labor restrictions in Britain had little effect in reducing child labor there. See Clark Nardinelli, "Child Labor and the Factory Acts," *Journal of Economic History* 40 (1980): 739–55.

129. For a discussion and summary of state laws, see Moehling, "State Child Labor Laws and the Decline of Child Labor."

130. For a more detailed discussion, see Somin, "Federalism and Property Rights," 60–64.

131. For a good recent summary of this conventional wisdom, see Douglas Laycock, "Protecting Liberty in a Federal System: The US Experience," in *Patterns of Regionalism and Federalism: Lessons for the UK*, ed. Jorg Fedtke and B. S. Markesisinis (London: Hart, 2006), 121–45.

132. William H. Riker, *Federalism: Origin, Operation, Significance* (Boston: Little, Brown, 1964), 152–53, 55; Riker later developed a less negative view of American federalism. See William H. Riker, *The Development of American Federalism* (Boston: Kluwer Academic Publishers, 1987), xii–xiii.

133. See Arthur Zilversmit, *The First Emancipation: The Abolition of Slavery in the North* (Chicago: University of Chicago Press, 1967); Joanne Pope Melish, *Disowning Slavery: Gradual Emancipation and 'Race' in New England 1780–1860* (Ithaca: Cornell University Press, 1998). The state of Vermont had abolished slavery even before it became a state in 1791. Melish, *Disowning Slavery*, 64.

134. Some northern states and abolitionists even resisted the Fugitive Slave Acts on "states' rights" grounds. See Robert Kaczorowski, "The Tragic Irony of American Federalism: National Sovereignty Versus State Sovereignty in Slavery and Freedom," *University of Kansas Law Review* 45 (1997): 1015–61, 1034–40.

135. James M. McPherson, *Battle Cry of Freedom: The Civil War Era* (New York: Oxford University Press, 1988), 497.

136. For a brief review of the record, see Lynn Baker and Ernest Young, "Federalism and the Double Standard of Judicial Review," *Duke Law Journal* 51 (2001): 75–164, at 143–47.

137. For an overview of segregationist federal policies during this period, see Desmond King, *Separate and Unequal: African-Americans and the US Federal Government*, rev. ed. (New York: Oxford University Press, 2007).

138. See Roger Daniels, *Concentration Camps, USA: The Japanese Americans and World War II* (New York: Holt, Rinehart & Wilson, 1971); Sarah Barringer Gordon, *The Mormon Question: Polygamy and Constitutional Conflict in Nineteenth-Century America* (Chapel Hill: University of North Carolina Press, 2002).

139. See the discussion of early twentieth century African-American migration earlier in this chapter.

140. See generally Stephen Clark, "Progressive Federalism? A Gay Liberationist Perspective," *Albany Law Review* 66 (2003): 719–57.

141. For an overview covering many such cases, see Luis Moreno and César Colino, eds., *Diversity and Unity in Federal Countries* (Montreal and Kingston: McGill-Queen's University Press, 2010); see also Dawn Brancati, *Peace By Design: Managing Intrastate Conflict through Decentralization* (New York: Oxford University Press, 2009).

142. See Gerken, "A New Progressive Federalism."

143. For well-known arguments that the political safeguards of federalism make judicial intervention unnecessary in the United States, see Larry D. Kramer, "Putting the Politics Back into the Political Safeguards of Federalism," *Columbia Law Review* 100 (2000), 215–311; Jesse H. Choper, *Judicial Review and the National Political Process* (Chicago: University of Chicago Press, 1980); Jesse H. Choper, "The Scope of National Power Vis-à-Vis the States: The Dispensability of Judicial Review," *Yale Law Journal* 86 (1977), 1552–84; Herbert J. Wechsler, "The Political Safeguards of Federalism: The Role of the States in the Composition and Selection of the Federal Government," *Columbia Law Review* 54 (1954), 543–64.

144. These points are elaborated in greater detail in McGinnis and Somin, "Federalism vs. States' Rights."

145. See ibid. and Weingast, "The Economic Role of Political Institutions"; see also James Buchanan and Geoffrey Brennan, *The Power to Tax: Analytical Foundations of a Fiscal Constitution* (Cambridge: Cambridge University Press, 1980), 214–15; Jonathan Rodden, *Hamilton's Paradox: The Promise and Peril of Fiscal Federalism* (New York: Cambridge University Press, 2006), ch. 4.

146. See Barry Weingast, "Second Generation Fiscal Federalism: Implications for Decentralized Democratic Governance and Economic Development," draft paper (2007), 13–16, 42–43.

147. See ibid.; see also Somin, "Closing the Pandora's Box of Federalism."

148. See examples of such cases noted in Chapter 1 and Chapter 4.

149. For a particularly influential argument for the former, see Weingast, "The Economic Role of Political Institutions."

150. Ibid.; Somin, "Closing the Pandora's Box of Federalism."

151. For a recent restatement of that view, see Laycock, "Protecting Liberty in a Federal System."

152. Klarman, *From Jim Crow to Civil Rights*.

153. See Ilya Somin, "Tiebout Goes Global: International Migration as a Tool for Voting with Your Feet, *Missouri Law Review* 73 (2008): 1247–64; Somin, "Foot Voting, Federalism, and Political Freedom."

154. These two limitations of foot voting are discussed in Richard A. Epstein, "Exit Rights Under Federalism," *Law and Contemporary Problems* 55 (1992): 147–65. On the limitations of foot voting in protecting property rights in immobile assets such as land, see Somin, "Federalism and Property Rights," 57–66.

155. For a recent survey of the literature on the various considerations involved, see Larry Ribstein and Bruce Kobayashi, "The Economics of Federalism," in *The Economics of Federalism*, ed. Larry Ribstein and Bruce Kobayashi (New York: Edward Elgar, 2010).

156. See Richard Revesz, "Federalism and Interstate Environmental Externalities," *University of Pennsylvania Law Review* 144 (1996): 2341–2402. Many smaller-scale externalities, however, can be handled by negotiation between local governments. See

Thomas W. Merrill, "Golden Rules for Transboundary Pollution," *Duke Law Journal* 46 (1997): 931–1019.

157. See, e.g., Paul E. Peterson, *The Price of Federalism* (Washington, DC: Brookings Institution, 1995). For a critique of the conventional wisdom on this issue, see Frank H. Buckley and Margaret Brinig, "Welfare Magnets: The Race for the Top," *Supreme Court Economic Review* 5 (1997): 141–77.

CHAPTER SIX

1. Alexander M. Bickel, *The Least Dangerous Branch: The Supreme Court at the Bar of Politics* (New Haven: Yale University Press, 1962), 16.

2. For useful histories of the debate over the countermajoritarian difficulty, see Barry Friedman, "The Birth of an Academic Obsession: The History of the Countermajoritarian Difficulty, Part Five: " *Yale Law Journal* 112 (2002): 153; and G. Edward White, "The Arrival of History in Constitutional Scholarship," *Virginia Law Review* 88 (2002): 485, 523–607; see also Laura Kalman, *The Strange Career of Legal Liberalism* (New Haven: Yale University Press, 1996).

3. Barry Friedman, "The History of the Countermajoritarian Difficulty, Part One: The Road to Judicial Supremacy," *New York University Law Review* 73 (1998): 334.4. It was Bickel who coined the phrase "counter-majoritarian difficulty" in 1962. Ibid., 334–35. On the development of Bickel's views on the countermajoritarian difficulty, see Anthony T. Kronman, "Alexander Bickel's Philosophy of Prudence," *Yale Law Journal* 94 (1985): 1567; and John Moeller, "Alexander M. Bickel: Toward a Theory of Politics," *Journal of Politics* 47 (1985): 113.

5. Bickel, *The Least Dangerous Branch*, 16.

6. Ibid., 18.

7. For a few of the more notable recent works addressing the countermajoritarian difficulty, see Barry Friedman, *The Will of the People: How Public Opinion Has Influenced the Supreme Court and Shaped the Meaning of the Constitution* (New York: Farrar, Straus, and Giroux, 2009); Christopher Eisgruber, *Constitutional Self-Government* (Cambridge: Harvard University Press, 2001); Paul W. Kahn, *Legitimacy and History: Self-Government in American Constitutional Theory* (New Haven: Yale University Press, 1992); Terri Jennings Peretti, *In Defense of a Political Court* (Princeton, NJ: Princeton University Press, 1999); Jed Rubenfeld, *Freedom and Time: A Theory of Constitutional Self-Government* (New Haven: Yale University Press 2001); Mark Tushnet, *Taking the Constitution Away from the Courts* (Princeton, NJ: Princeton University Press, 1999); Larry D. Kramer, *The People Themselves: Popular Constitutionalism and Judicial Review* (New York: Oxford University Press, 2004); Jeremy Waldron, *Law and Disagreement* (New York: Oxford University Press, 1999); Rachel E. Barkow, "More Supreme Than Court? The Fall of the Political Question Doctrine and the Rise of Judicial Supremacy," *Columbia Law Review* 102 (2002): 237; Steven G. Calabresi, "Textualism and the Countermajoritarian Difficulty," *George Washington Law Review* 66 (1998): 1373; Friedman, "The Birth of an Academic Obsession"; Friedman, "The History of the Countermajoritarian Difficulty"; Larry D. Kramer, "The Supreme Court 2000 Term Foreword: We the Court," *Harvard Law Review* 115 (2001): 4; Edward L. Rubin, "Getting Past Democracy," *University of Pennsylvania Law Review* 149 (2001): 711.

8. For advocacy of the abolition of judicial review by a prominent liberal legal scholar, see Tushnet, *Taking the Constitution Away from the Courts*. Kramer, "The Supreme

Court 2000 Term Foreword: We the Court," comes close to reaching the same conclusion. For a similar argument by a noted conservative, see, e.g., Robert H. Bork, *Slouching Toward Gomorrah* (New York: Regan Books, 1996), 196. For proposals to alleviate the countermajoritarian difficulty by severely restricting judicial review without eliminating it entirely, see, e.g., Raoul Berger, *Government by Judiciary* (Cambridge: Harvard University Press, 1977); Cass R. Sunstein, *One Case at a Time: Judicial Minimalism at the Supreme Court* (Cambridge: Harvard University Press 2000); Barkow, "More Supreme Than Court?"; Neal Kumar Katyal, "Legislative Constitutional Interpretation," *Duke Law Journal* 50 (2001): 1335, 1358–94.

9. Robert H. Bork, "The Impossibility of Finding Welfare Rights in the Constitution," *Washington University Law Quarterly* 1979 (1979): 697. It is worth noting that Bork wrote these words years before he came to believe that judicial review should be abolished entirely, a position first expressed in print in 1996. See Bork, *Slouching Toward Gomorrah*, 117.

10. Katyal, "Legislative Constitutional Interpretation," 1340.

11. For an example of such an argument, see Robert H. Bork, *The Tempting of America* (New York: Free Press, 1990), 2–3. For a summary of the evidence that this fear is overblown, see generally Peretti, *In Defense of a Political Court.*

12. See Chapter 2.

13. See the analysis in Chapter 3.

14. See R. Douglas Arnold, *The Logic of Congressional Action* (New Haven: Yale University Press, 1990), 70–87, 239–41, 270–72; Michael X. Delli Carpini and Scott Keeter, *What Americans Know About Politics and Why It Matters* (New Haven: Yale University Press), 78–86; Somin, "Voter Ignorance and the Democratic Ideal," *Critical Review* 12 (1998): 413–58, at 431–33.

15. See Lawrence Jacobs and Robert Shapiro, *Politicians Don't Pander* (Princeton, NJ: Princeton University Press, 2000), 75–294. See also my review of this book, Ilya Somin, "Do Politicians Pander?," *Critical Review* 14 (2001) 147–59.

16. Ilya Somin, "Voter Knowledge and Constitutional Change: Assessing the New Deal Experience," *William and Mary Law Review* 45 (2003): 595.

17. Bruce Ackerman, *We the People: Foundations* (Cambridge: Belknap Press, 1991). For my criticism of Ackerman's argument, see Ilya Somin, "Voter Knowledge and Constitutional Change," 607–11.

18. See the works cited in note 7.

19. "Jackson Calls Court Curb on Democracy; Says Law Reviews Block United Functioning," *New York Times*, October 13, 1937, 6. See generally Robert H. Jackson, *The Struggle for Judicial Supremacy* (New York: Octagon, 1941).

20. *United States v. Virginia*, 518 U.S. 515, 601 (1996) (Scalia, J., dissenting); see also *Romer v. Evans*, 517 U.S. 620, 636, 653 (1996) (Scalia, J., dissenting) (chastising the Court majority for preventing the issue of the status of homosexuality from being resolved by "normal democratic means" and for overruling the will of "a majority of Colorodans"); *Planned Parenthood v. Casey*, 505 U.S. 833, 1002 (1992) (Scalia, J., concurring and dissenting) (criticizing the Court for "foreclosing all democratic outlet for the deep passions this issue [abortion] arouses"); see generally Antonin M. Scalia, *A Matter of Interpretation* (Princeton, NJ: Princeton University Press, 1997).

21. See, e.g, *United States v. Morrison*, 529 U.S. 598, 649 (2000) (Souter, J., dissenting) (arguing that federalism issues are best settled by Congress, in part because of its "identity with the people"); *United States v. Lopez*, 514 U.S. 549, 604 (1995) (Souter, J., dissenting) (chastising Court majority for ignoring benefits of "Congress's political accountability" to the people in determining federalism issues). See also Stephen Breyer, *Active Liberty: Interpreting Our Democratic Constitution* (New York: Knopf, 2005), 39–85.

22. See Barry Friedman, "Dialogue and Judicial Review," *Michigan Law Review* 91 (1993): 577–682, at 630, which makes a strong argument to the effect that there is no countermajoritarian problem with overruling legislation that reflects solely the will of the legislators and not that of the people.

23. Ibid.

24. See, e.g., Lino A. Graglia, *Disaster by Decree: The Supreme Court Decisions on Race and the Schools* (Ithaca: Cornell University Press, 1976), 282–83; Donald L. Horowitz, *The Courts and Social Policy* (Washington, DC: Brookings Institution Press, 1977).

25. See, e.g., Gerald N. Rosenberg, *The Hollow Hope: Can Courts Bring About Social Change?* (Chicago: University of Chicago Press, 1991), 13–15, 21; Robert A. Dahl, "Decision Making in a Democracy: The Supreme Court as National Policy Maker," *Journal of Public Law* 6 (1957): 279. However, a substantial literature has called Rosenberg and Dahl's theses into question. See David J. Garrow, *Liberty and Sexuality: The Right to Privacy and the Making of Roe v. Wade* (Berkeley: University of California Press, 1994); R. Shep Melnick, *Between the Lines* 236 (Washington, DC: Brookings Institution Press, 1994); David J. Garrow, "Hopelessly Hollow History: Revisionist Devaluing of Brown v. Board of Education," *Virginia Law Review* 80 (1994): 151, 151–52; Ronald Kahn, "The Supreme Court as a (Counter) Majoritarian Institution: Misperceptions of the Warren, Burger, and Rehnquist Courts," *Detroit College of Law Review* 1994 (1994): 1, 21–58; Michael J. Klarman, "Brown, Racial Change, and the Civil Rights Movement," *Virginia Law Review* 80 (1994): 7; Mark Tushnet, "The Significance of Brown v. Board of Education," *Virginia Law Review* 80 (1994): 173, 175–77.

26. For prominent defenses of originalism, see Bork, *The Tempting of America*, 143–69; Akhil R. Amar, "The Document and the Doctrine," *Harvard Law Review* 114 (2000): 26, 133–34; and Randy E. Barnett, "An Originalism for Nonoriginalists," *Loyola Law Review* 45 (1999): 611, 654. See also Randy E. Barnett, *Restoring the Lost Constitution: The Presumption of Liberty* (Princeton, NJ: Princeton University Press, 2004); Berger, *Government by Judiciary*; Antonin Scalia, "Originalism: The Lesser Evil," *University of Cincinnati Law Review* 57 (1989): 849. For well-known criticisms, see generally Paul Brest, "The Misconceived Quest for the Original Understanding," *Boston University Law Review* 60 (1980): 204; H. Jefferson Powell, "Rules for Originalists," *Virginia Law Review* 73 (1987): 659.

27. See the discussion of retrospective voting in Chapter 4.

28. Ibid.

29. Ibid.

30. Delli Carpini and Keeter, *What Americans Know About Politics*, 80.

31. See *United States v. Eichman*, 496 U.S. 310, 310–11 (1990), which invalidated a federal anti-flag burning law; and *Texas v. Johnson*, 491 U.S. 397, 397 (1989), which struck down a Texas state law prohibiting flag burning.

32. A July 1990 *Times Mirror* survey showed that 52 percent of respondents knew that the Supreme Court had held anti-flag-burning laws to be unconstitutional. Somin, "Political Ignorance and the Countermajoritarian Difficulty," 1333. A June 1990 ABC News survey found that 58 percent of respondents supported a constitutional amendment to reverse the Supreme Court's decision. Ibid.

33. See the discussion in Chapter 4.

34. See, e.g., Calabresi, "Textualism and the Countermajoritarian Difficulty."

35. See, e.g., Ronald Dworkin, *Freedom's Law* (Cambridge: Harvard University Press, 1996); Ronald Dworkin, *Taking Rights Seriously* (Cambridge: Harvard University Press, 1977); Michael J. Perry, *The Constitution, the Courts, and Human Rights* (New Haven: Yale University Press, 1982).

36. Barkow, "More Supreme Than Court?"

37. See, e.g., Sunstein, *One Case at a Time*.

38. Bickel, *The Least Dangerous Branch*, 111–98; Alexander M. Bickel, "The Supreme Court 1960 Term Foreword: The Passive Virtues," *Harvard Law Review* 75 (1961): 40.

39. See Chapter 2; see also Somin, "Voter Ignorance and the Democratic Ideal," 435–38.

40. This argument was first advanced in Somin, "Voter Ignorance and the Democratic Ideal," 431–35; see also the discussion in Chapter 5.

41. Somin, "Voter Ignorance and the Democratic Ideal," 431–35.

42. Ibid., 431.

43. See Chapter 5.

44. Robert Higgs, *Crisis and Leviathan: Critical Episodes in the Growth of American Government* (New York: Oxford University Press, 1987), 20–34.

45. See Chapter 5.

46. See, e.g., *R.A.V. v. St. Paul*, 505 U.S. 377, 382 (1992) which held that "[c]ontent-based regulations [of speech] are presumptively invalid" under the First Amendment.

47. See, e.g., *Watson v. Jones*, 80 U.S. (13 Wall.) 679, 728 (1871), which established the principle that government must not intervene in internal church disputes because "[t]he law knows no heresy, and is committed to the support of no dogma, the establishment of no sect."

48. Richard A. Epstein, *Takings: Private Property and Eminent Domain* (Cambridge: Harvard University Press, 1985), 281. Obviously, these effects would occur only if the Court not only accepted Epstein's position but also had sufficient leverage to force the other branches of government to obey its decision.

49. *United States v. Morrison*, 529 U.S. 598, 613 (2000).

50. John Hart Ely, *Democracy and Distrust* (Cambridge: Harvard University Press, 1980), 87.

51. Somin, "Voter Ignorance and the Democratic Ideal," 434–35.

52. See, e.g., *Missouri v. Jenkins*, 495 U.S. 33, 57–58 (1990), which partially upheld a district court decision that took control of a Kansas City school district away from local government and ordered tax increases for purposes of alleviating school segregation. The Supreme Court further limited judicial control of Kansas City schools in a follow-up case, *Missouri v. Jenkins*, 515 U.S. 70, 101–02 (1995).

53. Malcolm Feeley and Edward Rubin, *Judicial Policy Making and the Modern State* (New York: Oxford University Press, 1998).

54. See, e.g., *Jenkins*, 495 U.S., 36–45, which describes how the district court ordered the creation of a new tax system and various changes in school district policy.

55. Adrian Vermeule, "Centralization and the Commerce Clause," *Environmental Law Report* 33 (2001): 11,334; Adrian Vermeule, "Does Commerce Clause Review Have Perverse Effects?" *Villanova Law Review* 46 (2001): 1325, 1325.

56. 531 U.S. 1046 (2000).

57. See *United States v. Morrison*, 529 U.S. 598, 649 (2000) (Souter, J., dissenting) (arguing that federalism issues are best settled by Congress, in part because of its "identity with the people"); *United States v. Lopez*, 514 U.S. 549, 604 (1995) (Souter, J., dissenting) (chastising the Court majority for ignoring the benefits of "Congress's political accountability" to the people in determining federalism issues).

58. For academic criticism of the Court's federalism decisions on countermajoritarian grounds, see, for example, Larry D. Kramer, "Putting the Politics Back into the Political Safeguards of Federalism," *Columbia Law Review* 100 (2000): 215, 293; Larry D. Kramer, "The Supreme Court 2000 Term Foreword: We the Court"; William P. Marshall, "Conservatives and the Seven Sins of Judicial Activism," *University of Colorado Law Review* 73 (2002): 1217, 1226–28; Robert Post and Reva Siegel, "Equal Protection by Law: Federal Antidiscrimination Legislation After Morrison and Kimel," *Yale Law Journal* 110 (2000): 441, 523; Peter M. Shane, "Federalism's 'Old Deal': What's Right and Wrong With Conservative Judicial Activism," *Villanova Law Review* 45 (2000): 201, 223–25; and John T. Noonan Jr., *Narrowing the Nation's Power: The Supreme Court Sides with the States* (Berkeley: University of California Press, 2002).

59. *Gonzales v. Raich*, 545 U.S. 1 (2005). For my analysis of *Raich*, see Ilya Somin, "*Gonzales v. Raich*: Federalism as a Casualty of the War on Drugs," *Cornell Journal of Law and Public Policy* 15 (2006): 507–49.

60. 132 S.Ct. 2566 (2012). For a variety of perspectives on this case, see Gillian Metzger, Trevor Morrison, and Nathaniel Persily, eds., *The Health Care Case: The Supreme Court's Decision and Its Implications* (New York: Oxford University Press, 2013).

61. The classic arguments against judicial enforcement of federalism are those of Jesse Choper and Herbert Wechsler. See generally Jesse H. Choper, *Judicial Review and the National Political Process* (Chicago: University of Chicago Press, 1980); Jesse H. Choper, "The Scope of National Power Vis-à-Vis the States: The Dispensability of Judicial Review," *Yale Law Journal* 86 (1977): 1552; Herbert J. Wechsler, "The Political Safeguards of Federalism: The Role of the States in the Composition and Selection of the Federal Government," *Columbia Law Review* 54 (1954): 543. Some recent authors have defended the Choper-Wechler position. See Bradford R. Clark, "Separation of Powers as a Safeguard of Federalism," *Texas Law Review* 79 (2001): 1321; Kramer, "Putting the Politics Back"; Shane, "Federalism's 'Old Deal.'" Others have attacked it. See Lynn A. Baker and Ernest A. Young, "Federalism and the Double Standard of Judicial Review," *Duke Law Journal* 51 (2001): 75; Saikrishna B. Prakash and John C. Yoo, "The Puzzling Persistence of Process-Based Federalism Theories," *Texas Law Review* 79 (2001): 1459. For my own criticisms of Choper-Wechsler, see Ilya Somin, "Closing the Pandora's Box of Federalism: The Case for Judicial Restriction of Federal Subsidies to State Governments," *Georgetown Law Journal* 90 (2002): 461–502, 494–97, and John O. McGinnis and Ilya

Somin, "Federalism vs. States' Rights: A Defense of Judicial Review in a Federal System," *Northwestern University Law Review* 99 (2004): 89–130.

62. For a useful brief summary of the main advantages claimed for federalism, see Michael W. McConnell, "Federalism: Evaluating the Founders' Design," *University of Chicago Law Review* 54 (1987): 1484, 1493–1500.

63. For a summary of the benefits of interstate competition, see Thomas R. Dye, *American Federalism: Competition Among Governments* (Lanham, MD: Lexington, 1990), 1–33; see also Somin, "Closing the Pandora's Box of Federalism," 468–69, and the discussion in Chapter 5.

64. The classic work on this point is Charles M. Tiebout, "A Pure Theory of Local Expenditures," *Journal of Political Economy* 65 (1956): 41; see also the discussion in Somin, "Closing the Pandora's Box of Federalism," 464–65.

65. See the discussion in Chapter 2; see also Somin, "Voter Ignorance and the Democratic Ideal," 417–18; Angus Campbell, Philip Converse, Donald Stokes, and Warren Miller, *The American Voter* (New York: John Wiley & Sons, 1960); W. Russell Neumann, *The Paradox of Mass Politics* (Cambridge: Harvard University Press, 1986); Philip Converse, "The Nature of Belief Systems in Mass Publics," in *Ideology and Discontent*, ed. David Apter (New York: Free Press, 1964); M. Kent Jennings, "Ideological Thinking Among Mass Publics and Political Elites," *Public Opinion Quarterly* 56 (1992): 419–41.

66. For a thorough survey, see Linda Bennett and Stephen Bennett, *Living with Leviathan: Americans Coming to Terms with Big Government* (Lawrence: University Press of Kansas, 1990).

67. See Chapter 1.

68. Robert J. Kaczorowski, "The Tragic Irony of American Federalism: National Sovereignty Versus State Sovereignty in Slavery and Freedom," *University of Kansas Law Review* 45 (1997): 1015–61, 1025–40.

69. Ibid., 1034–40; Somin, "Closing the Pandora's Box of Federalism," 467. See also the discussion of the interaction between racism and federalism in Chapter 5.

70. Somin, "Closing the Pandora's Box of Federalism," 461–62.

71. Virtually all federal grants to state governments have had attached conditions since the abolition of the General Revenue Sharing program in 1986. Ibid., 462.

72. For detailed discussion of the federalism issues raised by federal grants to state governments, see Somin, "Closing the Pandora's Box of Federalism." See also Lynn A. Baker, "The Spending Power and the Federalist Revival," *Chapman Law Review* 4 (2001): 195.

73. *Printz v. United States*, 521 U.S. 898 (1997); *New York v. United States*, 505 U.S. 144 (1992).

74. *United States v. Morrison*, 529 U.S. 598 (2000); *United States v. Lopez*, 514 U.S. 549 (1995).

75. Calabresi, "Textualism and the Countermajoritarian Difficulty," 1382–83; see also Steven G. Calabresi, "The Structural Constitution and the Countermajoritarian Difficulty," *Harvard Journal of Law and Public Policy* 22 (1998): 3, 6–8.

76. Robert A. Dahl, *Democracy and Its Critics* (New Haven: Yale University Press, 1989), 119–22.

77. See, e.g., Richard A. Epstein, "Exit Rights Under Federalism," *Law and Contemporary Problems* 55 (1992): 147, 154–59; see also the discussion of these issues in Chapter 5.

CHAPTER SEVEN

1. Thomas Jefferson, "Letter to William C. Jarvis, Sept. 28, 1820," in *The Writings of Thomas Jefferson*, Vol. 15, ed. Andrew Lipscomb and Albert Bergh (Washington, DC: 1904), 278.

2. See the discussion of these points in Chapter 2.

3. Jefferson, "Letter to William C. Jarvis."

4. John Stuart Mill, *Considerations on Representative Government* (Indianapolis: Bobbs-Merrill, 1958 [1861]), ch. X.

5. Milton Friedman, *Capitalism and Freedom* (Chicago: University of Chicago Press, 1962), 86–89.

6. For a recent defense of the idea that increased investment in civic education can generate not only increases in political knowledge but also increased civic engagement generally, see Ben Berger, *Attention Deficit Democracy: The Paradox of Civic Engagement* (Princeton, NJ: Princeton University Press, 2011), 153–57.

7. See, e.g., data compiled in Chapter 2; see also Michael X. Delli Carpini and Scott Keeter, *What Americans Know About Politics and Why It Matters* (New Haven: Yale University Press, 1996), 184–85; Scott L. Althaus, *Collective Preferences in Democratic Politics* (New York: Cambridge University Press, 2003), 68, 134–36; Norman Nie, et al., *Education and Democratic Citizenship in America* (Chicago: University of Chicago Press, 1996), ch. 2.

8. See the studies cited in Chapter 1.

9. Nie, et al., *Education and Democratic Citizenship in America*, 116–17; see also William A. Galston, "Political Knowledge, Political Engagement, and Civic Education," *Annual Review of Political Science* 4 (2001): 217–34.

10. Delli Carpini and Keeter, *What Americans Know About Politics*, 197–98.

11. See Michael Flynn, *Are We Getting Smarter? Rising IQ in the Twenty-First Century* (New York: Cambridge University Press, 2012).

12. Nie, et al, *Education and Democratic Citizenship in America*, 39–58, 187–88.

13. Bryan Caplan and Stephen C. Miller, "Intelligence Makes People Think Like Economists: Evidence from the General Social Survey," *Intelligence* 38 (2010): 636–47.

14. See the discussion of altruism and incentives to acquire political information in Chapter 3.

15. John Stuart Mill, *On Liberty*, ed. David Spitz (New York: Norton, 1975 [1859]), 98.

16. See, e.g., Eugen Weber, *Peasants into Frenchmen* (Stanford: Stanford University Press, 1976); E. G. West, *Education and the State*, 3rd ed. (Indianapolis: Liberty Press, 1994), 84–107; and John R. Lott Jr., "An Explanation for Public Provision of Schooling: The Importance of Indoctrination," *Journal of Law and Economics* 33 (1990): 199–231.

17. See, e.g., Diane Ravitch, *The Language Police: How Pressure Groups Restrict What Students Learn* (New York: Knopf, 2003).

18. Ibid., 71.

19. Ibid., chs. 6–7.

20. See Alberto Alesina and Nicola Fuchs-Schuendeln, "Goodbye Lenin (or Not?): The Effects of Communism on Peoples' Preferences," *American Economic Review* 97 (2007): 507–28.

21. See Jamie Terence Kelly, *Framing Democracy: A Behavioral Approach to Democratic Theory* (Princeton: Princeton University Press, 2012), 119–22.

22. For possible suggestions backed by data, see Galston, "Political Knowledge, Political Engagement, and Civic Education," 225–32.

23. For a recent review of the evidence, see Eric A. Hanushek, *Schoolhouses, Courthouses, and Statehouses: Solving the Funding-Achievement Puzzle in America's Public Schools* (Princeton, NJ: Princeton University Press, 2009).

24. See Terry Moe and John Chubb, *Liberating Learning: Technology, Politics, and the Future of American Education* (San Francisco: Jossey-Bass, 2009).

25. David E. Campbell, "Making Democratic Education Work," in *Charters, Vouchers, and Public Education*, ed. Paul E. Peterson and David E. Campbell (Washington, DC: Brookings Institution, 2001), 254–55.

26. Friedman, *Capitalism and Freedom*, ch. 5.; Mill, *On Liberty*, 98–99.

27. For a review of the political obstacles facing vouchers, see Terry M. Moe, *Schools, Vouchers and the American Public* (Washington, DC: Brookings Institution, 2001). For a discussion of the role of teachers' unions in effectively preventing the enactment of anything more than small-scale private school voucher programs, see Terry M. Moe, *Special Interest: Teachers Unions and America's Public Schools* (Washington, DC: Brookings Institution Press, 2011), 327–30.

28. Bruce Ackerman and James S. Fishkin, *Deliberation Day* (New Haven: Yale University Press, 2004); see also James S. Fishkin, "Deliberative Democracy and Constitutions," *Social Philosophy and Policy* 28 (2011): 242–60, at 257–58.

29. Ackerman and Fishkin, *Deliberation Day*, 9.

30. Lawrence Jacobs, Fay Lomax Cook, and Michael X. Delli Carpini, *Talking Together: Public Deliberation and Political Participation in America* (Chicago: University of Chicago Press, 2009), 37.

31. See the discussion in Chapter 4.

32. Diana Mutz, *Hearing the Other Side: Deliberative Versus Participatory Democracy* (New York: Cambridge University Press, 2006), 29–41.

33. Ackerman and Fishkin, *Deliberation Day*, ch. 3.

34. Ibid., 17.

35. Ibid.

36. See, e.g., James S Fishkin, *When the People Speak: Deliberative Democracy and Public Consultation* (New York: Oxford University Press, 2009); James S. Fishkin, *The Voice of the People* (New Haven: Yale University Press, 1997); James S. Fishkin, *Democracy and Deliberation: New Directions for Democratic Reform* (New Haven: Yale University Press, 1991); Robert Luskin, et al., "Considered Opinions: Deliberative Polling in the UK," *British Journal of Political Science* 32 (2002): 455–78.

37. Ackerman and Fishkin, *Deliberation Day*, 226.

38. For related criticisms of the Deliberation Day proposal, see Guido Pincione and Fernando Teson, *Rational Choice and Democratic Deliberation* (New York: Cambridge University Press, 2006), 95–97; and Arthur Lupia, "The Wrong Tack," *Legal Affairs*, January-February 2004, http://www.legalaffairs.org/issues/January-February-2004/feature_lupia_janfeb04.msp.

39. See Chapter 4.

40. Ackerman and Fishkin, *Deliberation Day*, 25–29. The candidates will have previously been asked to announce two to four major issues they intend to focus on, one month before Deliberation Day (ibid., 24).

41. Ibid. 24–37.

42. For a discussion of some others, see Jacobs, et al., *Talking Together*, ch. 7. See also Robert E. Goodin, *Innovating Democracy: Democratic Theory and Practice After the Deliberative Turn* (New York: Oxford University Press, 2008).

43. For a more detailed discussion of these problems as applied to structured deliberation proposals in general, see Ilya Somin, "Deliberative Democracy and Political Ignorance," *Critical Review* 22 (2010): 253–79, 268–69. See also Mark Pennington, "Democracy and the Deliberative Conceit," *Critical Review* 22 (2010): 159–85.

44. Mill, *Considerations on Representative Government.*

45. Ibid., 142.

46. See Pam Belluck, "States Face Decisions on Who Is Mentally Fit to Vote," *New York Times*, June 19, 2007.

47. See Solomon Skolnick, *The Great American Citizenship Quiz: Could You Pass Your Own Country's Citizenship Test?* (New York: Walker & Co., 2005).

48. Ibid.

49. See the discussion in the Introduction.

50. Bryan Caplan, *The Myth of the Rational Voter: Why Democracies Choose Bad Policies* (Princeton, NJ: Princeton University Press, 2007), 197. For a recent philosophical defense of the idea that knowledge-based restrictions on voting may be justified, see Jason Brennan, "The Right to a Competent Electorate," *Philosophical Quarterly* 61 (2011): 700–24.

51. See Alex Keyssar, *The Right to Vote* (New York: Basic Books, 2000), 111–16, 141–46.

52. Caplan, *Myth of the Rational Voter*, 148–53, 198.

53. See the discussion in Chapter 4.

54. The exclusion of convicted felons from voting, which seems to be accepted by the public, is an exception that proves the rule. Some four million people are prevented from voting because of felon disenfranchisement laws. Keyssar, *Right to Vote*, 308. Presumably, felon exclusion is popular because felons are perceived as morally corrupt people who have forfeited their right to vote through their own actions. There is no popular consensus that merely being an ignorant voter is comparably blameworthy.

55. See Stephen Breyer, *Breaking the Vicious Circle: Toward Effective Risk Regulation* (Cambridge: Harvard University Press, 1993), ch. 3; Cass Sunstein, *Risk and Reason: Safety, Law and the Environment* (New York: Oxford University Press, 2002).

56. See the discussion in Chapter 6.

57. See Breyer, *Breaking the Vicious Circle*, ch. 2; Sunstein, *Risk and Reason*, 25–52.

58. For a review of the relevant literature, see Dennis C. Mueller, *Public Choice III* (New York: Cambridge University Press, 2003), 347–53.

59. Cass R. Sunstein and Timur Kuran, "Availability Cascades and Risk Regulation," *Stanford Law Review* 51 (1999): 683–768.

60. F. A. Hayek, "The Use of Knowledge in Society, *American Economic Review* 4 (1945): 519–30.

61. See Eric Crampton, "Public Health and the New Paternalism," *Policy* (September 15, 2009), http://www.cis.org.au/publications/policy-magazine/article/2661-public-health-and-the-new-paternalism. For evidence that most smokers actually *overestimate* the risks of smoking, see W. Kip Viscusi, *Smoking: Making the Risky Decision* (Cambridge: Oxford University Press, 1992).

62. For arguments along these lines, see, e.g., Thomas E. Patterson, *The Vanishing Voter: Public Involvement in an Age of Uncertainty* (New York: Vintage, 2003), ch. 3; Thomas Patterson, *Out of Order* (New York: Vintage, 1994); Stephen J. Farnsworth and

S. Robert Lichter, *The Nightly News Nightmare: Network Television's Coverage of U.S. Presidential Elections, 1988–2004,* 2nd ed. (New York: Rowman & Littlefield, 2007). For a survey and critique of such arguments, see Doris Graber, "The Media and Democracy: Beyond Myths and Stereotypes," *Annual Review of Political Science* 6 (2003): 139–60.

63. See, e.g., Patterson, *Out of Order*; Farnsworth and Lichter, *Nightly News Nightmare.*

64. See the discussion in Chapter 1.

65. See, e.g., Markus Prior, "News vs. Entertainment: How Increasing Media Choice Widens Gaps in Political Knowledge and Turnout," *American Journal of Political Science* 49 (2005): 577–92; see also John Hindman, *The Myth of Digital Democracy* (Princeton, NJ: Princeton University Press, 2008), 60–61.

66. See Markus Prior, *Post-Broadcast Democracy: How Media Choice Increases Inequality in Political Involvement and Polarizes Elections* (New York: Cambridge University Press, 2007), chs. 4 and 8; Prior, "News vs. Entertainment."

67. See Shanto Iyengar, et al., "Cross-National vs. Individual-Level Differences in Political Information: A Media Systems Perspective," *Journal of Elections, Public Opinion, and Parties* 20 (2010): 291–309.

68. See ibid., 299. This study found that Americans answered 78 percent of domestic knowledge questions correctly, compared with 75 percent for British respondents, 83 percent for Finns, and 85 percent for Danes. By contrast, the American respondents answered only 40 percent of international questions correctly, compared with scores ranging from 65 percent to 69 percent for the other three countries.

69. See the discussion earlier in this chapter.

70. See the first section of this chapter.

71. See, e.g., Kelly, *Framing Democracy,* 106–07.

72. See Chapter 3.

73. See Prior, *Post-Broadcast Democracy,* chs. 4, 8; Prior, "News vs. Entertainment."

74. For an optimistic take on the possibility of increasing political knowledge through new technological developments, including ones that improve information processing, see John O. McGinnis, *Accelerating Democracy* (Princeton, NJ: Princeton University Press, 2013).

75. This is my main reservation about the otherwise persuasive technological optimism of McGinnis, *Accelerating Democracy.* The potential advances he outlines mostly reduce the cost of disseminating and acquiring information, but not the time and effort needed to learn it and analyze it. In that respect, they have much in common with the advances of the last fifty years, which have done little to increase political knowledge, despite their numerous other beneficial effects.

76. See, e.g., Michael Abramowicz, *Predictocracy: Market Mechanisms for Public and Private Decisionmaking* (New Haven: Yale University Press, 2008); McGinnis, *Accelerating Democracy,* ch. 4.

77. See Steve Schaeffer, "Intrade Closets to US Bettors, Bowing to Pressure from Regulators," *Forbes,* November 27, 2012, http://www.forbes.com/sites/steveschaefer/2012/11/27/cftc-takes-aim-at-intrade-files-suit-going-after-prediction-market.

78. See Chapter 5.

79. Arthur Lupia and Markus Prior, "Money, Time and Political Knowledge: Distinguishing Quick Recall and Political Learning Skills," *American Political Science Review* 52 (2008), 169–83.

80. Ibid., 174.

81. Ibid., 177. For another recent study reporting increases in correct answers in response to financial rewards, see John Bullock, Alan Gerber, and Gregory Huber, "Partisan Bias in Responses to Factual Questions," paper presented at the Western Political Science Association, March 2010.

82. See the third section of this chapter.

CONCLUSION

1. F. A. Hayek, *The Constitution of Liberty* (Chicago: University of Chicago Press, 1960), 115–16.

2. See the discussion of retrospective voting in Chapter 4.

3. For arguments that narrowly targeted protectionism can sometimes increase national welfare, while emphasizing that free trade is superior in the vast majority of cases, see, e.g., Paul Krugman, *Pop Internationalism* (Cambridge: MIT Press, 1996)

4. See Bryan Caplan, *The Myth of the Rational Voter: Why Democracies Choose Bad Policies* (Princeton, NJ: Princeton University Press, 2007), 36–39.

5. Siegel-Gale survey, September 18, 2009, http://www.siegelgale.com/2009/09/18/new-poll-americans-still-confused-by-president-obama%E2%80%99s-health-care-plan/.

6. See Wolf Linder, *Swiss Democracy* (New York: St. Martin's Press, 1994), ch. 2.

7. All four rank in the top thirty countries in per capita GDP, with Liechtenstein and Luxembourg ranking first and third respectively. See Central Intelligence Agency, *The World Fact Book* (Washington, DC: Central Intelligence Agency, 2009), https://www.cia.gov/library/publications/the-world-factbook/rankorder/2004rank.html.

8. The classic analysis is Robert Dahl and Edward Tufte, *Size and Democracy* (Stanford: Stanford University Press, 1973).

9. Caplan, *Myth of the Rational Voter*, ch. 4.

10. See Jane Kelsey, *The New Zealand Experiment: A World Model for Structural Adjustment* (Auckland: Auckland University Press, 1995).

11. James Gwartney and Robert Lawson, *Economic Freedom of the World: 2009 Annual Report* (Washington, DC: Cato Institute, 2009), 145.

12. See David Henderson, "Canada's Budget Triumph," Mercatus Center working paper no. 10-52, George Mason University (2010).

13. As of 2007, the United States had a 7.88 rating in the economic freedom index, compared to 8.03 for Ireland, 8.19 for Switzerland, and 8.30 for New Zealand. Gwartney and Lawson, *Economic Freedom of the World*, 112, 145, 172, 185. In fairness, it should be pointed out that public spending in Ireland also went up massively as a result of the financial crisis, just as it did in the United States.

14. Canada's score was in 2007 7.85, virtually identical to the 7.88 posted by the United States. Gwartney and Lawson, *Economic Freedom of the World: 2009 Annual Report*, 73. By 2009, Canada (7.78) ranked slightly ahead of the United States (7.58). James Gwartney, Robert Lawson, and Joshua Hall, *Economic Freedom of the World: 2011 Annual Report* (Washington, DC: Cato Institute, 2011), 49, 161.

15. *Washington Post*-ABC News Poll, January 12–15, 2010, http://www.washingtonpost.com/wp-srv/politics/polls/postpoll_011610.html.

16. Ibid.

17. Frank Newport, "Americans More Likely to Say Government Doing Too Much," Gallup Politics, September 21, 2009, http://www.gallup.com/poll/123101/americans-likely-say-government-doing-too-much.aspx.

18. CNN exit poll, November 7, 2012, http://www.cnn.com/election/2012/results/race/president#exit-polls.

19. Pew Research Foundation, "Public Wants Changes in Entitlements, Not Changes in Benefits," July 7, 2011, http://www.people-press.org/2011/07/07/section-1-impressions-of-entitlement-programs.

20. See, e.g., Samuel DeCanio, "State Autonomy and American Political Development: How Mass Democracy Promoted State Power," *Studies in American Political Development* 19 (2005): 117–136.

21. See Chapter 2.

22. See discussion in Chapter 2 and Ilya Somin, "Voter Ignorance and the Democratic Ideal," *Critical Review* 12 (1998): 413–58, at 438–42.

23. See Chapter 5. For a rare recognition of this possibility in earlier literature, see Guido Pincione and Fernando Teson, *Rational Choice and Democratic Deliberation: A Theory of Discourse Failure* (New York: Cambridge University Press, 2006), 242–45.

24. For the data on increasing IQ scores, see Michael Flynn, *Are We Getting Smarter? Rising IQ in the Twenty-First Century* (New York: Cambridge University Press, 2012), 6.

25. See Chapter 1.

26. See the discussion in the Introduction.

Index